The
CHURCH
in the
WAY

THE CHURCH IN THE WAY

by James E. Dittes

Charles Scribner's Sons ◆ NEW YORK

Preface

The churches of the land are filled but, we are told, they are filled for the wrong reasons. Those who write books about the church today explain that people fill pews and rosters out of fear or out of monstrous self-confidence, to enhance reputation in the community or to restore a sagging self-esteem, to develop professional and business contacts or to escape from the tribulations of profession and business. We are told that people go in search of guaranteed friendships or psychological refurbishing at less cost than country club or psychiatrist, or just because—like raising three children in a split-level house with a weedless front yard—it's "the thing to do." But, say our modern prophets, they are not in the churches because they have been gripped by the Holy Spirit, been compelled by the promises and commands of the gospel, or begun earnest search for the direction of God in their lives.

Ministers—some of them, some of the time—feel the dilemma even more keenly than the book-writing prophets. The minister should feel heartened at the outward signs of a flourishing church. But he may equally often feel disheartened by the stubbornness with which people resist his efforts to inspire them to a vital expression of faith. They attend services and meetings, but they don't seem to "get" the main point. The people are in the church but they do not comprise a church. And if they are not a church, how can he be a minister?

So the minister's ears are tuned to hear the voices of our times, which assure us that God, and God's future work among His people, is not in these churches. As he listens, his feelings vacillate between envious longing for the promised greener pastures of the "new minis- tries" and irritation at being reminded so callously of his plight.

This book proposes to enter the debate over the validity and vital- ity of the institutional parish church, and to take the currently un- popular side—the affirmative. It also proposes to speak to the plight of those ministers who feel, to some degree, impeded by unready laymen and an unwieldy organizational structure from exercising that ministry to which they feel called.

To the debaters and to the ministers, the book offers some bold hypotheses:

1. *The church can become a living parable.* The desperate search within the church for meaning and faithfulness may be the best possible preparation for men to find meaning and faithfulness in the world. The struggle in the church against irrelevant and futile busy-ness, empty forms, half-commitment, and misunderstanding— the very struggle that makes some want to abandon the existing form of church as hopeless—may guide and goad men to combat the futil- ity, emptiness, and half-commitment of our world. To abandon this struggle by avoiding the forms that occasion it may be to abdicate the responsibility and to forsake the particular mission of the church for our times.

2. *Intransigence can be a form of disguising and expressing reli- gious pilgrimage.* The layman's (or the minister's) unreadiness to participate in the church's true mission and ministry, and the vigor with which he attaches himself to the peripheral, the incidental, and even the distracting among church forms and activities seem to pose discouraging obstacles to faithful ministry. But this seeming unreadi- ness and misdirected vigor may sometimes reveal a vitality, a positive though tortuous engagement with faithful ministry, which is actually an ally of a minister's highest purposes.

3. In brief, combining these two possibilities, the resistance which seems most to thwart ministry *may* be the best occasion for ministry. When the church seems most in the way, it may be most

in the Way of Him who is met at the cross of the crowded ways of life.

For people are still in the churches, and so is the minister. They and he will probably stay there for the foreseeable future. I cite this stubborn fact not in order to counsel reconciliation with the inevitable (although this would not be out of place in the face of contemporary literature on the church, which so often overlooks it). Rather, this stubborn fact—that the people *are* in the churches—is important because it raises the possibility that the attraction of persons to the church is neither so flimsy nor so irrelevant to the proper image of the church as is sometimes assumed. If people are not obviously gathered for the loftiest of self-conscious spiritual purposes that prophets and ministers can most admire, nevertheless that which does bring them and keep them there cannot be casually dismissed. Although their reaction to the highest that the church and the minister hold before them may be agonizingly compounded of misunderstanding, pettiness, and rebuff, it is still a reaction. There is still encounter. These behaviors are evidence of their response to the encounter, not evidence that they have missed it. If the minister has offered the best expression of the word and will of God that he can, then their response—however different from what the minister expects or wants—deserves to be thought the best response to that word and will which they can make.

Their response, resistive as it seems, may be vital spiritual pilgrimage in disguise. Maybe we are fooled by the disguise when we see *only* busy-ness, sociability, and blunting of impact. Perhaps this is the way that busy, sociable, and blasé American suburbanites express their encounter with the verities of the church and its gospel. Perhaps the disguise is also expression. If one can see through the disguise, maybe one can find expressed in it the longings, gropings, confessions, and affirmations of genuine and vigorous religious pilgrimage. Perhaps the layman's place in the church is best symbolized by his fondness for the back pews—he is in the church, but as far from altar and pulpit as possible. Does he keep his distance from word and grace because he is indifferent and proud, stubborn and unconcerned, uninformed and uninvolved, or because he is all too apprehending and apprehensive, though perhaps not consciously so, of the meaning of the word and the altar? Is the space between layman and the "front" of the church an exasperating emptiness (as the minister usually sees it), a gap to be closed by instructing and cajoling? Or is the distance defined and charged by the vital encounter between layman and his awesome perception of God's claims, which keep him bound just so—in the church, but at a distance? If the latter, the distance represents a vitality of engagement which is to be celebrated and captured.

These, then, are the hypotheses offered for testing in the conventional parish churches of our time. The book (1) states and illustrates these hypotheses; (2) seeks to make them seem plausible enough to be worth trying; (3) suggests clues and rules by which a minister might "see through" or "decode" the resistive disguise-expressions to find their meaning; and (4) proposes ways of responding and ministering in terms that the resistance itself suggests.

This is genuine hypothesis. It is not here argued, Pollyanalike, that all obstacles to the church's ministry are to be embraced as blessings in disguise. It is to suggest, rather, that this may sometimes be true, perhaps often enough to be worth considering and testing when one confronts resistance. It may be true more often than it is recognized by ministers, in their justified sense of annoyance, or by prophetic book-writers, with their singleminded awareness of the church's deficiencies. Ministers, and prophets too, are invited to look at specific instances and to see for themselves whether and when such interpretation as here hypothesized may be appropriate.

For ministers only

This book is intended for a limited audience: ministers and prospective ministers who acknowledge as real the kinds of bewilderment and frustrations—resistances to their ministry—described in the opening paragraphs.

It is common to write in the prefaces of books for ministers that they are written for ministers and "interested educated laymen." This has a plaintive, apologetic tone, as though there were something not quite proper about ministers having particular professional problems, viewpoints, and concerns more or less peculiar to their particular role, and as though there were something equally improper about writing for such restricted professional concerns. This book is not written for laymen—unless they want to look over a minister's shoulder in order to see things, including themselves as layman, as (I think) a minister sees them. This book is stanchly intended to be read from the perspective of a parish minister and—even more narrowly—from the perspective of those ministers today who view their labors with uncertainty, frustration, but persistence.

The vigorous current public debate about the proper role of church and ministry in our times must seem to many ministers a pale imitation of the personal debate they have waged within themselves, ever since they first began to feel called to this vocation, as to exactly what is most required and expected of them. Over the span of decades, what are the specific directions and goals for themselves and for the institutions and people in their charge? In each daily encounter, what is the most appropriate, most helpful, most faithful response that one can make? It is in the nature of the vocation, as confident as one may feel about his general calling, never to be certain about the specific actions and daily decisions he finds himself making. It also seems to be in the nature of the profession to feel perpetually impeded from realizing whatever objectives one does find formulated. The institution and the people—those laymen for whom this book is not written—that he loves, serves, and for whom he dreams visions sometimes become a millstone, defying him to move a step. But he persists, resilient and with spasmodic faith that he is still accompanied by God.

It is for ministers who hold some such attitudes as these—perhaps complemented or complicated by many other attitudes, perhaps accompanied also by many moments or moods of satisfaction and thanksgiving in their vocation—that this book is written. It assumes that their hopeful persistence may get them into, and perhaps through, the book. In the face of, and even in using, the particular intransigencies and frustrations which they experience, it tries to suggest some possible lines of direction and of strategy. It recognizes that these too are inevitably partial, perhaps as misleading as helpful, and perhaps as likely to lead to new uncertainties and frustrations as great as those it would speak to.

If attempts to apply these hypotheses turn up difficulties and deficiencies, that is to be expected. If these in turn suggest refinements, or even refutation, this is welcome. If refinements and rejoinder provide an enrichment of what is now recognized about the church and the ministry, the present exercise will have served a gratifying purpose in provoking them.

A psychological perspective

In terms of the distinctions by which libraries and curricula, authors and teachers are usually divided, this book might be classified as an application of *psychology of religion* to problems of *pastoral theology*.

The psychological perspective which is brought to bear is a blend of many elements. The central thesis, as stated above, is borrowed directly from the concept of *resistance* in psychotherapy, as this is understood by the psychoanalytic approach to therapy. This concept implies two general "dynamic" or Freudian understandings of personality which are presupposed here. One focuses on intra-psychic *conflict*; most important matters of life involve the tension between competing personal motives or attitudes or inclinations. This fact is important here because of the inference it permits that when we see one strong tendency (such as an avoidance or blunting of the church's mission) we may suppose a competing tendency (such as a keen sensitivity to the church's mission) also to be present, even though not visible. Perhaps in many religious matters this ambivalence becomes what we call "awe." The other general understanding has to do with the particular type of conflict involved in *rationalization*, the maneuver of making one's behavior, however prompted, seem closely congruent with norms and with the demands of objective circumstances. This is important to this book, since resistance is a kind of acted-out rationalization. Rationalization and resistance stand on two legs, the inner promptings and the "objective reality." No rationalization is pure invention; it refers plausibly to actual facts. But neither is it ever totally congruent with objective facts, and the gap in congruence becomes the evidence that inner meaning is also betrayed by the rationalization.

Other psychological themes prominent in the book are attributable to Carl Rogers and to John Dollard and Neal Miller. From Rogers comes the confident understanding that persons have available far more resources for healing and maturation than most of us suppose and that they can use these resources when provided circumstances of support and freedom. From Dollard and Miller comes the restatement of some of the mechanisms of personality with the precision of "neo-behaviorism" and with the social awareness of "ego psychology." Particular use is made of their analysis of conflict and of "cue-producing responses." More general insights from social psychology and from psychology of religion also find their place, especially in connection with analysis of particular illustrations. About these illustrations a word now needs to be said.

A perspective, not a prescription

The primary purpose of the book is to suggest a perspective, a point of view, a framework for analysis of certain types of situations. The book is not a manual of what to do in those situations. It is the fruit of a kind of theoretical, even armchair, if you will, venturesomeness, not the fruit of years of successful experience. It is offered not as empirically confirmed fact of wide generalizability, but as a plausible hypothesis, with enough anecdotal and analogical support to warrant attention. Case examples are presented in order to illustrate ways in which the perspectives and categories suggested here could be applied, not to demonstrate successful outcomes when they are applied. In most of the cases, in fact, the perspectives and analysis here suggested were not applied at the time the incidents occurred. The suggestions here constitute simply proposals, and hypotheses. The main intention, then, is to influence perception, to increase "sensitivity," to enhance the possibility that a reader may see a future situation in a different perspective.

The reflection or perspective which this book hopes to offer presupposes exactly the conditions that it suggests the minister can count on when *he* offers reflection and perspective to his people. I am aware that the reader knows infinitely more than I do about any particular situation, its people and problems and possibilities, and about his own purposes and abilities and limitations. The writer of a book, like a minister, can offer a kind of freshly objective point of view. But not much more. If the perspective seems illuminating, the reader, like the parishioners, can be counted on to find ways of adapting and making use of it in ways that would not even occur to the author.

In this connection, a word is in order about the "case" illustrations with which the presentation is sprinkled. These represent a range of fidelity to actual data. One, that of Mrs. A in Chapter II, is presented as a verbatim transcript of a tape-recorded interview. Some are reconstructions from memory, or from memory plus report, of actual incidents. Others are reconstructions of actual incidents, up to a point; the beginning of an episode is reported as accurately as possible, but a new and "happy" ending has been proposed, to illustrate how a minister following the perspectives of this book might have responded differently. Still others are not reports of any actual single incident, but are constructions—fictional, if you like—based on a variety of experiences and observations; they are cast in the form of episodes which are hopefully "true to life" and clearer than more abstract presentation. The language with which each case is presented should imply which type it is. But the distinction does not seem greatly important. The book presents a hypothesis; and the cases are offered not as evidence for the hypothesis, but as illustration of it. The cases are more "predictions" than reports, predictions of what may be discovered if the perspectives of the book are applied to such instances.

Reactionary or only psychological?

This exercise will be regarded by many as hopelessly conservative. Since they will mean this as a rebuke, and since the word can mean so many different things, let me try to explain here two of the meanings they are likely to have in mind when they call this conservative.

In the first place, this is a discussion of the church, its mission and ministry, from a psychological rather than a sociological perspective; and most progressive, adventurous, and exciting discussions of the church these days are written from a stanchly sociological position. Sociology is concerned with the surges and pulses of life that one finds so dramatically unfolding about him as he grows up and leaves home—power centers, political decisions, economic forces, class struggles, industrialization, urbanization. By contrast, psychology is concerned with matters one would leave behind when he grows up—individuals trying to get along with each other amicably in the intense intimacy of family life, trying to master childish fears, trying so terribly self-consciously to determine a coherent set of guiding principles and patterns of conduct that can pass as one's "identity."

From our perspective in the mid-sixties, psychology is what was offered in the forties and fifties, largely in terms of pastoral counseling, as a basis for the church's mission and ministry.

Yet it may not oversimplify recent history to suggest that there is a healthy alternation in this country in this century between the dominance of psychological and sociological perspectives among those concerned with the church who pay any attention at all to the social sciences. Each rises up in turn to provide correctives for the inevitable abstractions and partialness of the other. The first two decades of the century belonged largely to the psychologists of religion, and their prime focus was the religious education of individuals, all in a context of liberal optimism. Then, still in the optimistic mood, came the social gospel. In the sobered, realistic mood of the postwar years, psychology offered the theologian help in defining the sinfulness of man and offered the pastor help in mending this sinfulness with the tools of therapy and counseling. Now has come the contemporary concern to define the church's mission and ministry in relation to the forces of public life as the sociologist analyzes them.

Allowing two decades for each stage in this apocalyptic calculation, this book is thirteen years premature to usher in the twenty-year reign of psychology that will climax the century! Thus, it will more likely be seen as a throwback to the era just ended.

The reader ought to recognize how much of the contemporary debate over the proper mission of the church boils down to a kind of debate that psychologists and sociologists have always had between themselves, and philosophers long before them: Which is the more fundamental reality, social processes or individual processes; the public or the private; the economic, political, and other social forces of men as collectivities, or the passions, hopes, and fears of men as individuals? The intimate interaction between social and individual is acknowledged by all. But the question still poses itself: In the nature of things, which are relatively more determinative and which more derivative? Do collective processes more reflect or determine the individual? Do individual processes more reflect or determine the collective?

If you want to change, to reform, to "Christianize," where is it more strategic to apply force? If you can make individuals feel more secure, more responsible, more sensitive to both God's assurances and His demands, will this open and move them to effective alteration of our institutions and systems, to make *them* more reflective and responsive to God's will? If persons know love at home or in the household of faith, in the suburbs though this be, are they more likely to foster it among the segments of collectivity in which they drudge, or over which they preside? Or must one start directly with collectivities and the public sphere, believing that only as these become more responsive to God's will can men as individuals find the assurance and the direction which God places before them? [1]

The public and collective or the private and personal? In principle, many parts of this answer might be settled empirically; we can try to find out. Indeed, the movements of past decades—social gospel,

---

[1] Perhaps the ecstatic celebrations of political, technological, economic, and other social structures within modern urban society have reached such an exaggerated pace that they have already burned up the twenty-year life span I have allowed them in less than half that time. Harvey Cox (*The Secular City*, [New York: Macmillan, 1965]) finds that the accomplishment of such structures is the climax of the liberating word of God, exercised previously, but imperfectly, in the Exodus and in Easter. But it may also be that such pretentious idealization of the structures of the city is only a regression to the situation of Babel—a considerably more primitive stage in man's spiritual pilgrimage than either the Exodus or the Resurrection.

pastoral psychology—can be interpreted in just these terms, as grand experiments which demonstrate the possibilites and the limitations of group-oriented, or private-oriented strategies. But because we lack clear empirical conclusions, the decision is now made by each person according to whatever variety of personal (rebellious, conformist, repressive, projective, etc.) and public influences he is subject to.

In the second place, and more significantly I think, a conservative luster—attention to the status quo and to the beneficial functions of the status quo—is an inevitable by-product of the particular task here attempted. I have set myself the task of analyzing some of the psychological functions of the characteristic American Protestant contemporary parish church; hence, attention to the status quo. I have also set myself the task of finding similarities between the parish church and the institution of psychotherapy; hence, emphasis on the beneficial characteristics of the church. This is admittedly a partial picture. If one set out to try a comprehensive analysis, even from a psychological point of view, of the functions of the typical American Protestant parish, he would have to include much that would be judged from most standpoints as undesirable. If I have chosen a path of analysis that issues in largely favorable evaluations of the existing parish church, this must reflect my judgment that criticism, which can be so easily heard, needs a counterbalancing word.

Our ministers and theology students may be restless and painfully aware of the countless ways in which their church falls short of the intentions and missions to which God calls His people at this time. They may forsee how much the church may transform its structures in the decades and centuries ahead. Yet, they will probably spend their careers in the same kind of conventional parish churches in which they grew up. They deserve some help in understanding how their church and ministry can serve—not in spite of, but indeed because of, the frustrations they feel—to goad and prepare men for active engagement in responsible, faithful, and effective Christian ministry in the world of today.

Acknowledgments

Appreciation is due at least five ministers for showing me, each in a different way, the potential vitality of the parish church, James B. Ashbrook, Browne Barr, Buckner Coe, D. Alan Keighley, and James B. Nelson. They may or may not recognize or approve anything in the book. But their ministries, and their reflections on their ministries, have dramatized for me the excitement and power of the church which this book tries, in its own way to be sure, to interpret. Searching guidance has also come from my colleagues in study at the Yale Divinity School, especially those who have sat around the table in recent years in the course on the work of the parish minister.

Opportunity for writing was provided in part by support from the John Simon Guggenheim Memorial Foundation, the Italian Fulbright Commission, and a sabbatical leave from Yale University. The manuscript has been helped by editorial suggestions made by James B. Ashbrook and Mrs. Elizabeth Powers. It has also benefited from this and innumerable other forms of help given by my wife.

Perhaps the pages that follow reflect the fact, too, that many of them were written in Rome at a time when the spirit of John XXIII still exerted an unmistakable hold on the city and its people—Papa Giovanni, who in aspiring most to be a "good shepherd" moved hierarchies and enlivened structures.

Table of Contents

Table of Contents

The
CHURCH
in the
WAY

I

The Relevance
of Being Irrelevant

The church, we are told frequently, is futilely irrelevant and can save itself and regain its mission only by radical renunciation of its present forms. The church is portrayed as dragged along on the march of time, too busy preserving its own structures and operating its own machinery even to notice the direction of the march, much less to affect its course.

But if this is the true picture of the American Protestant church, what could be more relevant to the plight of men and institutions in our culture? For the haunting predicament of our times is the sensation of irrelevance, impotence, and futility before the forces that seem to engulf us. How can one stand up and count for something without being swept away? If the church participates in this predicament of our times, thank God that He has placed it in the world where it can share precisely in the crises and futilities of the world— not as an aloof observer, but as a full participant, and, by His grace, as a guide.

Yet those who most urge the church to "become relevant" often seem peculiarly unable to accept it when the church obviously shares this overwhelming predicament of our time. They complain in almost the same breath that the church is irrelevant and that it is over-relevant; that it escapes the machineries and dilemmas of the culture around it, and that it is caught too much in them.

Ironically, those whose slogan, if not their god, is "relevance" may be the ones who most risk being swept along passively and blindly by the march of time. It sometimes seems as though they would preserve Christianity in the world by baptizing as "Christian" whatever they find thriving in the world: psychotherapy, urban renewal, sexual revolution, now even secularism itself, and finally atheism.

The church is indeed locked in struggle for its very soul against the temptation to disengage from the world and to seek sanctuary in its own islands of peaceful piety and in preoccupation with its own internal affairs. But this very struggle must also be the struggle of its members. Each man, if he is to save his soul, must find ways of keeping the gospel and himself engaged with the vital forces of life he daily confronts. His temptation, like the church's temptation, is to withdraw the gospel and himself—at least the creative centers of his life—into a quiet or distracting personal haven symbolized by the suburbs, the frantic merry-go-round of chauffeuring the family and tinkering with the lawn mower. But how is a man to get the nudge and the guidance and the faith that he needs to continue his struggle for relevance and engagement unless he sees his church desperately and frankly engaged in its struggle? The suburban captivity of the churches is precisely their point of participation in a major dilemma of current life and their opportunity of giving guidance in men's struggle with this dilemma.

When we are told by friendly and unfriendly challengers of the church that the church must break free of its captivity to the cultural context so as to avoid the dilemmas of irrelevance, we must be suspicious. Would such "reforms" in fact enhance the relevance of the church or drastically reduce it? We are told to shed the constricting forms. No more couples' clubs struggling, sometimes successfully, more often unsuccessfully, to find the courage and the means to make their oganizational life and program significantly faithful to the gospel. No more busy machinery of committee meetings struggling, sometimes successfully, more often unsuccessfully, to remain open to God's claim in the midst of bickering over budget and business. No more conventional 11:00 A.M. worship services attended by complacent, well-dressed suburbanites who still half hope, half fear that they may be gripped by God in the midst of their conventionality and complacency.

But the task of discerning and responding to God's claims is, for most American Protestants, in the very midst of the impotent, mechanical conventionality and futility of their lives, in exactly the conditions characterizing couples' clubs, budget committees, and conventional worship assemblies. It may be our hope, and the promise of God, that in the clubs and committees and conventionalities within the church may exist seeds and sparks of salvation, which need to be nourished there first—if salvation is ever to be found in the clubs and committees and conventionalities outside the church.

Finding a sample of worldliness in the church is no guarantee that worldliness out of the church will be transformed. First it needs to be transformed in the church. But before this can happen, it must be acknowledged and accepted in the church. This book insists on acknowledging the seeming deficiencies and hindrances of the parish as important and valid opportunities for ministry.

It takes this point of view from combining two clues within the practice of psychotherapy, represented by the concepts "resistance" and "acceptance." One clue is the technique of identifying resistance and exploiting it for therapeutic purposes, especially as this technique has been developed in Freudian psychoanalysis. Therapy often heals a person for return to the world by focusing precisely on those impediments with which he obstructs the conduct of therapy itself. The other clue is the recognition, emphasized by Rogerian therapy, that healing and transformation proceed from the "acceptance" of the unwelcome and the disturbing. This should be true not only when the disruptions affect remote affairs "in the world," but also even when they intrude into the arena (therapy, and by inference, the church) that is supposed to be enough different from the world to accomplish healing.

Is "relevance" sometimes an evasion?

We have a right to ask the churches' challengers: Who is most guilty of escaping into illusion and irrelevance? For there is a grave risk that the seeming "relevance" of special ventures, such as direct social action, *may* be an evasion of the responsibility to respond to God in one's own station and to set right the affairs of one's own life. The great crusade to attack the devil on his home ground is particularly alluring and also demonically spurious just when the devil is busy in one's own home ground.

Our folk wisdom, in a mixture of gossip and truth, is full of accounts of clinical psychologists with unhappy marriages and disturbed children, of pacifists violent and bitter in pursuit of their cause, of social actionists campaigning for civil liberties while running roughshod over democratic rights in their own organization, of evangelists with wayward piety and moral standards, and so on—men relentlessly pressing in public a battle that they have abandoned in private.

A minister finds himself impatient and irked by the seeming superficialities which preoccupy his encounter with his people. He is unable to see, in these encounters in narthex or committee room or on the telephone, persons engaged in the same personal struggles or confronting the same theological questions that he can recognize when he meets them for counseling or in study groups. He sees the ordinary church encounters as obstacles rather than as expressions of the ultimate issues of life. It is no surprise, then, when one such man feels himself called to be chaplain in a private mental hospital, another turns to college teaching, and another becomes a social worker. Meeting searching patients, students and families, and untroubled by parish ministry, he can be "relevant" all the time. Or is he evading engagement with life as it is actually lived and struggled by the vast majority? Is he reserving his ministry only for those isolated few who meet his prerequisites of psychological and intellectual sophistication?

SEEKING RELEVANCE IN PASTORAL COUNSELING. Since World War II, pastoral counseling has appealed to many clergymen as a means of achieving relevance and effectiveness. Some may have made their ministries highly specialized in counseling because this seemed to them *the* way to have a significant impact on the lives of others. In the counseling interview is the sense of touching other's lives where the struggles and hopes are, and of reaching them with a healing response; such a sense is often lacking in a minister's experience outside counseling.

A book offering psychological insight into the work of a minister may in our time still be misunderstood as to its purpose, especially a book that takes its key from a concept of psychotherapy. But to endeavor to enhance psychological sensitivity of ministers is not to ask them to become psychotherapists, or even to become more proficient counselors.

It is my belief that the same exciting drama found in counseling, the same fulfilling sense of touching people effectively where they really are is available to a minister in an enviable and unique array of opportunities. Individual personal counseling happens to be only one way a minister may develop and use psychological sensitivity. Far from urging ministers to do more and better counseling, this book intends just the opposite. It wants to develop some psychological sense of the meaning and drama within the *full* range of encounters a minister has with his people—as minister.

SEEKING RELEVANCE IN SOCIAL ACTION. Sometimes direct social action, or talk about social issues, seems to promise guaranteed relevance. It may make it possible to overlook the realities of the immediate neighborhood in favor of the glamours of the more remote reaches of one's community. Problems in the suburbs may be trivial and discouragingly egocentric, but they are there and have within them the kernel of basic dilemmas. When the smoke from one man's incinerator or the noise from one man's lawn mower disturbs another family's picnic—or one church's bells or traffic disturbs another church's worship—there are, within the petty haggling, the same basic issues of men's responsible life under God and with neighbor as are raised in more socially significant issues. We may regret the energy squandered on such trivial issues, especially when it is to the exclusion of more urgent matters. But we also must be wary lest we assume too easily that personal and community salvation is achieved when particular, dramatic social issues are settled. We must not underestimate the evil in the backyard smoke or overestimate the relevance of racial problems in the center of the city.

To question the appeal of the dramatic or the remote is not to raise suspicion of motivation or to pose a contrast between Pharisee and publican—though sometimes these issues may also be involved. The intent is, rather, to take seriously the implication of Jesus' searching gaze at subtle human tendencies immediately at hand, to the discomfort of those who find more comfort in the overt and dramatic. Perhaps we need to hear words like these today: "You have heard it said that thou shalt establish love and justice in Mississippi, Africa, and your city schools. But I say that love and justice must obtain even between next-door neighbors and among church committee members."

Perhaps all intensely but narrowly motivated persons in the church, those who find special ministries with minorities of especially responsive people, run the risk of becoming the beatniks of the church, protesting against irrelevance and disengagement by disengaging themselves still more into isolated individualistic "Greenwich Villages." Perhaps worse than the "suburban captivity" of the churches is their captivity in "the village." The throb of campus, counseling center, inner city, hospital, or other isolated village—including, one must add, a seminary faculty—is sometimes mistaken for the essential heartbeat of contemporary life. But, just as the pulse is best felt in the extremities after it has pushed its way through much tissue, so is the genuinely living heartbeat of our time that which pushes life through the sometimes flabby, sometimes muscular tissues of involvement in the major roles of life: in vocation, in family, and in widening concentric circles of community.

This will seem incomprehensible to persons fervently engaged in ministry in factory, city hall, tenement, hospital emergency room and clinic waiting room, African villages and Asian hovels, buses in Alabama and Evanston, and all the other points of desperate, almost hopeless human need. Such ministers inevitably and genuinely feel that those within the walls of suburban churches and seminaries are hopelessly cloistered in secluded refuge and isolated sanctuary. From the point of view of those in crisis ministry, the conventional minister *is* cloistered. How odd, and maybe even unkind, to suggest that the crisis minister, responding so directly to urgent, immediate tugs of human plight, suffers his own form of isolation and cloistering. But in fact, the move to the crisis ministry may not be too different from the appeal monasticism has exerted on able and dedicated men throughout the centuries: renunciation of the humdrum conventionality and comforts for the sake of sharply focused, undistracted obedience and tasks. Nothing here is intended to challenge the validity of such specialized crisis ministry. We can only salute it. But we must question the claim that it is normative for the church of our times.

SOME THEOLOGICAL CORRECTIVES

1. Church as "incarnation"

It is not special distortion and sin—as the critics would see it—that makes the church vulnerable to tendencies and temptation to retreat into a self-justifying, self-preoccupied haven. It is, rather, part of the church's intended status that it share just such temptations of the world—just as the church is the continuing body of the incarnate Christ fully human. God's redemptive forces cannot reach and redeem men apart from a fully human incarnate Christ; neither can they reach and redeem men apart from a church that in its own life fully knows and fully shares their trials and temptations.

Do we not hear echoes of Gnosticism and related heresies in the impatience that the church of Christ has a physical, psychological, and social body, not essentially distinguishable from the other institutional bodies of its time or immune to all the ills of such bodies? Any "incarnation" of the mission and fellowship of the people of Christ into particular forms and organizations and patterns is thought by some necessarily to pervert and distort. As with Puritanism of other kinds, any body is thought to defile the purity of the spirit.

Such a view is implied in the attitude of the minister who sharply distinguishes all the administrative and organizational activities from his "pure" or "true" ministry (which may be variously defined as preaching, study, community leadership, pastoral care, etc.). He resents the former because they keep him from the latter. Or, at best, he tolerates the former as an evil necessary to permit the latter.

In this dualistic thinking, he may feel that most of his energies are spent in the "preliminaries" with little chance to employ his real training and calling. He would lead worship and Bible study, but first he must persuade people to attend and then instruct them in how to worship and study. As a Sunday school teacher, he must first solve the "discipline" problems of gaining and holding attention before he can teach. Similarly, as a leader of adult groups, he must recruit members, develop morale, instruct in fundamentals before he can lead fruitful discussion. Before he can engage in effective counseling relations with intimate impact on others' lives, he must engage in the seemingly superficial, unrewarding work of establishing "precounseling" relationships, so that parishioners come to trust and seek him as counselor. He must train people to understand his proper role as minister and theirs as laymen before he and they can begin to function in these roles. He feels that most of his effort is spent cranking and repairing, and he does not perceive either of these tasks as part of the driver's role for which he feels called.

The two common solutions to this dilemma, opposite though they are, both preserve the Gnosticlike dualism, with a disparagement of the daily activities of the church and minister as preliminary and superficially remote from the grander activities of the "real" ministry. One solution is to become preoccupied, perhaps even obsessed, with the machinery as machinery. So we have the expert administrators and technicians in each phase of church life. They do not understand their efficient prowess to be directly relevant to goals of ministry but, rather, to be indirectly instrumental. Their work is to be blessed with an invocation at the outset of the meeting and is a necessary means for others to address the "real" ends of church and ministry. Means and ends are distinguished. The other reaction is to dismiss summarily the mechanical procedures, to damn the machinery and structures of the church as "irrelevant," to dispense with the hampering body, and to set free the otherwise captive spirit and purposes of the church. Again, means and ends are distinguished, this time more drastically.

In both cases, whether procedures and structures are compulsively served or phobically evaded, they are evaluated as *mere* machinery.

They are not seen as intrinsically or organically related to the major mission of the church. Both are avoiding the problem of finding means of effective ministry in whatever situations, more often than not, frustrating situations, of machinery and structure that each day may bring.[1]

A TYPOLOGY OF "BODY-SPIRIT" UNDERSTANDINGS. In the writings and mood of our time are varying degrees of impatience with the "body" of the church. By "body" is meant here the social structure and administrative organization of the church and the fact that it too often betrays human, selfish motivations, pettiness, and shortsightedness. Let us consider five points along the continuum from "rejection" to "acceptance" of this "body."

a. There is the extreme view that any body contradicts the mission and fellowship of the church, its spirit. The more body, the more defilement. The implied corollary may or may not be made explicit, that the spirit, the true expression of the church can, does, and should exist without any such body. This view seems to be implied, for example, in writings by Emil Brunner. It is a common misinterpretation of the language of Romans 8. The "spirit" or "essence" of the church is like a butterfly. When you want to capture and preserve it, your net and pin destroy much if not the essence of its flitting gaiety. You cannot capture, even to measure, an atomic electron without disrupting exactly the characteristics you want to measure. You cannot capture wind in a bottle. The problem is not that some structures and forms become distorted and sinful but, rather, that all structure, per se, distorts. Any attempt to manifest or express or detect the church in particular visible or usable forms contradicts and distorts the essential nature of the church.

b. Some may not be so drastic or graphic about describing the distortions occasioned by the body of the church. But their emphasis, such as in Karl Barth and Dietrich Bonhoeffer, on an idealized and

[1] It may be that in particular ways the ecumenical movement partakes of both these ways of isolating "means" from "ends." On the one hand, there are some hints of preoccupation with the procedures and machinery of unity. On the other hand, there may be some tendency to gloss over as too troublesome the diversity and plurality which, in reality, comprise the rich fabric of contemporary life.

thoroughly spiritualized church, suggests that it is able to exist and function without need of any "body." Whether they intend it or not, the effect of their view is to encourage impatience with body.

c. A more subtle and complex view holds that only some, not all, forms of body distort and pervert the church. Such a view raises, of course, the problem of the criterion. On what grounds will some forms be judged as appropriate expressions of the church and others as perversions of it? This is a question never satisfactorily addressed except in the most abstract or obvious categories. The usual practice seems to be the suggestion that although, in principle, some forms of the church are not perversions, in fact, all the known forms do seem to be distortions and perversions. So the practical effect of this view may be the same as the more extreme one cited above.

d. Another view suggests a parallelism or peaceful coexistence between "body" and "spirit." This seems to be, for example, the major emphasis of James Gustafson. This also seems to be a heritage of Barth, whether intended or not, of H. Richard Niebuhr, and also of Søren Kierkegaard. On the one hand is the institutional church, and on the other the real church, but without clear intersection or interaction between the two. Analysis of one is not necessarily relevant to participation in the other. The true mark of the church, the expression of God, may occur in the most unlikely places within or without the institutional church. In practical effect, this view suggests a disparagement of the manifest "body" of the church.

e. In contrast to the above views, what is to be suggested in this book of course assumes the view that the bodily expressions are necessary to the fulfillment of the church's mission and fellowship. More than a tolerated necessity, they are an intrinsic part. We do not condescendingly acknowledge that, alas, God's activities in this world must compromise with its nature. Rather, we insist that God's activities in this world must—because of the nature of His activities, not because of the nature of the world—employ and exploit precisely the imperfections of the bodily forms of the world. To save, Christ—the new Adam—had to assume precisely the form and predicament of the old Adam. The church is the continuation of His saving work, even—or especially—the church with the most annoying of bodily necessities, phoning, arranging, recruiting, and all the rest.

2. The secular church

Along with Gnostic echoes, many of the cries of "irrelevance" carry overtones dissonant with important principles established by the Reformers; for they seem to require a church comprised of the elect (who have already solved the problem—by joining a study group, for example—of how to retain loyalty to their faith in the midst of their lives), rather than a group of sinners still seeking justification. And they would have the church, in its organizational and actual life, aspire to a holier and purer status, aloof from the ordinary realities of the "secular world." It is particularly ironic, even irking, to find those who most celebrate the structures of the secular world the most annoyed with structures within the church.

The Reformers attacked the wall of separation between the "secular" and the "sacred." Their principles are invoked by the critic when he urges the church to "enter" the world, but ignored by him when it appears that the realities of the "secular" are also part of the church.

The Reformers' doctrines of vocation and of the priesthood of all believers are invoked enthusiastically to promote the ministry of the laity, in which the laymen are encouraged to functions and roles they once thought reserved for the ordained clergy. But the same doctrines are neglected when it comes to seeing the plight and status of the ordained clergy as not essentially different from the layman. For if other vocations share responsibilities and opportunities with the ministry, so does the ministry share with other vocations all the dilemmas and ambiguities that beset the Christian trying to respond to God in his own world and calling.

If the minister and church are not unique or special in their calling by God, neither are they exempt from the predicament of trying to express that calling in the sinful world. When the minister finds that his life as minister, or that the chief deacon's life as deacon, or that

the life of the women's society as a Christian group is fully in need of
God's divine wrath and forgiveness, he ought to be no more surprised—or resentful, or tempted to escape—than when he finds that
rare housewife or businessman or physician or clergyman coming
close to a genuine expression of Christian vocation. His own calling
and ministry may—at the very least—lie just as much in meeting the
needs of the former as in evading the former and seeking sanctuary in
the company of the latter. Someone has commented that the ministry seems to be the only profession in which men complain about
finding customers or clients immediately at hand!

3. Church as new creation

If distinctions between "body" and "spirit" and between secular
and sacred are false and misleading, so is the distinction between the
creative and the redemptive actions of God. These forces are seen in
distortion unless they are seen in continuity with one another. God
does not create in one mode or one moment and then save in another. He transforms chaos into life, formlessness into meaning,
alienation into union, and these actions may sometimes be viewed as
creation, sometimes as redemption. The Hebrews' account of creation echoes, in its imagery, the memory of their saving in the Exodus:
the spirit of God moving across the darkness and void (as it had
before them in the wilderness), dividing the waters (as before
Pharaoh's hosts), bringing light out of darkness and a people out of
the bare earth to be set in a garden to the east. At the same time, the
language of salvation, in Old Testament and New, makes clear that
redemption is a fulfillment of life, not an escape from it. Salvation
and revelation are not found apart from the very structures of creation. Nor is any moment of creation remote from the redemptive
actions of God.

Such perspective is judgment on the minister who sees much of his
work, even though regretfully, as a kind of mechanical preparation,
creating forms, constituency or programs, for the redeeming word
that is to follow. Foundation-laying is no less an occasion for building
the Kingdom than is placing the keystone. The moments of develop-

ing order out of chaos, form out of disparity, vigor out of lethargy are in and of themselves as valid occasions for saving ministry as the occasions for which these may seem only preliminary.

Such perspective is judgment also on the critic who sees the church exercising saving ministry only as it abandons and escapes the living patterns of its existence. For it is in working *in*, not *out of* (*with*, not *against*) the actualities of life—perverted and distorted though they are—that transformation comes. God is far more likely than not to be working within the events of history, however unlikely they may seem in and of themselves. Events, however isolated or even however demonic they may seem, are still the living stuff out of which God fashions His purposes. But this Christian affirmation is much easier to apply to the remote than to the intimate events of history. It is easier to attribute meaning and importance to distant matters than to the personally involving. If there is anything harder than seeing the thundering Assyrian armies as God's instrument, it is recognizing occasions of His purposes in the petty tactics by which one organizes and supplies one's own army.

Indeed, it may be especially in the bleakest—not the exalted—moments of our created existence that a saving comes. If this apocalyptic truth is relevant, the church's own crisis of irrelevance may be especially welcome as the locus in which God's word for this irrelevant and lost generation may be heard. If anything is less likely than that God's word may be spoken and heard in a middle-class congregation, it is that this word may be spoken and heard among those who have contrived to escape from the crisis of contemporary middle-class complacence.

Perhaps it is the response of a Bonhoeffer or a Frankl to his concentration camp experiences that is the epitome of what is suggested here for the lesser evils and frustrations of a parish ministry. This book suggests that the proper response to failures and to obstacles is neither to curse them nor to evade them, but rather to ask their meaning, to learn the redemptive possibilities disclosed in them.

In the world in which only God is sovereign, not even an ordained minister can presume to schedule the means by which God's will is to be heard and expressed. The very profession of the minister is to respond to his calling responsibly and to plan, carefully, intelligently, and responsibly, the ways in which he will endeavor to carry on his ministry effectively. But it is also part of his Christian faith to remain open to the creative, redemptive richness of God and to recognize that the thwarting of one's own carefully arranged plans may well be the occasion for still greater ministry.

THEME OF THE BOOK:
OBSTACLES AS OCCASIONS FOR MINISTRY

The discussion of irrelevance is only to illustrate and to introduce the more general argument of this book. The preceding has not been intended primarily as a pep talk to churchmen to stay at their task or as a *tu quoque* slap at the church's critics. A more fundamental and radical tool of analysis has been intended. If "irrelevance" seems to plague a minister and to frustrate his ministry, this irrelevance may be the very occasion and vehicle for exercising precisely the form and goals of ministry he found frustrating. So it has been argued. But this book makes bold to argue the more general point: *Whatever the internal obstacle to the purposes of the church and its ministry, this obstacle presents precisely the occasion for a realization of those purposes.* Obstacles do not arise accidentally, capriciously, or meaninglessly. They are evoked out of the interaction between purposes and the stuff of human experiences to which the purposes apply. The obstacle discloses, therefore, precisely the dynamic and fruitful point of interaction between the purposes and the "objects" of the purposes. Like the enigmatic bottle, which is half empty but also half full, a cover conceals, but also reveals the contours it drapes. Particular purposes and objectives of the ministry evoke resistances and obstruction which are not random but specifically pertinent to them.

If a budget committee insists on getting bogged down in trivial procedural issues, avoiding the larger issues of stewardship; if a congregation insists on "enjoying" the sermon and picking up irrelevant tangents of illustration; or if they adore the christening gown of the baby to the disregard of any meaning of the sacrament of baptism; if a fifth-grade boy in church school refuses to sit still to listen to the lesson; if the layman insists on treating the minister with a deferential attitude complete with 10 per cent discount and suppression of dirty stories, denying his own conception of his calling and involvement in the affairs of the world—all these situations are obstacles and frustration to the true ministry of the gospel. But they are also the "acting out" in immediately accessible situations of the very conditions to which the minister would speak.

Such obstacles are not merely evidence of a general "sinfulness," requiring a blanket denunciation and a general summons to renewed fidelity to the church and its gospel. They are not merely instrumental problems, requiring instrumental and administrative solutions—rearranging situations, recruiting, organizing, training people more effectively. They are not deliberate attacks or frustrations for the sake of attack or frustration, requiring angry counterattack. Rather, they are occasions of specific response by particular persons to particular presentations of the church's message, mission, and ministry. They are meaningful events, disclosing to those with eyes to see how that portion of message, mission, or ministry is having impact on these particular persons, and inviting further ministry.

All of life is continuous, and the sins and needs demonstrated within the structures of the church life are likely to be the very ones that are prominent in all life and to which the minister is attempting to address himself. It is just that within the church life they loom so large and are so personally frustrating for the minister that he often cannot recognize them as opportunities for ministry, but only as obstructions.

If means and ends cannot be arbitrarily separated, neither can obstacles and ends. Any objective finds means consistently and intrinsically related with it. So does any objective find its obstacles intrinsically related with it. Procedural problems disclose, and often become the agency for solving, substantive issues.

This is true in legislative bodies in which major issues of policy are often fought and settled in terms of such procedural questions as arranging the agenda, seating delegates, referring to committee, or settling the tangle of procedural motions which nearly smother the main motion. The seemingly irrelevant and intrusive "point of order, Mr. Chairman" or "I move to amend the amendment" becomes— usually by intent, sometimes not—the occasion for addressing and determining the main issue. Amateurs in political matters may be amazed or amused at the lumbering, tortuous machinery of parliamentary procedure which, to them, seems only to be unnecessarily delaying a decisive vote on the real question. And they are correspondingly startled or suspicious when the "decisive vote on the real question," finally reached, proceeds quickly and perfunctorily, the outcome of the issue, of course, having long since been settled in the "obstructive" parliamentary machinery. (It is ironic that persons who understand this process in political matters with sophistication and even admiration are sometimes the most impatient—like the amateurs—with the "preliminary" machinery of church life, which seems to them to defer and impede coming to grips with "real" issues in the church's mission.)

In the writing of books, like this one, the providing of illustrations, like this one, may seem to the author a cumbersome compromise with readers' requirements and an unwelcome intrusion into his otherwise smooth, consecutive flow of thought. Or "illustrations" may become the occasion by which the author discovers and makes clear to himself what he is trying to say. So, it is proposed here, it may be with the purposes of the church and its ministry, that the seeming obstacles to these purposes may be—not in disguise, but in stark actuality—the occasions for realizing these purposes.

Another analogy may be helpful. History is sometimes written as having turned on accidental events. For example, Theodore H. White [2] sees the presidential campaign of 1960 turning on the first television debate between Nixon and Kennedy. In turn, he sees the outcome of this debate as dependent on what many persons might regard as accidental irrelevancies: the complexion and composure of the two candidates, their respective debating "styles," the ways they had chosen to spend the day before the debate (Nixon in rest and seclusion, and Kennedy in an intense "tutorial skull session"). Surely,

[2] *The Making of the President, 1960* (New York: Atheneum Publishers, 1961).

it might be contended, such personal and essentially trivial differences between the two men should not determine the outcome of a national election, which should be decided on the basis of the major issues of policy that are at stake. But one needs to reflect carefully on just how irrelevant these "personal" characteristics actually are to the "real" issues in the choice of leadership. White's analysis makes clear that Kennedy's style of preparation and delivery, which in turn made possible his composure, was based on concern for communication with the national audience, on meticulous attention to detail and data, and on exhaustive analysis of how best to exploit the present occasion. Further, White makes clear that Nixon's unhealthy appearance and complexion was a consequence of decisions he had made earlier, often against strong advice and with "his instinct as solitary leader," on how to invest his campaigning time. Such differences between the men in style of operation and decision-making, which emerged in the debates as relatively superficial "image" differences, are more than casually relevant to abilities of national leadership and to the direction of policy. The superficialities to which the television audience allegedly responded were trustworthy and perhaps unconsciously perceived "symptoms" of more fundamental matters.

"Image" may refer to reflection or representation in intense miniature, as through a lens, and in this sense the "image" cast in a television debate, as incidental or accidental as it first seems, may nevertheless be a meaningful and faithful clue to the "reality" lying behind it. Response to the "image" may in truth be a legitimate and informed response to the realities that have projected it. Within the life of the church, too, that which seems trivial and that which seems obstructive—the minister so often finds these in the same event—may often turn out to be a meaningful concrete "image" of the major realities to which he would address himself.

The analogy of resistance in psychotherapy

This book finds its theme suggested principally by a clue within the theory and practice of psychotherapy: the problem of identification and use of "resistance." To each encounter with a patient the psychotherapist comes loaded with interpretations, expectations, and plans. Whatever his school of therapy, he has notions about what is wrong with the patient and about what he and the patient must do as a remedy. These are born out of his training and general experience with patients, and also out of any past associations with this particular patient. But despite his expert wisdom and rapport with the patient, in any particular session of therapy the psychotherapist is likely to find his interpretations rebuffed and, even more significantly, the very procedures of healing blocked and hindered. The patient, in his objective, stubborn "otherness," answers back; the therapist and/or the patient thereby learns more about this patient and about the procedures necessary for his healing. Chapter II will consider this problem in considerable detail as it appears in psychotherapy and counseling. The rest of the book will attempt to develop the implications for church and ministry.

It should be clear, however, that only as an analogy or a model is the experience and theory of therapy looked to. It is not contended here that the ministry of the church should be or is like therapy, that it should share either the same goals or the same procedures as therapy. It is simply proposed that the general pattern—healing purposes and talents first confronting, but then *using*, stubborn obstacles—suggests enough similarity to provide helpful insight for the church. The potential help is greater because these dynamics have been studied with some care in psychotherapy.

This is hardly the first time that aspects of counseling or psychotherapy have been advanced as models for the church. This is not surprising, since whatever the differences, there are obvious similarities. Both are concerned with transformations of persons at deep levels of their existence, within the context of trusting personal relationships. Even closer parallels between the natures of the two transformations have been drawn, and are probably warranted.

But virtually all discussions of the nature and purposes of the church that have tried to draw from experiences of psychotherapy have drawn on a single dimension of the experience, one emphasized by a single school of contemporary American psychotherapists. This focus has been on the therapeutic benefits of the context of "acceptance" provided by the therapist or the counselor. This has been developed almost to the point of cliché: the therapist provides a permissive, threat-free atmosphere in which the patient feels unconditional, highly regarding acceptance of himself as a person. In this context, he gradually is able to drop the defensive modes of reaction and thought which have developed in response to nonacceptance in the past and which have become the symptoms and impediments in his life. The therapist provides this acceptance, and so should the church for similar reasons. Such an insight is important and valid. Chapter III of this book is, in a sense, another presentation of this point of view, and all that is said in the book presupposes that some such relationship exists in therapy and in the church.

But acceptance is only one ingredient of psychotherapy. It is assumed as essential by Freudian psychoanalysts and by most other schools. It has been elevated by Carl Rogers and his school of therapy to a prime position, which has had a major impact on American pastoral psychology. But in the emphasis on acceptance, other elements of psychotherapy have been neglected. What happens when the therapist is proficient and sensitive, when therapist and patient have established rapport and trust, yet things still do not go right? It is then that the psychoanalytically oriented therapist looks to such "resistance" by the patient, first, for the important and purposive (though unconscious) meaning it may have for him and, second, for occasion to exploit this resistance for the healing purposes of the therapy. This book proposes that such unwelcome and unprovoked resistance in the church may be similar enough that the minister may learn from the therapist how to understand it and how to exploit it for the purposes of church and ministry.

The identification and use of resistance has no place within Rogers' system; if anything, its occurrence is taken as a rebuke to the therapist, as evidence of mistakes on his part. Interestingly enough, this is also the way resistance is understood by the minister. With his emphasis on the importance of defective *inter*personal relations as origins for difficulty and of the trusting *inter*personal relations in therapy as occasion for healing, Rogers has been less aware of *intra*personal conflicts. He has slighted the possibility that these may erupt as resistance in therapy because of the difficulties that have brought the patient to therapy and quite beyond the influence of the therapist and his "acceptance" of the patient. Yet the disagreement between analytic and Rogerian views may be more apparent than real. The coping with resistance, which is a central ingredient within the Freudian tradition of psychotherapy, may also be understood within a Rogerian framework. It extends the "acceptance" of the patient even to the impediments the patient places before his therapist. These are not to be denied or rebuked any more than the disruptions that occur outside of therapy and which he only reports to the therapist.

Other analogies

Although the central theme of this book takes its clue primarily from the arena of psychotherapy, other analogies also come to mind. One of these is from the arena of marriage, where increased realism and deromanticizing have made us aware that more of the intimacy and the sharing of the marriage relationship is achieved in the acknowledgment than in the denial of the frustrations within the marriage. Dissensions and frustrations, even between themselves, are an important part of the life which the couple has agreed to share. And even though such frustrations disrupt intimacy at a superficial level, their sharing enhances the bond of marriage at a more fundamental level. An example is the case of a couple who despaired of each other's company to the point of mutually insisting one year that they take separate, month-long vacations. In one sense, this is a symptom of a break and a breakdown in the relationship. On the other hand, the couple found this situation a new and useful occasion for sharing. If all they could agree on was to disagree, this was still agreement. If the only thing they shared was this degree of rupture, this was still something they shared. They found themselves joking about it, with each other and in the presence of friends. It became, in a sense, the badge of their identity as a couple. Certainly not as desirable a badge as some, but nevertheless a real mark of their identity: they were the couple who took separate, month-long vacations. And from this candid moment of sharing, perhaps the first in their marriage, others followed.

Dorothy Baruch points out in *Sex in Marriage* [3] that newly married couples, led on by our culture to overexpect fulfillment and intimacy from sex, usually find failure and disappointment in their early sexual experience. But this very experience of disappointment and failure—candidly shared—can become the occasion for richer intimacy and stronger bonds than they might have imagined could accrue from sexual "success."

Consider another analogy, this time from the history of science. Discoveries are often "stumbled on," as we like to say. But for every such discovery, how many potential discoveries are lost to those who kick and curse the obstacles they stumble over in their relentless pursuit of an objective? Picture Newton heaving away the apple which disturbed his mathematical ponderings. Most of us would have. How many people before, and even since, Sir Alexander Fleming would have cursed in disgust the mold that someone had negligently allowed to grow in the laboratory? How many young astonomers were rebuked for their consistent differences in reporting sightings—until these individual differences themselves were taken seriously, explanations were sought to account for them, and the science of psychology was born? How much Pavlov missed because he knew it only as an inconvenient laboratory procedural difficulty that his dogs had to be hungry before he could condition their salivation—and thereby missed insight into the role of internal motivation in the "conditioning" process.

The same thing is true in engineering problems, in which the theoretical issues of "pure" science may be discovered and settled in the course of "mere" engineering applications. A man who longs for the uncluttered, undistracted freedom to address some "basic" problems in his field may come to discover that, in attending to the cluttering, distracting, immediately demanding "practical" problems, he has in fact been working on the basic ones. The development of policy for a government, or any other institution, may be aided by

[3] Dorothy Baruch and Hyman Miller, *Sex in Marriage: New Understandings* (New York: Harper & Row, 1962).

leisurely reflection on fundamentals, but it may be still more decisively and trenchantly developed in the course of the pressing decisions which seem to impede the leisurely reflection.

Another analogy comes to mind from the realm of child development. For the child, the points of growth are the points of difficulty. It is at the points of frustrating and conflict-filled encounter that he discovers how things are in his world and determines how he can best respond and develop his own identity. The frustrating stresses of life not only motivate but guide the development of his own personality. The prototypical model emphasized in theoretical discussion of "ego" psychology is the point of the first major frustration of life, when the breast or bottle is denied while the infant is still hungry and wants to suck. This is the point at which he may begin to discover himself as a discrete identity. So long as the nipple is invariably there to match his needs, his sensation must be that he himself is continuous with it. The frustration imposes a sensation of his own particular uniqueness, and the beginnings of personality development.

Then there is the old joke about the cub reporter who was assigned to cover a bridge-opening ceremony but complained to his editor that he couldn't get a story because the bridge collapsed. When sights are so narrowly trained on one means of reaching a goal, the larger event fulfilling the same goal may loom only as frustration. This book proposes that we try tracing back from the frustration to discern the larger fulfillment.

Different ways to view obstacles

When a minister finds goals frustrated—as when his people seem stubbornly unable or unwilling to live out their common life in the faithful mission to which they have been called—he may respond variously. (1) He may be most aware of the distance the people are from the goal, and he may regard this distance as one to be denounced in despair or as a gap to be closed by scolding, instructing, administrative maneuvering, or any other means. Perhaps this view is most prominent among theological students, their professors, the authors of their textbooks, newly ordained ministers, and former ministers. (2) He may be most aware and grateful that the people have traveled some distance toward the goal. If they don't understand stewardship or practice mission as they ought to, one still needs to recognize and celebrate as much understanding and faithfulness as they do show in their own way. Maybe the goals need to be redefined and reinterpreted more "realistically." Perhaps this view is most prominent among veteran ministers. (3) This book suggests a view that takes the distance from the goal seriously—so seriously as to regard it as potentially meaningful. The gap may not be a void to be filled by instruction and maneuvering. The gap itself may be a dynamic and meaningful engagement with the goal.

If people are not at the goal, this third view asks the question "Why not?" It does not rule out the possibility that the first, prophetic view above may be right: the people have not been sufficiently goaded or guided to the goal. It does not rule out the possibility of the second, conservative view: the goal has been stated unrealistically for these people. But it considers, as a plausible hypothesis to be explored in any instance, the possibility that the people are already perceptive of the goal and responsive to it—resistively. There may be engagement and involvement between people and goals, maybe even intense involvement, not immediately visible, but discernible. It happens to be an involvement that puts, even pushes, the people some distance from the goal. But from this resistive posture, one may read its meaning, the engagement the people do have with the goals, the forces that keep them at a distance. We now turn to a more thorough consideration of meaning in resistance.

THE "MEANING" OF RESISTIVE REACTIONS

The kind of meaning and occasion for ministry that is here claimed for obstructive reactions can perhaps be clarified by a type of more formal analysis, complete with diagram. Any event, including obstructions in church life, is the product of three distinguishable influences. The "meaning" of the event, insofar as it can be looked for in orgins, may be found in any one or in all three. The three may contribute in varying degrees to any particular event. The "meaning" of one event may be found largely in one of these components, that of another event in another component.

Labeling these three influences is precarious, and the present purpose is not so much to insist on the precise and clear definition of each of the components as to insist on the distinction among them, a distinction which we believe can be recognized even when the three general areas of influences are only approximately defined. We shall refer to this distinction throughout the following chapters.

1. There are, first, and sometimes overlooked in "psychological" discussions, the *situational*, objective, external, environmental, realistic influences or sources for the event—the top line in the diagram

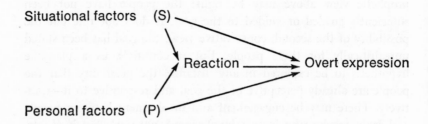

Situational factors   (S)

Reaction ——→ Overt expression

Personal factors   (P)

seen here. For example, the rambling, seemingly irrelevant meandering of a Bible study group or the Board of Deacons may, in part, reflect a number of objective factors. The material for the discussion may have been presented unclearly. (What is "objective" for one person's behavior may in turn be the consequence of "subjective" factors in another person's.) The material for discussion may be so complex as to require wide-ranging consideration from many points of view; rapid conclusion, though desirable for the sake of efficiency or a "successful" meeting, might be quite unrealistic to the actual material at hand. The material presented for discussion may be, in fact, irrelevant or otherwise unsuited for the persons asked to discuss it: their response is the most adaptive and realistic possible under the circumstances; they act lost because they are lost. Such a relation between the objective situation and the responsive event is essentially independent of the particular persons involved. Presumably any more or less normal persons with the same general background and experience would respond in approximately the same way to the objective situation. To the degree that the event or behavior is the consequence of this objective situation, nothing personal or idiosyncratic is revealed about the persons who are involved. It is appropriate to read the "meaning" of the event in terms of what it says about the objective situation that has provoked it. This is the kind of "meaning" assumed when people recommend situational solutions to problems, such as better agenda, more preparation, different personnel, bigger budgets.

2. Any event is also the consequence, to some degree, of the relatively persistent characteristics of the person or group producing the behavior—the bottom line in the diagram. They are simply "that kind of person" or have these "habits" or those "traits." They are people beset by particular aspirations or fears or "problems." These *personal* predispositions would more or less similarly affect their behavior in any situation; their influence on the events is not limited to the particular stimulus situation. It is appropriate to read the "meaning" of their response in terms, so far as this component is concerned, of the personal characteristics of the individuals or groups involved. This is the kind of "meaning" assumed, for example, when a minister looks for pastoral needs as they may be uncovered by administrative contacts, or attends to political realities within a church, or deals with the prejudices of particular persons or groups. The point is as simple as discovering what people are like by observing their behavior across a variety of situations.

Thus, for example, the meandering of the discusson group or the deacons' meeting may reflect their unreadiness, in intellectual ability or experience with disciplined discussion, to engage in the kind of discussion proposed. It may reflect their individual preoccupation with personal concerns, which intrude and dominate a discussion without regard for the announced topic, or without regard for the concerns expressed by others. It may reflect something about the interpersonal relations within the group: for example, a tendency for one person to ignore rebelliously the remarks of another; or the condescending way one (perhaps a husband) tries to explain or explain away the contribution of another (perhaps his wife). It may reflect a general mistrust of the minister or a reluctance to participate in the church. (This borders on the third component to be discussed below, but it is included here because it is a more general, persistent characteristic, independent of the particular situation and particular purposes immediately at hand.)

3. Any event is also the result of the *reaction* of a particular person or group to a particular situation—the middle of the diagram. The first two components are both extremely important, and it would be a foolish minister who did not attempt to try to reflect on episodes, especially troubling and frustrating episodes, to learn what "meaning" may be there, in either of these senses, which could enlighten and guide his future ministry. But this book is not concerned essentially with either of these components. It is concerned with the third type of meaning, the interaction of the first two.

Any event, of course, is likely to contain all three of these "meanings," to be a consequence of all kinds of influences. To be able to discern a meaning in one sense easily is not a reason for searching or for not searching for a meaning in one of the other two senses. On the other hand, in some instances neither the objective nor the purely personal meaning may be compellingly obvious. These may be the situations in which the third component needs to be given special consideration. To the degree that an event or an episode or behavior cannot be thoroughly or convincingly "explained" as an appropriate response to the objective circumstances (top line), or as simply an expression of the persistent personality characteristics of the persons (bottom line), this is the point at which we especially look at that component which consists of the interaction (middle line) of the circumstantial and the personal in a particular situation.

The expression which an event gives of a particular person's or group's *reaction* to a particular situation is both more intense and more subtle than either of the other two components, which are the "direct" expression of situational or personal factors. It is more intense because there is here, in relatively narrow focus, the imprint of how this particular situation impinges on these particular persons;

or how they, with their own individual backgrounds and personal concerns, perceive, receive, and respond to the objective stimulus. This is obviously the point of intense and intimate relevance for the heart of the ministry; how the word, in the particular fashion that it is being communicated through this minister, this congregation, and this institutional church (top line) is perceived and responded to by these particular persons (bottom line) in this particular time and place. What has been heard? What has been missed? What needs to be said and done next?

The reaction is more subtle and obscured because its expression is blunted and disguised by the fact that it takes place internally (center of diagram) and is expressed in overt behavior only indirectly (right of diagram).[4] We distinguish here two types of "behavior," one implicit and unobservable, but nevertheless quite real; the other explicit and visible. When confronted by a religious stimulus, a person does have a distinct reaction, as for example, a guilty pang, and the reaction does issue in some kind of overt event, for example, sudden, rapid speech. But the reaction itself is internal and usually not expressed directly; and the overt event, which the reaction prompts, may not permit easy inference as to what the reaction was.

The *behavioral expression* of the reaction is restricted by many factors. One is the ability and the experience of the persons in expressing themselves. Few of us have well-developed repertories of words and actions for communicating directly and accurately the reactions within us which may be most important to us, our fundamental fears and hopes, disappointments and self-doubts and aspirations, our sense of our relation to God and to other people. Perhaps just to ·the degree that a reaction touches central and important chords of life, its expression is obscured by this poverty of articulation.

Expression is also restricted by various socializing and inhibiting influences which affect the social acceptability of expressions, again

---

[4] The author is here indebted to John Dollard and Neal E. Miller's analysis of cue-producing responses in *Personality and Psychotherapy* (New York: McGraw-Hill Book Co., 1950).

putting severe restriction on direct expression of many of the most intimate and important reactions persons may experience. In other words, for most of the crucially important reactions of our lives, our culture neither provides nor even permits the means of direct expression. The intensity seems to be too much to bear. These two factors may often be so strong that a reaction cannot find expression even in a person's private consciousness.

But most significantly for the purposes of this book is the limitation to expression that is imposed by the limited "raw materials" of any particular situation. A "guilt pang" aroused during a committee meeting may be expressed within that meeting, but with behavior appropriate to the meeting and to the roles the persons have within it. These preclude direct, overt expression. In a committee meeting, people cannot suddenly start behaving as though they were in individual confessionals or even as though they were in a Bible study group. They must still use the procedures of the committee meeting and the intended topic of its business with which to express their reactions. A pastoral counseling session or a Bible study group would provide "raw materials" which might express the "guilt pang" more "naturally" and in a way more easily interpretable. To code or translate guilt feelings into the procedures and topic of the committee meeting may require more devious and obscure links, which make it difficult to decode and translate back in order to infer the guilt from the behavior. But the contention of this book is that people do regularly and consistently, even though unconsciously, accomplish such coding; and further, that there is ample "raw material" in any situation within the church, including business meetings, with which people can express their religious reactions. Just as any event in the church is potentially capable of eliciting an important and meaningful reaction relevant to the purposes of church and ministry, any event is capable of providing means for expressing that reaction.

RESISTANCE AND RESPONSE WITHIN ONE ROLE

Perhaps another kind of consideration, referring to the roles of a clergyman, will help to make clearer that the argument of the book is of an intrinsic and necessary relation between the frustration and the realization of any particular objective of church or ministry.

It is sometimes suggested that a minister should be alert to pastoral or teaching opportunities in the course of pursuing administrative affairs. Administrative phone calls or committee meetings, secondary and even frustrating as they may seem to the minister, may be important and even exclusive points of contact with people which make it possible for the minister to pursue the pastoral or teaching ministry that he regards as primary. Another common suggestion is for the minister to make use of the pastoral or administrative "interruptions" in his sermon preparation in order to provide insight or illustration for his sermon. Such suggestions are valid and important, but they are not the point being made here. Such recommendations are based primarily on the multiplicity of the minister's roles, relationships, and purposes. They emphasize that there are many fronts, and a battle lost is not the war lost. A setback or inconvenience in terms of one purpose may be the occasion for developing and serving another purpose. If one type of role or relationship cannot be pursued, another can. In terms of the diagram (see p. 26), the minister can shift from the top (S) line to the bottom (P) line.

In such instances the relationships between frustration and advance are accidental. There is no necessary or "meaningful" connection between the frustration and the opportunity, between S and P. For example, in the course of administrative phoning or committee meeting, the pastor *may* make contacts, build rapport, and learn something of personal pastoral needs which enable a subsequent counseling ministry. Or he *may* even introduce something like counseling into the course of the phoning or the meeting. But there is no particular connection between the original purpose of the phoning or the meeting and the subsequent counseling. The contact, knowledge, and rapport could as well come from any other association with the persons involved. From this point of view, the phoning and the meeting become something of an arbitrary pretext.

True, the relation between frustration of initial purposes and new opportunity for ministry may not always be accidental or arbitrary. For example, an administrative phone call may be required by the failure of a lay official to keep an assignment and the failure in turn may be the consequence of important personal or family pastoral needs, which the phone call reveals. But even this connection between the impediment and the opportunity is based on the multiplicity of relations between the minister and layman. Each has several roles in relation to the other, and upon the breakdown of one, each can shift to another.

What is proposed here is an application to a *single role or purpose*. It is suggested that the impediments encountered as a minister goes about a single role or purpose reveal the likely fruitful opportunities for achieving that purpose. All that is proposed here supposes that the minister and/or his congregation have specific purposes and objectives for particular situations. The more specific and clearly defined is such purpose, the more plausible and possible the kind of analysis and response proposed here becomes.

SOME EXAMPLES

Here are there brief examples of how the discernment and achievement of ministry can begin with the seeming obstacle of the moment. Additional examples appear in the final chapter, following more systematically there the pattern of analysis offered in the intervening chapters.

Budget Committee

One fall a minister asked a budget committee to defer the usual procedure of making allocations in budget estimates until after they had spent a session or two in serious, theological reflection on the nature and mission of the church. It was his purpose to start a pattern of making the official deliberations of the church more responsibly and more profoundly related to its theological bases. The members agreed, with apparent eagerness, and did in fact study in advance several materials the pastor supplied, including copies of two recent sermons in which he had tried to state his own position.

But the discussion session, on which the minister was counting so highly, became completely dominated for an hour by procedural and tangential conversation. Some members raised passing questions about the source and authority of some of the materials they had seen. Others made brief speeches endorsing highly the idea of the discussions—but not advancing them substantively. Another took off from the need for more money to begin a discussion of the strategy of educating and canvassing members, a topic on which others joined wholeheartedly. Another made a few discouraging speeches about the difficulty of educating the church members into their responsibilities. Another added a historical appendix to this speech, recounting the history of past attempts. This led to discussion about being more democratic and involving more church members in the budget decision as a strategy for educating them and enlisting their fuller support. This led to other and prolonged discussion about the procedures and how budget decisions are made. The minister, aided sometimes by the senior trustee, tried several times to direct the discussion to the agreed substantive questions. But each time, without any open resistance or objection, the discussion was immediately deflected and sidetracked.

To this not uncommon frustrating experience, several responses are possible. One minister might persist in the straightforward attempt to direct the discussion into more serious reflection. Another might feel the need to become more adept at discussion-leading procedures. Such solutions share the "dualistic" assumption that getting the discussion going is a prerequisite to an effective theological or religious experience for these leaders. The minister is prepared to discuss theological issues, but finds, as he feels it, that before he can do this he must spend much effort, time, and skill—which he may not feel that he has—just in getting a discussion going. He must get out and crank up before he can start driving. Such solutions regard the difficulty as having only "situational" meaning.

But there is another way of regarding this discrepancy between intent and execution. This is to ask whether there is not some significance in the discrepancy—in the very irrelevance—which is itself of primary importance, not merely of instrumental significance with reference to some other objectives. This meeting is where these persons' attempts to live lives as Christians in the church are now being made. Their attempts are *here in this committee meeting,* not in the better educational, social service, pastoral program, and evangelistic witness to the church and to the community about which they are supposed to be talking. If one is starting to learn to think theologically about important events in his life, why not start with the event at hand?

This particular minister not only asked himself about the significance of the present dilemma, but also asked the committee members to share this inquiry. He pointed out that they had embarked with some consensus on an enterprise that they had not been able to accomplish, and he expressed his curiosity—not his hostility—about this discrepancy. The committee members acknowledged the discrepancy and some reported that they, too, had felt subconsciously frustrated and had even begun to blame one another for getting bogged down. But now, with this commonly shared predicament open for discussion, they began to consider the problem more consciously and more carefully. Some confessed a sense of intellectual inadequacy, symbolized by, but not necessarily resulting from, their awareness of the minister's greater knowledge and expertise in theological affairs. One went so far as to relate this to the inadequacy he felt in prayer, the lack of "goodness enough" to approach holy things. These "confessions" were not directly dealt with by the minister or by other members; but in the telling they found a certain "acceptance" and were presumably cut down to realistic size. The committee members also acknowledged the greater ease and even security that they found in dealing with the relatively trivial and more familiar procedural questions. They confessed their greater inclination to take this easy path. It is not too far-fetched to suggest that they began to experience something of both the judgment and the grace of God on their immediate personal and shared life, as budget committee.

After such a session of theologically oriented self-reflection on their shared experience, they did not in their subsequent sessions turn much more easily or readily to the kind of general and over-all theological discussion which the minister had originally hoped for.

The minister did note, however, that they showed far more sensitivity and perceptiveness with respect to particular aspects of the church's educational and evangelistic and missionary program—exactly the kind of sensitivity which the minister had hoped to induce by the theological discussion. But instead it appeared to have come from a kind of experience—mild, to be sure—of personal faith, which they now wanted to share and express.

Sunday school

When Sunday school teachers find problems and want help or want out, they usually describe the difficulty as a "discipline" problem. They feel competent and prepared—sometimes very carefully prepared week by week—to teach the lesson, but before they can get to teaching they feel an almost insurmountable barrier to be crossed, the task of gaining decorum and attention. This is a separate task from that of teaching a Sunday school lesson, as they see it, related to the latter only in a kind of time sequence: attention must be gained before the lesson can be taught. The great distinctions they feel between the task of discipline and the task of teaching are betrayed in nothing so much as in the kind of help which they ask. Sometimes they want special training on the problems of discipline, separate from training on the problem of teaching. Sometimes they ask for another person, often a parent, to serve as a kind of policeman so that the teacher can teach.

Once I consented to conduct a special teacher-training session on "discipline," called as an emergency session in the middle of the year, well after the regular "teacher" training sessions in the fall. I began by leading a discussion on the goals of teaching. This seemed so remote from the problem of discipline that the minister shortly whispered to me a concerned reminder, fearing that I had confused the topic, and knowing how deeply troubled over discipline problems were some of his teachers. But I persisted in drawing the teachers out into stating their purposes in being teachers. They were able to state quite clearly a number of objectives in such terms as getting the children to understand the love and demands of God and their own responsibilities. They understood well the many helpful teaching aids and strategies suggested by their curriculum materials.

But as they talked, they discovered that the very dimensions of life (and God's sovereignty over it) which they wanted to talk about in the classroom as "teachers" were being actually acted out in the classroom in connection with "discipline problems." One teacher had been disheartened by having a carefully planned dramatization of the Prodigal Son disrupted by two boys who broke from the group and wrestled in the corner; she suddenly discovered—with an audible "aha"—that she had had a real-life "play within a play" right there in her room. Instead of having to stage the story in terms of remote and distant personalities and language, her class had actually staged the same parable for her. Or rather, they had given her the start for the story, but she had failed to follow through with her part. Now she said, "I hope they both come next week and act up again. I'll leave them in their 'alien land' and make life at 'home' attractive. When they repent—and they probably will if I leave them alone—I'll give them the job everybody always wants, marking my attendance for me. Then we'll have a ruckus from the good children. And then we'll have something to talk about that they will understand and remember for a long time, because it has been real." I do not know whether this teacher's plans for the next week worked out as she suddenly discovered they might. But I do know that *whatever* real-life parables her class may have presented her, she was more ready to discern and to help them discern the meaning within the actual experience which they shared.

"Playing it by ear" to hear the word within the immediate encounter is far more difficult than recruiting a policeman to stand guard while one recites carefully prepared words. But it is possibly an effective way for students and teachers to begin to learn to live their lives under God.

Stereotyped on a pedestal

One of the minister's major hurdles to being relevant is the stereotyping our culture provides for him in holding him high on the shelf away from the hurly-burly of real encounter. "Whenever I want to have a pleasant or an involving or serious conversation with a stranger, I try to avoid the subject of my vocation as long as possible," one minister writes, probably on behalf of most. "My laymen close up their liquor cabinets, hide their ashtrays, and switch from stories and shop talk when they invite me," reports another. This kind of emasculation, this kind of enforced 4-D exemption from all of life, may seem an insurmountable barrier to the minister who yearns to share in the vital, throbbing predicaments of life, with the feeling that he can shed some illumination on them.

There are several common ways of attacking this barrier so as to get on the "inside" as a participant, rather than be left outside as an observer. Some ministers are known to make a direct assault, parading drinks, stories, and locker-room conversation ostentatiously. Others may try a more plaintive plea for acceptance as "one of the boys." Some may take the occasion of every offered 10 per cent discount or every apology for profanity as the time for a sermon on the proper role of the minister. Some ministers make an earnest effort to understand the actual business dilemmas of their parishioners and make pastoral calls on the commuter trains or at the office. Most work hard to make their sermons "relevant" to the actual lives of their hearers, as well as they understand them. All such solutions betray the dualistic "one-two" strategy of attacking *first* the *obstacle* to pave the way for *later ministry*. The minister feels that he must first establish his role before he can function within this role to minister.

But is there not important meaning in this stereotyping itself which makes it immediately an occasion for understanding and for ministry, rather than simply an obstacle to be overcome before ministry can begin? Is the minister unique in being pigeonholed and taken as a stereotype? Or is this not the haunting predicament of most men in our automated, bureaucratized age? What disturbs salesmen, executives, and laborers more than being taken as cogs and interchangeable parts, rather than as the individuals they are? When the minister is stereotyped by his seat partner on the plane or by his parishioners in their living rooms, instead of being made irrelevant, he is being permitted or forced to share the very dilemma which makes his life relevant to theirs.

He can point this out, not as a challenge but as a matter of mutual interest and an object for reflection. "Actually I don't feel myself quite as you seem to see me, . . . but I'll bet you have that happen to you a lot too, don't you?" Here, unseen for being so close and perhaps for being so personally involving, is a point for very significant contact and interpretation and ministry. The minister doesn't have to work his way—by strategy and lecture and prolonged self-interpretation—into a position of relevancy. He is thrust into it by his own particular participation in life—if he can only recognize it.

The stereotyping may have still further meaning, intimately relevant to the individual's religious quest and to the minister's place in it. The distance which the minister feels in the stereotyping may be, in some sense and probably unconsciously, intended. Whether he likes it or not, the minister may represent for the stranger or for the parishioner a symbol of holiness or goodness or responsibility, which makes the other uncomfortable, and from which he wants to retreat. "Excuse me for swearing, Reverend" may be a modern and impoverished equivalent of "I heard the sound of thee in the garden, and I was afraid, because I was naked; and I hid myself" (Gen. 3:10) or "Master, I knew you to be a hard man . . . so I was afraid and I went and hid your talent in the ground; here you have what is yours" (Matt. 25:24 f.). The most immediate, intimate, and important fact of such a man's feeling of his status before God (a formless but familiar compound of guilts, doubts, fears, and angers) may be represented in just this reaction of putting himself at a distance from God's representative.

Why not use, then, the living text rather than go through the arduous task—recruit, enlist, educate, hold interest—necessary to bring this man before the written text? A minister might struggle through a lifetime of desperate attempts at relevance in preaching, teaching, and calling to gain access to such a man's soul and not come one-tenth as close as he inadvertently is in this distressing moment of being put off as irrelevant. If a muffled disclosure has been made in the usual defenses called forth by the immediacy of the personal encounter, the minister only need start with this encounter in order to follow the disclosure back through the defenses to come closer to its roots and meaning. "Actually I don't feel myself quite as you seem to see me. . . . I wonder why the difference?" This is no guaranteed formula for breaking through to intimate ministry. But it is the right starting point, because it recognizes the existing relationship to be as valid, sacred, propitious, and redeemed a moment for ministry as any more conventional and comfortable occasion into which a minister might conspire to convert the present moment.

SOME BASES OF RESISTANCE TO RESISTANCE

This introductory chapter will end with a coda, which proposes to take the chapter seriously enough to suggest that difficulties in accepting its viewpoint may themselves comprise a kind of resistance which can be profitably reflected upon. But if the pages which now follow are consistent in intent with the theme of the book, they are faithless in execution to much of the book's substance. The relation which exists between me and the reader does not permit us to explore his own understanding of the meaning of his reactions. It does not even permit us to consider his reactions, but only my suppositions as to what they are. Rather than showing respect for the reader and his reactions (which exploration of resistance ought to do), these pages may seem to confirm his worst suspicions about the aggressive and imperious use of psychologizing. Nevertheless I think the following reactions are common enough and important enough to be worth discussing, even with the limited conditions imposed by a writer-reader relationship.

Conflict is unwelcome and unaccustomed

We are not accustomed to finding positive meaning in disruption, but only to regard it as something to be overcome. From earliest childhood, we are persistently trained to deny, to shun, to undo conflict in any form. We are not trained to accept, to understand, or to use conflict. Peace and harmony become the norm as to what is acceptable and constructive, whether in the family, between nations, or in the church. When hostilities break out between children, or between nations, or when the ministry of the church runs into obstruction, then our first impulse is to attack the disturbance. "Stop fighting" or "stop fighting *me*," we insist, and we seem to imply that only a return to the state of harmony will make insight and progress possible. Hostilities between children as between nations have their causes and their meanings which cry out for recognition and attention, and so does disruption and obstruction within a church. But a minister facing resistance is understandably no more inclined to search out and address any meaning within it than is a harried parent confronting his quarreling children or a fearful world trying to keep down outbreaks of warfare. If we can just keep armies on their own side of the border, separate children into different rooms, eliminate the resistance among those laymen, then we can operate in manageably familiar and tranquil terms. And in so doing, we ignore the discovery and the opportunity potentially within disruption.

It seems curious that social commentators on the church who are most impatient with disruptive tensions within it are those who display a realistic acceptance of tensions within society. They know and admire the process by which social, political, and economic forces must clash and spark if they are to achieve a resolution. They urge the church's participation in just such give and take in the "world," and they properly find the church deficient when its clergy and members retreat from this turmoil into such haven as the suburbs allegedly provide. But for these same commentators the norm within the church would seem to be one of harmony and tranquility, without contending forces, some demonic, some faithful, competing for attention and allegiance.

A form of pride

It may betray a certain kind of narrowness and pride to regard a frustrating experience as frustrating, and it may require a humility to see it as having objective meaning apart from one's own frustration.

For frustration implies a reference and a criterion in the actor's own intentions. When a minister enters the pulpit, or a committee meeting, or a counseling session, or a study group, it is with certain general goals and commitments and with specific intentions for these particular circumstances. But he must wrestle—wrestle with ideas, with the moods, fears, and dreams of others, with the intentions of others, with all the stubborn realities of the circumstances he would engage —wrestle, if not for a blessing, at least for some hint of fulfillment of his intentions. When the sign of fulfillment fails, a minister may be most keenly conscious of his own intentions as the reference mark, and therefore feel frustrated, and regard these stubborn realities of the situation only in their role as frustrators of his intentions.

On the other hand, he may discover that when the situation "answers back," it needs to be heeded with respect, as a supplement, a corrective, and perhaps ultimately a completion of his intentions.

For the "stuff" with which a minister deals—people, ideas, ideals, institutions—is not passive and inert material, ready, like the potter's clay, to be shaped by the minister. This is true even though most discussions in seminaries and in ministerial-training literature seem to imply that all depends on the insights and skills of the minister. The purposes of God and the prospects of His service are continually being revealed to the minister and are never possessed by him. This "stuff" about which the minister develops and exercises intentions— the moods and motives, the whimsies and wiles of people, their dreams and dreads, their responsibilities and irresponsibilities, the structures and clashes of groups, their forms and formalisms, commitments and conceptions, ideas and ideals—this "stuff" is active, reactive, insistent, and sooner or later must have the last word.

For in all likelihood this "stuff" has also had the first word. The minister's general aims and his particular strategies have been found initially in encounter with this stubborn otherness of ideas and individuals and institutions. The present goals and intentions with which he now so strongly identifies have not always been his. He has acquired them from confronting people and situations in the past and from reflection on such confrontations. If he chooses to regard these experiences and reflections as "revelation" he must be prepared for still new revelation. New encounters are really only new stages in this never-ending process of forming goals and formulating strategies out of repeated exchange and encounter with this active "stuff." When this "stuff" answers back to our ventures and probing, it offers a positive message, a new instruction, a new basis for shaping, a message unlikely to be inconsistent with the objectives and intentions which we have formulated. The new message is most likely to be a fuller extension of what we have learned from past messages, a correction of partialness, an illumination of darkness, an opening of new possibilities. Attending to resistance requires no more and no less than a willingness to let reality "answer back."

But this willingness comes hard. When reality answers back to his intentions and strategies, the minister may, as the saying goes, "take it personally" as an assault on the plans in which he has invested so much of himself and therefore as a challenge to him as a person. Initially dependent for insight and guidance, one easily rises up to a kind of independence from which he would comprehend all, command all, tolerate no rebuff, accept no further instruction. From such an adolescence, only a few of us in only a few segments of our lives manage a more humble maturity. But such pride is necessarily and inevitably our lot. Men must formulate objectives, even in their partialness, and they must invest themselves in these formulations, or else they can never act or accept a responsible role. When new encounters do not produce frustration and clash, there is no occasion for novelty and correction, expansion and fulfillment.

Undue humility

On the other hand, if a form of pride and arrogance can make a minister fail to respect the meaning in the resistance he faces, so can a type of unwarranted humility and self-deprecation. To respect the resistance as important and meaningful is to assume that the ministry which provoked it is important and meaningful. This is not always easy for a minister, discouraged by this very resistance, to assume about his own work. It is to suppose that the church really is "in the world," that it is touching relevantly sensitive and central points of life, that it is taken seriously enough by people that they resist it, that its ministry is impinging with enough impact to provoke resistive re-action. It is to claim a greater seriousness and relevance for people's lives than a minister often feels justified in assuming his ministry has.

This book suggests, to take an extreme example, that when a congregation seems to show neglect and casualness toward the minister's words and the church's mission this may sometimes be more purposive and serious than it seems. The indifference or other resistance may be an unconscious attempt to blunt the minister's message, just because it is registering too well, too close for comfort. But to accept such a possibility may contradict a minister's own dis-couraged or humble self-image. Ministers often report a feeling of standing on the sidelines, of being out of touch with the vigorous centers of personal and social life, even when an objective appraisal of their work finds that this is not so. There may be at least three bases for such feelings.

1. Clergymen are subject to a number of social influences to make them feel "set aside" quite as much as "set apart." Folklore still commonly supposes a minister to be excluded from such human characteristics as concern for money, anger, sexual temptation, polit-ical opinions, family spats, etc.; society institutionalizes the exclusion in such forms as the 4-D draft deferments and the 10 per cent store discounts, and the inevitable rituals of alarm when a minister appears in a divorce court or a mental hospital. From his first announcement of his vocational plans as a boy, he has experienced such forms of social exclusion and isolation, both from adults and from his peers. It may also be true in some cases that a boy who feels "out of it" socially is attracted toward the ministry in part just because its role does seem to fit and confirm this image which he already has of himself. This degree of social isolation which the clergy role provides may be one reason that a minister has difficulty in accepting the hypothesis that his ministry may have more relevance and more impact than is most obviously apparent, and why he is so ready to accept—or to make—the popular accusation of the day that the church is irrelevant.

2. Another reason may be the inherent difficulty in the ministry of "seeing results." The nature of the vocation's purposes is such that

there is seldom clearly discernible evidence of achievement of purposes—unless a minister is driven, as some are, to counting attendance and budget to provide this sense of achievement. The effects of ministry, whether it is dealing with social forms or with individuals, tend to be subtle, long range, and measurable at best only by slight degrees of relative change. A clergyman may well envy most of the members of his congregation, both men and women, who can count the tangible fruits of their labors at the end of a day, or at the end of a decade. And he may accordingly have some reason to feel less vitally engaged with the realities of the world, and hence vulnerable to suspicions of irrelevance, futility, and impotence.

3. The clergy role also provides the temptation for the minister to feel unduly responsible personally for the program of the church and the success of its ministry. This, in turn, offers further difficulties in accepting the importance and impact of the church's ministry, as, for example, in provoking meaningful resistance. The minister who feels that his own admittedly puny efforts are responsible for carrying the enterprise along is more timid and less confident about acknowledging the importance of that enterprise than is a minister who feels the enterprise dependent on resources far exceeding his own.

It may be ironic that the "nonreligious" psychotherapist may display this latter kind of "faith" at least as readily as a minister. When the psychotherapist encounters a patient's resistance toward the enterprise of therapy, he has no difficulty in taking it seriously, because he does not take it personally. He is prepared to believe that very important emotions and attitudes in the patient's life may be evoked by relatively trivial events within the therapy situation. But he can believe this because he also knows that the structures and conditions of psychotherapy which are more or less intended to provoke just such critical emotions are not of his making (see Chap. II); and he knows that the patient's responses to therapy—both resistive and healing—disclose dynamic inner resources of power and richness beyond his own making, even beyond his own ken. If a therapist felt that all reactions to therapy were reactions to his own doings, he would, of course, be as paralyzed as some ministers, unable to regard these immediate reactions as vital, important, and central.

Resistance in Psychotherapy

A person must be strongly motivated before he becomes willing and able to suffer the stigma, expense, inconvenience, anguish, and labor that are the cost of being a patient in psychotherapy. Before he will endure the prolonged torment of psychotherapy, he must feel strong motivations—usually compounded of his own painful sense of disruption in his life at certain crucial points, the sometimes prodding, sometimes pleading wishes of other persons important to him, his sense of duty to these others, his desire to please them, his confidence or hope in the remedy that therapy can offer. Most people are unhappy with themselves to some degree and would like to be different. But one has to "hurt" a lot before he undertakes psychotherapy.

As part of his commitment to engage in psychotherapy, the patient makes many subsidiary commitments, which he understands are essential to successful therapy. He agrees to come regularly at appointed times to the consultation room, to speak candidly about emotionally significant matters, to reflect thoughtfully about them, and to work toward maturing changes in himself. The therapist, in turn, uses all his skills to provide a context and encouragement for the patient to accomplish these commitments.

Yet—despite the patient's strong motivation, despite his commit-

45

ment to carry on all that is necessary for his therapy, despite his obvious and demonstrated ability to do this, despite the therapist's skillful and earnest effort to help him, it typically happens that the patient appears to be sabotaging his own therapy. He is tardy for his appointed hour or he misses it altogether, without adequate excuse. He speaks guardedly, not freely, though he knows only candor can help him, and even after he has been made to feel free to speak. He occupies the hour with trivial talk or with silence. He shows remarkable and uncharacteristic stubbornness and stupidity in his inability to perceive or to understand significant things about himself. He suddenly becomes fuzzy or sluggish in his accounts, after having shown an ability to be lucid and concise. He shows every sign of having—along with motives to pursue therapy successfully, to get well, and to change—motives to avoid the requirements of therapy and perhaps even to avoid change in himself.

"The neurotic patient is in conflict, impelled to approach certain goals but yet afraid to do so, urged to act on impulse but yet unable to act. . . . Thus the patient partly cooperates, perhaps one should say *mostly* cooperates but also he partly resists." [1]

This chapter is about such *resistance*. It is about the behavior that blocks and impedes the process of psychotherapy despite the patient's earnest motives to do well and despite the best therapeutic environment. It is about the way in which the therapist—and the patient—consider and respond to such resistance. It is about the process by which resistance becomes not a frustration of therapeutic goals, but the very instrument by which therapy most effectively works. "The core of the therapeutic process consists in overcoming the resistance." [2]

Ambivalence toward important goals is not unique to psychotherapy. Nor is the experience of self-deceiving maneuvers. It should not seem strange to those familiar with Christian theology that there lie within a person persistent and stubborn forces working to contra-

---

[1] John Dollard and B. F. Auld, Jr., *Scoring Human Motives* (New Haven: Yale University Press, 1959), p. 140.

[2] P. M. Symonds, *Dynamics of Psychotherapy* (New York: Grune and Stratton, 1957), p. 306.

dict his own, recognized best interest. Nor will parish ministers be surprised to hear that people resist being helped, that carefully arranged plans and schedules sometimes break down. What is unique in psychotherapy—but also, this book suggests, a possible pattern for churches and ministers occasionally to venture—is the therapeutic exploitation of these obstructions when they appear.

RESISTANCE IN PSYCHOTHERAPY

Blocks to progress

Consider a typical situation from the point of view of a counselor or therapist.[3] He has committed himself, years of training, and his career to the task of helping people to "solve their problems" and to develop into more mature, responsible, and happy persons. He is approached by a troubled person who is able to identify, in some degree, the nature of his distress and the direction in which he would like to change. He wishes to become a client of the counselor's (or a patient of the therapist's). After some preliminary conversation and mutual inquiry, they make, in effect, a bargain. Sometimes this is more explicit than other times, but it is nevertheless a firm agreement. They have a common goal, the remedy of the client's distress and his maturing development, and they agree to work as partners toward this end. The client agrees to meet with the counselor regularly and to work at the task of reviewing freely and appraising thoughtfully the relevant elements of his life, his thoughts, and his feelings. (He may also agree to pay fees, to accept medication or hospitalization, to join some particular outside groups, or to refrain from medication or outside social entanglements; to share the topics considered during counseling with important persons at home, or to refrain from such sharing, etc.) For his part of the contract, the counselor agrees to meet with the client, to give him unrestricted attention, and to exercise his talents and skills to the best of his wisdom and ability. Depending somewhat on his particular training and theoretical commitment, the therapist may exercise his skills in

[3] These two terms are used interchangeably throughout, as are "client" and "patient."

different ways. He may emphasize the provision of a receptive, permissive, accepting, threat-free atmosphere for the counselee; or insightful attention and interpretation of dynamically relevant portions of the patient's thoughts and feelings; or other skills and strategies he believes will aid the client to reach his goals.

After such a covenant is made, the work proceeds and likely makes some noticeable progress toward release of the clients's distress or other objectives. But at some point before long, progress stops. The client does not continue to improve. He may even have a relapse or develop more serious difficulties. Instead of doing his agreed-on work, he may ask the counselor to take on more work, such as by insisting that the counselor provide advice or analysis. He may spend his time scolding the counselor. He may grossly and baldly misperceive the counselor's gestures of acceptance, such as by interpreting silence as evidence of ill-will or laziness. Instead of talking freely about the significant things in his life, he may speak about the weather, or about trivial details of his daily life, or about someone else's feelings, or about the counselor's feelings. He may discuss something he has read or heard. He may report what someone else, another counselor or his wife, has told him about his feelings. He may enter into intellectual discussions about the theories of therapy or of symptoms. He may bring in carefully rehearsed and prepared reports about himself, rather than permitting spontaneous and free recount. He may stubbornly refuse to see or may disagree with some of the most obvious reflections which the counselor makes about him—reflections that any neutral observer would agree are only restatements of what the client himself has said.

The frustrating problems may seem even more procedural and irrelevant to the main course of counseling when they involve the trivia of administrative matters. The client may have problems about the fee or about meeting at the appropriate times. He may occupy much time and energy in explaining why the particular hour was inconvenient and in trying to arrange a more suitable appointment time. The client, in short, abandons the type of behavior which can—as he has already seen—accomplish his professed objectives. The counselor cannot honestly perceive any way in which he has failed to live up to his part of the contract, or any way in which he is responsible for the client's defecting. He has worked conscientiously and sensitively.

In such a circumstance the natural and understandable feeling of a counselor is chagrin and frustration, perhaps mingled with anger and guilt. The client is not doing his work. Here is a *procedural* problem relating to his behavior in therapy which must now be solved before work and progress can continue on the original *substantive* problem concerning his anxiety, relations with his wife, work habits, or whatever. This procedural problem might well seem to call for new and different, perhaps drastic, tactics by the counselor in contrast to those he uses when counseling is flowing along as it should. How can the client be put back on the track, doing his work so that counseling can proceed and the counselor can do the kind of work he has agreed and is trained to do? Communicating acceptance and making interpretive analysis are fine when counseling is proceeding, but how can counseling be begun again, so that these strategies can be used? Must one scold, cajole, instruct, tease?

No great effort is needed at this point to draw the parallel between the plight of such a counselor and the common plight of the clergyman. In the foregoing paragraphs, "minister" may be read for "counselor." The minister, too, has committed himself to certain goals and has entered into implicit contract with others, the congregation, who share the goals and who agree to make certain efforts, even sacrifices, in a reciprocal and cooperative role with the minister. The minister, too, often has good reason to feel that his partners in the contract are failing, even obstructing, him and their common goal. The minister has reason to feel that this presents a new type of procedural, sometimes trivially administrative, problem, which has to be solved before he and his partners can get back to their true task of working at the real ultimate goal.

Resistance viewed simply as another symptom

An alternative understanding of such resistance is available. This would see such obstruction by the client not as reason for the coun-

selor's guilt, not as trivial, incidental, or irrelevant to the main purpose, not as occasion for a different strategy by the counselor, certainly not as occasion for scolding or rebuking or manipulating the
client to get him back on the track. Rather, the fact of the resistance,
and its particular form, is seen as intimately and dynamically related
to the underlying "problems" of the client and to the purposes of the
therapy. The patient has problems in being a "good patient" precisely for the same reasons that he has problems in being an effective
husband, or executive, or whatever. He finds it as difficult and as
conflictful to realize his own purposes and ideals and commitments in
therapy as in these other areas. The particular difficulties which have
plagued and disrupted his life to the point of causing him to seek or
to accept therapy continue just as disruptive and conflict-laden as he
tries to address himself to therapy. To be able to understand and
interpret the resistance in therapy is to understand and interpret
something of the basic "problem." To remedy the resistance is to
remedy an instance of the basic "problem." Above all, then, the
counselor's response to the resistance is not different from his response to any other instance of the client's disturbance and distress.

It should not surprise a psychologically sensitive counselor to find
that a client's behavior in therapy is disrupted, inefficient, and beset
with ambivalence and conflict, any more than it should surprise a
clergyman to find "sinners" in his church. If a person could ideally
adopt the role of a patient, effectively, maturely, and adaptably
without getting in his own way, without frustrating his and others'
objectives, he wouldn't need to be a patient. If the patient could
face, without flinching or defense, the feelings and facts of his life
which provoke resistance in therapy, then he could handle these outside of therapy and wouldn't be there. Elements of his life which are
not problematic and conflictful and disruptive outside of therapy are
not likely to be so within therapy. "The client's resistances are the
main reason for giving him therapeutic help." [4]

Is not something like this also true of the church? Whether we
view people from a theological or a psychological perspective, there is
an important sense in which we can say that they are in the church

---

[4] Symonds, op. cit., p. 306.

because they "need" to be, or perhaps more accurately, because they know they need to be. If in their lives without the church, difficulties, contradictions, estrangements, and conflicts are not disturbing or prominent, persons are not so likely to be within the church, where the same difficulties, contradictions, estrangements, and conflicts persist. This is true even if one has a more cynical understanding of the basis for some church participation and is aware of such motives as pleasing one's wife or mother, or establishing oneself in the community. Such motives, in enough intensity to produce vigorous church participation, may themselves represent stresses and conflicts which are likely to emerge in church life.

Rather than fought as frustrating, these instances of disruption may be welcomed by the therapist or counselor. They are welcomed as immediate and intimate instances of the problems and therefore as most easily accessible for examination and remedy. Why search in memories for problems to analyze when there is a rich, three-dimensional instance right at hand? Whatever particular strategy and attitudes the counselor may be committed to as a way of coping with a client's difficulties, these can be employed no less effectively, and probably more so, on instances of resistance than on recalled, "second-hand" experiences. If identification and reflection and acceptance are a major strategy, they can be used with resistance. If interpretation and analysis are employed, they too can be used with resistance.

"Each patient from the beginning shows what may be called his baseline of resistances. These are defenses determined by the patient's psychological past. The long-range aim of therapy is to gradually overcome some of these initial obstacles, while the short-range aim is to modify whatever increases take place from the baseline as therapy progresses, i.e., intercurrent resistances." [5]

Difficulties in exploring resistance

At least three related problems may handicap a counselor's (or a minister's) constructive use of resistance, but none of these is neces-

[5] Kenneth M. Colby, *Primer for Psychotherapists* (New York: Random House, 1951), p. 96.

sary or insurmountable. First, it is sometimes difficult simply to identify the resistive behavior for what it is. It is too close, too immediate to see in objective perspective. The patient's sudden chattering, sudden silence, or sudden change in topic is too pressing, too demanding of some immediate response from the therapist. Up close and on the spot, as the therapist is, closely following and responding to the patient, it is harder to keep the "third ear" tuned to the meanings of what goes on than it is in the leisure of afterthought and reflection. It may seem just like so much chattering or silence or a new topic, rather than like a piece of behavior of some important significance to the therapy.

Second, it is difficult to recognize that the resistive behavior, even when correctly appraised as resistance, can be dynamically relevant to the major themes of therapy. The patient has come to therapy with a particular set of problems, perhaps his relations with his wife. He and the therapist may have begun to suppose that these problems are related to other themes, perhaps his difficulty in "accepting himself," perhaps his early relations with his mother, or perhaps something else. But it is difficult to see that there may be any connection ·between these and the patient's outbreak of discussion about the trivial events of the afternoon or about some abstract theory of therapy. In principle, the therapist may accept as theoretically likely that all of the patient's behavior—resistive chattering about trivia as well as substantive accounts of emotional reactions to important events—is dynamically related. But the principle is hard to adhere to when the prospective relation is obscure. He may believe theoretically that all events in therapy, though separated on the surface, are actually outcroppings from the same iceberg. But when one abruptly bumps into trees, it is particularly difficult to discern any pattern they may have as part of the larger forest; it is even harder to suppose that these trees, just because they seem to block the way, may carry special clues to the paths and boundaries of the whole forest. It is more tempting to swing an ax, if possible, to remove them.

As an analogy for this difficulty, the reader is invited to ask himself whether he was not distracted by the above juxtaposition of two figures of speech, the iceberg and the forest. Mixed metaphors are disconcerting for their superficial dissimilarity. As readily clear as their meaning may otherwise be, it is obscured when the reader's mind is asked to jump, as in this case from ocean to woodland. Even as familiar as these two figures are, to the point of cliché, and even as similar as are their points (immediate appearance vs. basic reality) the superficial differences may still be disturbing; readers are likely to be more aware of these superficial differences than of underlying communality.[6]

The minister has similar difficulty in perceiving or even in supposing any significant or functional relation between the major themes and purposes of the church and any particular forms of resistance which he may encounter in the life of the congregation. In the general and abstract way presented above, it is easy to accept the interpretation that disruptive resistance in the church testifies to the sinfulness of persons, or their "need," or their alienation, or some such general formulation. So can the therapist similarly accept the notion that resistive behavior in therapy is evidence of the general illness of the patient. But it is far more difficult for the minister or therapist to see the more specific relevance between the particular form and occasion of resistance and the particular goals or purposes or problems to which he wishes to address himself. It is relatively easy, though not always so, to accept the relevance of resistance in principle. It is excruciatingly difficult to discern the relevance in any particular instance, in which the resistive behavior strikes one as so obviously meaningless, so frustratingly irrelevant, so purely disruptive.

The third potential difficulty in responding to resistance enhances the first two. This is based on the fact that the therapist, or the minister, himself is involved. It is partly his partnership and his task which is being disrupted, his goals which are being frustrated. To the degree that he feels involved, it is more difficult for him to see the resistive behavior fully in terms of its dynamic significance in the life of the client.

But these three "resistances" to the use of resistance themselves

---

[6] The reader is also invited, as an analogy for the therapeutic power of insight, to reread the troublesome paragraph on icebergs and trees to see whether the present attention to the "problem" does not help him to dissipate or "solve" it.

need to be seen in the same light that we suggest any immediate problem requires. They do not justify special or novel attention, but ought to be seen as wholly representative of the total counseling transaction. If a counselor has difficulty, in connection with resistance, in perceiving the central dynamic element of the counselee's experience, or if he has difficulty in keeping his own feelings from intruding, these problems probably arise more generally in counseling. They ought to be looked at, and one might as well start in connection with his response to resistance.

A case example: Miss N

Perhaps an example will be useful to illustrate the general characteristics of resistance and its potential handling in counseling. Following this section, we shall consider in more theoretical detail, and with another case, how resistances may represent significant characteristics or "problems" in the counselee's life.

This example will be taken from the second hour of counseling with a young woman who sought counseling because of the generally unsatisfactory and unsatisfying character of her relations with men. She can't seem to keep the friendship of men whom she likes. This counselee was particularly insightful and articulate so that this episode of resistance was compressed and can be presented here in a brief account. With another client, essentially the same interaction might be extended over a longer conversation.

At one point, Miss N, normally articulate and fluent, interrupts an account of relations with her former boyfriend to tell of a recent occasion on which she has written a note to the boy's mother, now terminally ill with cancer. The relevance of telling about the note is not clear. It is not connected with her declared "problem," relations with men, or with the immediate topic of the boyfriend. Therefore it seems a kind of intrusion or interruption to the progress of the counseling to that point, a digression from the problem to be discussed. Furthermore, her telling of the note is prolonged, wandering, repetitious, and boring. The account simply does not seem to have a point or a direction. She intersperses, in seemingly random fashion, remarks about the woman's personality, the content of the note, the woman's medical history, the circumstances of the note's writing, the woman's attitude toward death, her own attitude toward death, and other miscellaneous associations to this incident.

The counselor feels slightly irritated by this interruption in what has been a dynamically promising line of counseling, and especially by the prolonged array of trivia and the boring, inarticulate way that it is presented. His first inclination is to shut off the story abruptly, pointing out that it seems an irrelevant interruption, and to urge the client to get back to the important and promising discussion of the relations with the boyfriend; that, after all, is what she wanted counseling about.

USE OF FORM AND CONTENT OF RESISTANCE. He suppresses these inclinations and instead raises the question, both in his own mind and for the client, about the likely meaning of the client's telling of this incident in this way. He points out first that her behavior seems uncharacteristic and something of a "problem."

Counselor: You sure are beating around the bush on this one. What's going on?

He makes his remark in a way which presupposes and preserves the fairly congenial and warm relation they had established. He does this primarily by making her behavior a matter of puzzle and curiosity, an attitude they can share; any form of mild rebuke or criticism would have put them on opposite sides. Her response accepts it as a problem and a mystery.

Counselee: Yeah, I can't seem to find the handle of what I want to say. I don't know. . . .

The counselor replies by more explicitly setting the problem as he sees it. (This was in the second hour of counseling. In a later hour, this would have been unnecessary. The woman would have become accustomed to raising the question clearly and explicitly for herself, once the counselor had called attention to the behavior.)

Counselor: I was wondering why you have so much trouble telling me now about writing a note to Mrs. Hagan.

The counselor pointedly uses "me" and "now" to remind both of them that the question is not with respect just to the isolated account of the note, but that the account has a particular context which may be crucial to understanding the puzzling, resistive behavior. The "trouble" she's having may have something to do with the immediate situation she is in—namely, the conversation with the counselor. The client's reply acknowledges this. It also indicates that she has been feeling a certain subjective mood in the course of the account which she had no occasion to mention before the counselor's intervention, but now has no difficulty reporting.

Counselee: I guess I'm afraid my halo is showing.

She is embarrassed over having launched an account in which she presents herself as a particularly gracious, thoughtful, and even courageous person for writing a note under such circumstances. Her difficulties in speaking, in "finding the handle," are an attempt to disguise and blunt what seems to her as undue self-glorification. This is now a theme of potential dynamic significance. It is one of a half dozen possibilities the counselor vaguely had in his own mind when he first called attention to the resistance. But questions still remain as to the significance of such "embarrassment" for this young woman. It is worth discussing more. The counselor can indicate his interest in a general way and thereby invite her to continue. One way is for the counselor to reflect his understanding (as this paragraph just has) of what the counselee has said. This counselor chooses to do this but also to go on with a more direct question.

Counselor: Are you afraid it will dazzle me or you?
Counselee: You, I guess. I'm afraid it may look like I'm trying to impress you.
Counselor: Is that bad?
Counselee: Yes, I always push myself too soon and too fast.

The discussion continued about her fear of being too forward, especially in relations with men. This proved eventually related to a number of themes of important significance in this woman's personality and her difficulties. These included her feelings of unworthiness, especially her fear of inadequacy in connection with men (against which she was compensating by "pushing," but which she was also expressing by inhibiting the pushing), her past and present relations with her mother, whose own dominating manner she feared to imitate (a factor, of course, not unconnected with her own self-misgivings). All these were behind her irritating rambling and were discovered by following the clue which the rambling provided that something was "up." The rambling did, after all, have a psychological meaning immediately and directly relevant to her original problem of relations with men. By more clearly understanding something about this rambling in therapy, she more clearly understood something about the problem which brought her to therapy. Further, beyond understanding, by "working through" and reducing the fears which prompted the rambling, she dissipated a bit some of the fears which disrupted her relations with men.

USE OF FACT AND CONTENT OF RESISTANCE. The above exchange followed one aspect of the resistance, the rambling and the difficulty in speaking. What about the other aspect, the fact that the story of the note had interrupted an account of relations with the boyfriend and had, in fact, changed the topic from the original topic of counseling? A question about this could have been raised in the same way in which the counselor mentioned the rambling. But by now the counselor was more aware of the probable connection, between the conflict over "pushing" herself and the relation with the boyfriend. So he did not raise the question of the interruption in quite the open-ended, general way that he had first handled the rambling.

Counselor: Does this have something to do with why you broke off telling me about Steve?

This startled her at first. But yes, there had been an incident in which she felt she had been much too forward with Steve. In fact, it seemed crucial in breaking off the relation with him. She still felt considerable anxiety or guilt over her behavior then, even in telling about it now. The account of her relations with Steve had been moving toward this episode. But she had broken off recounting such an anxiety-provoking theme—only to illustrate it in her actual in-therapy behavior!

In summary, Miss N thus felt ambivalence over "forwardness," strong inclinations to be assertive, plus strong anxiety over such assertiveness. That this characteristic shows up in her actions in the live context of the counseling relationship, rather than as a report of an experience elsewhere, has a number of interrelated advantages. (1) It happened. With the anxiety she apparently felt about this characteristic, it might have taken her some time to disclose this verbally. The censors in the service of anxiety apparently operate more efficiently against thoughts than against behaviors. (2) It provided a focus and a specification. As counselor and counselee discussed the varied aspects of her misgivings about "pushing," both referred repeatedly to the actual episode and relationship which started this conversation. It forced a precision of insight not other-wise possible. (3) It provided a shared experience for future refer-ence. Material in later hours of therapy, where relevant, was related back to this episode and gained a certain immediacy and vividness. It also provided a kind of private vocabulary and set of convenient symbols. In the future in their shared private language, "Mrs. Hagan's note" meant "anxiety and inhibition over assertiveness." (4) It allowed for actual remedy. Thus exposed and discussed without punishing consequences, some of these exaggerated or unwarranted fears could be partially dispelled and extinguished. For example, it proved with the counselor not such a disastrous event to "push" or even talk about "pushing" as she had come to fear, based on her experience with her mother and certain boyfriends. The most imme-diate effectiveness was that after the reassuring "live" encounter, she was able to discuss the earlier episode of "forwardness" with the boyfriend which she had ten minutes earlier found too anxiety-provoking to mention. (5) This therapeutic benefit, modifying fears and apprehensions, in connection with an actual experience, offers much more favorable prospect of generalizing to life and experience outside therapy than if it had all happened in connection with second-hand verbalization.

Resistance in "administrative" relations

Another episode at the end of this same counseling hour grew out of "merely" administrative "trivia." The question came up of the time for the next appointment.

Counselor: Would three o'clock next Wednesday be all right?

Counselee: No, I'm supposed to meet with my YWCA group then. Oh! I could miss that.

Counselor: That's not necessary. Is three o'clock Thursday all right?

Counselee: Yes, that is okay. But I can skip the Y meeting on Wednesday, if that is better for you.

Counselor: That's not necessary—unless you feel some urgency about not delaying until Thursday.

Counselee: Since you suggested Wednesday first, that must be more convenient for you, so. . . .

Such a frustrating impasse is enough to make a counselor (or minister) long for the chance to stay at his counseling (or ministering) and to delegate the "administrative" affairs to a good secretary. But, alas, "administrative" affairs are not so easily separated from counseling (or ministering)—especially when they are frustrations and impediments.

In this case, the counselee is apparently again demonstrating her exaggerated fear of imposing herself on the counselor—and perhaps any man, or any person—and demonstrating the troublesome inefficiency and "problem" which this causes in her personal affairs. (As was eventually made clear, the exaggerated apprehension and inhibition of making even legitimate claims for herself—such as by accepting an appointment time freely offered her—grew out of her own unconscious recognition of the strong wishes she had to make severe demands. She had to lean over backward to protect herself against her impulses at this point. This was enhanced by the counselor's slightly passive role intended, as a matter of general policy, to make clear that the continuation of the counseling was the client's responsibility.) Such implications of this scheduling difficulty might have been discussed to therapeutic advantage, as in the previous episode.

However, one other important consideration occurred to the counselor. The time reserved for this counseling interview was virtually at an end. This type of "acting out" behavior could be understood—especially in the case of such an alert young woman who had just experienced the previous interpretation of resistance—as an unconscious bid for more attention. It could be interpreted as throwing the counselor the kind of bait which it is known he is attracted to; if anything is likely to make the counselor run over the appointed time, it is to produce a sample of this kind of behavior. Since it had begun to appear to the counselor that an important basis for her own fear of being too "pushy" and destructively dominating was her past success and her witness of her mother's success, the counselor was especially cautious about giving her one more reinforcement. He needed to be especially careful not to make her feel she could "destroy" his own integrity (by extending the agreed-on limits of time).

The counselor, therefore, resolved to use this episode for therapeutic benefit, by letting her realize that her own dominating impulses (expressed by the implicit bid for extra time) were not as universally or powerfully destructive as she may have unconsciously feared. He responded to her own "acting out" by "counteracting." He chose, at this time, not to turn the episode to therapeutic advantage by discussing it. Nor was it put down as the first item on the agenda for the next meeting. (It *was* recalled in a later session when the client began to recount a similar kind of episode with another person.)

Such an episode, based on "administrative" affairs which may at first seem outside counseling, may have peculiarly important value. Just because the events may seem outside the peculiar relationship of counseling, they may seem more "real." Just because the counselor and counselee have shared a real, "worldly" business encounter outside the special and perhaps artificial relationship of counseling, the episode may have an especially intense and demanding and representative nature and also become a good basis for generalization from counseling back into "real life."

A concluding reassurance

This may be a good time to try to make clear a reassuring qualification. It is not expected that the clergyman would exhibit the same intuitive insight into unconscious psychological meaning—even in his role as pastoral counselor—that is claimed for the counselor here. Nor is it expected that the typical church member is motivated or prepared to engage in the same kind of candid psychological introspection as described here. It is not expected that encounters in the context of the church necessarily result in therapylike self-confrontations. Therapy is discussed in this chapter only to provide a basis or model for the more general point—that apparent obstructions to a goal may turn out to be the best means for reaching that goal. If one of the goals, as in counseling, is candid self-understanding, then apparently resistive impediments to the goal may become the very vehicles for enhancing that self-understanding. If the objectives of ministry and church are formulated differently, then, it is suggested here, the apparent procedural obstacles to those goals may turn out to be the best bases for accomplishing those goals. Therapy and counseling are presented here as an initial model because they present one arena in which the general point of using resistances has been studied with some care.

(The reader may also recognize, however, that for me to include the above "reassuring" and explanatory paragraph may be inconsistent with the theme of this book. The point of that paragraph has already been made previously. The last paragraph implies that I believe that the reader may be saying to himself something like, "That's fine for the psychologist with all his intuition and training and for the bright girl who wants this kind of psychological interpretation and is good at it, but that's not me and my situation." If so, then this response should be identified as a kind of resistance and dealt with accordingly, not sloughed over with another reassuring explanation.

But if it is precarious enough to try to *identify* such remote and collective resistance among readers, the *interpretation* of such resistance would seem utterly foolhardy. There are so many possibilities. It could reflect self-despair. It could reflect irritation at the irrelevance of the presumptuous professorial authority. It could reflect a certain apprehension or antagonism about the aggressive intrusion or imperialism of psychological inquiry. The reader, if he feels so inclined, is invited to inquire for himself. The only point of the present remarks is to acknowledge that the preceding paragraph seems to contradict the theme of the book. But the contradiction is not an abandonment of the principle. It is simply a recognition that the conditions necessary for its implementation including, among other things, a minimum of acquaintance and trust (see Chap. III) are not necessarily achieved in the relationship of the writing and reading of books.)

THERAPY IS IN THE WORLD

It is a common misconception, sometimes even held by patients and by therapists (just as such a misconception is sometimes held of the church), that therapy is a retreat, a neutral situation aloof from the ebb and flow of "real life," a quiet, pleasant haven where one can go and relax while he *talks about* real life. There *are* some important, indeed crucial, differences between therapy and "real life." These are summarized in Chapter III. But there is no exemption from the stresses, fears, hopes, pressures, and the give and take of interpersonal relations. The therapeutic transaction is nothing if it is not a genuine "slice of life."

In fact, therapy is more than this. It is a concentrated portion of life. Based on an intense and consistent interpersonal relationship, with many of the common defense solutions distilled away, it becomes a crystal-clear focus for the client of his own conduct in life, especially in relation to important other persons, and especially in the face of a commitment to pursue an arduous task. The way in which therapy brings to focus and magnification characteristic personality and behavior patterns is one of the important reasons that therapy can offer effective remedy. A client can discover things about his reactions and can try out and practice new reactions before he has to take them into other arenas.

But the therapy situation is structured so as to do more than elicit representative and significant patterns of behavior. It makes impediments and blocks particularly likely. Intended to enhance eventually the effective functioning of the person, therapy is designed also to bring out his worst functioning. The many ways the client inadvertently disrupts relationships, gets in his own way and others', frustrates or sabotages his own goals, all the many ways his personal functioning is a "problem" for himself and for others—these are especially likely to be aroused by the conditions of therapy.

It was earlier pointed out that one who becomes a patient in therapy is likely to bring with him disruptive patterns and conflicts that may interfere with his attempts to be a patient, just as they have interfered with his attempts to fill other roles. We have said that the *patient is the same person* in therapy as out—perhaps "more so." Here we are calling attention to the conditions of therapy that are particularly likely to elicit disruptive patterns. Whatever his secret hopes for a haven and refuge, the patient finds that *therapy is just like life*—perhaps "more so." Whatever incapacitating and self-defeating ambivalences and conflicts he may have, they are likely to insinuate themselves into and be evoked by the particular conditions of therapy.

TWO REAL-LIFE INGREDIENTS. Psychotherapy reproduces in magnified miniature the two ingredients which make life both rich and problematic: (1) interpersonal relations to be developed, and (2) tasks to be completed. It is an intense and demanding interpersonal relationship which is defined and developed largely at the patient's own choice and pace. What happens in the relationship is all up to him. The patient assumes responsibility for a difficult and somewhat unfamiliar task, the continuing, thoughtful, and candid discussion of intimate and personal affairs. Again, the success of completing this task is left up to him.

These—*developing personal relationships* and *tackling tasks*—are two general arenas of life in which people, all people, in therapy or not, make trouble for themselves, arenas in which they fall short of their own aspirations because of problems within themselves. The more important, involving, intimate, and intense the relationship or the task, the more keenly aroused are our ambivalences. The persons and the projects which matter most to us, just because they matter and because they are most familiar, most evoke our reservations and antagonisms. This tends to be true, we suggest, for everyone, but for some more painfully than for others. Among those whose internal conflicts and antagonisms are particularly defeating of their own aspirations, some find their way to therapy. (They or others like them may also find their way to church.) Here is another person and another goal toward which they feel commitment and positive motivation. If not, they would not be there. Toward the therapist they feel some attraction, a desire to like and to be liked, to develop a close relationship. Toward the labor and goals of therapy they feel a strong determination to be successful. But the person and the task also evoke the large repertory of hesitations, antagonisms, apprehensions which the patient has come to feel about major figures and events in his life. His reaction to the therapist and to therapy is ambiguous, mixing the earnest with the resistive. The person and the task are novel, but they provide the patterns and structure for the familiar disruptions with which the person is beset.

In the closer scrutiny which the last half of this chapter gives to an instance of resistance and its relation with the "real life" behavior of the patient, emphasis will be upon reactions to the task of the therapy, rather than on reactions to the therapist. This is primarily for reasons of simplicity. Reactions to the therapist may range, in their ambivalence, along so many dimensions—love, anger, fear, dependence, rebellion, and many more—that they are difficult to discuss except with reference to specific cases. On the other hand, the reaction to the task of engaging in therapy, though it takes many individualized forms, tends to be along the single dimension of success vs. failure, commitment and effort vs. resistance. Something in general can be said about conflicted behavior along this single dimension. Another related reason for the focus is the greater likelihood of relevance for the church, where intense, though ambivalent commitment to a cause or task is more common than a demanding personal relation with the minister or a fellow member.[7]

PERMISSIVENESS ENHANCES DISRUPTIONS. Part of the focus provided by therapy on these ambivalences arises from the fact that all these demands are encountered in the context of a general support and personal assurance which preclude the patient's use of the most familiar and superficial defenses, such as simply avoiding the task. He finds himself involved to the point where the "reserve" defenses he keeps for more basic conflicts and resistances are invoked. Because the patient experiences more freedom to venture, he ventures right into the quicksand of his life, which he is cautious or fearful enough to avoid in less permissive situations.

RELATED TO THE WORLD IN TWO DIRECTIONS. The relations between disruptive reactions to therapy—resistances—and the "real-life" problems which they represent can be described as both centripetal and centrifugal.[8] Therapy brings to clear focus disruptive reaction patterns from a wide range of possible situations. Thus central and focused, they can be discerned and dealt with. But discernment and remedy generalize back from therapy centrifugally to a wide range of "real-life" situations. The fact that therapy is so intensely "in the world" is the basis for its being clue and key, the basis for discovery and precise diagnosis of difficulties and for healing and remedy.

LIKE THE CHURCH. The characterization of therapy here and in

[7] As anyone the least familiar with psychoanalytic writings will recognize, the term "transference" is frequently used to refer to phenomena here called "resistance." From Freud's earliest papers since, the two terms have been used somewhat interchangeably, with the distinction between them varyingly drawn by different writers. "Transference" has suffered even more than "resistance" from a multiplicity of definitions. Toward the end of Chapter III, we will take up some differences between the terms. Here it is appropriate to point out the tendency—and it is only a tendency, hardly a definitive distinction—for the following usages: "transference" refers to reactions generalized from past personal relations to the *person* of the therapist, especially those reactions which are negative and resistive; "resistance" refers to disruptive reactions to the *task* of therapy, especially as these are "transferred" from and representative of reactions to previous experiences.

[8] Roy Grinker, Helen MacGregor, Kate Selan, Annette Klein, Janet Kohrman, *Psychiatric Social Work: A Transactional Case Book* (New York: Basic Books, 1961).

Chapter III, that it is "in, but not of the world," is intended
deliberately to suggest a parallel with the situation of the Christian
church. Within the context of the church are brought to intense
focus precisely the kinds of crises and disruptions of personal and
interpersonal behavior which characterize life outside of the church
and in the world.[9] This is for many of the same reasons that apply to
therapy: the intensity of experience and relations, the concern with
intimate and charged personal concerns, the relative freedom which
precludes the more superficial defenses. Just as the redemptive work
of Christ presupposes His complete incarnation, so does the continuing redemptive work of his body in the church presuppose the
church's full-bodied participation in the impediments and disruptions
of the world.

A CASE EXAMPLE: MRS. A

This section continues that above and is an attempt to trace in some
psychodynamic detail the ways in which the resistances of therapy
represent precisely the critical conflicts and struggles which bring a
patient into therapy. The discussion is based on the transcript of a
portion of a single therapy hour. This case is chosen because so many
forms of resistance are concentrated within a single session and because enough else is known about this patient to be able to relate
these instances of resistance to the broader facts of her life.

Mrs. A was a young married woman with two small children. She
was seen in the psychiatric outpatient clinic of a city hospital. In the
first interview she presented an array of her difficulties. She described
general anxiety and fearfulness, and specific problems like reactions
to certain situations, such as taking her children on walks in the
neighborhood. She also described a great degree of compulsiveness in
her housekeeping. These general characteristics bothered her, but she
was coming to therapy primarily because of deteriorating relations
with her husband. Good rapport was established with the therapist,
and she showed both a strong motivation to overcome her difficulties

[9] The church, like therapy, also partakes of some important differences
from the world, which make it peculiarly effective in bringing about remedy.
These will be discussed in Chapter III.

and also an ability to talk about herself with some insight and understanding.

The transcript which follows is from the second hour, representing approximately the first twenty minutes and the last ten minutes of that hour. The intervening long recital of a stressful experience has been deleted.

The therapist began this hour in a relatively standard way for his school of therapy and this clinic. He asked the patient to add to the other commitments she had assumed in therapy an agreement to follow the rule of free association. After the therapist's initial instructions, the exchanges are numbered. Ellipses (. . .) represent pauses.

The transcript

Therapist: Last time I did a lot of the talking. I asked you a lot of questions, trying to get some information. From now on I may still ask a question occasionally, if there seems to be something I think I can help clear up. But the treatment for the most part will be asking you to say whatever comes into your mind. Now this may be a little bit different from what you are used to outside. I will be asking you, as you sit here, to say what comes to your mind, whatever it may be. If it seems to be something that somehow seems dirty or nasty or the sort of thing you wouldn't ordinarily say in other situations, I will still be asking you to say it here as it comes to your mind. Or if something comes to your mind about me which may be uncomplimentary, for example, or anything about me you might not tell me if you met me outside in a social situation, but I'm asking you to tell me if it comes to your mind in here. Do you think this is the kind of thing you can agree to?

1. *Mrs. A:* I can do my best.
    Therapist: Yes.
2. *Mrs. A:* You mean just when I'm sitting here just to mention anything that comes to my mind? . . . Just anything that pops in at all while I'm sitting here?
    Therapist: That's right.
3. *Mrs. A:* And I do most of the talking?

Therapist: Yes.

4.   *Mrs. A:* Do you want me to say now . . . ?

Therapist: Of course.

5.   *Mrs. A:* Well, right now I'm . . . I was real upset before I got here because the baby came down with an earache this afternoon and my husband was supposed to be at the house at three-thirty, so he . . . at three-thirty I couldn't get ready because the baby was fussing and crying and wanted me just to hold him . . . and uh . . . and I just couldn't get ready . . . and I'm the type that just has to be where I'm going on time; he's never there on time. And otherwise if I depend on myself I'm always on time, and to me that's something important, to be where I'm supposed to be on time. Well, he said he'd been watching the time at work and got involved in something, and when he looked it was twenty minutes of. So he came right up then. And so I was all upset when he got there because I couldn't see how he could possibly make it. And I wasn't sure, y'know, just how to get here from my house . . . I had a general idea, and find a parking place and everything . . . and I . . . it would take me much longer where if my husband just came and dropped me off, he'd know where he was going. And yet I didn't want him to do that because of the baby. So when he got there I was all upset . . . I said, just call him up and tell him I'm not coming, I'm just not coming. And so he says, no, he says, I'll wrap the baby up real warm and I'll drop you off, he says, it'll be much faster. So he dropped me off just now, but I insisted he could have gotten here a much faster way than he did, I mean just . . . the little petty things he does—everything seems to irritate me. My little boy had just come back from school and he was asking a lot of questions and I was hollering at him just because of the fact that I wasn't getting here on time. And, uh, then he couldn't find . . . he was going to turn down here and it was a one-way street and he had to go all the way around and . . . so that, right now, is what was on my mind when I walked in here (*laughs a little*).

But, uh . . . (*long pause*) . . . well, right now there's nothing more on my mind . . . but that, I guess I can't seem to get that off . . . I mean, once I think about something, but right now . . .

well, I just finished telling you . . . I mean, I can't think of anything else except what's on my mind immediately . . . what do I do now?

What is bothering me is uh . . . when I was standing outside, uh . . . is why am I coming over here and the others are coming over there to that place? I mean, when I got home I wondered why I wasn't going like the others were going but my husband didn't seem to think there was anything to it because they put . . . they do things differently, not to bother about it . . . but I just couldn't understand it. I just didn't know what to expect when I left here, and my husband asked me to ask you, and as for what was bothering me—bring it up. Well, uh, do they all come twice a week? Do they all come that often?

Therapist: I'm going to answer these questions in just a minute. You were wondering why you are coming here and not to the other place and you were wondering about twice a week, but first let me ask you what comes into your mind in connection with these questions.

6.   *Mrs. A:* Well, uh . . . I, uh, she said I would have to wait 'til summer, so just thought, well, that it wasn't anything too serious or anything. I figured, well, they'd put me in . . . maybe take them in order, more or less, that it might be crowded and that they would take the most serious cases first, so that was all right, that didn't bother me, so she called up and said to come the next week, well, then I was taken a little bit different from those others over there . . . and you asked me to come twice a week. And when I got out to the car, I was telling my husband on the way home that I know there's nothing seriously wrong, it's just some simple thing's the matter with me, and, well, why was I treated so differently and he didn't seem to think it was different, but y'know, it just preyed on my mind. . . . But I know there wasn't anything seriously wrong; if I'd thought I'd have been sure there wasn't anything really wrong. But if I wasn't sure of this I would have thought that there might have been something wrong. But I said it must have been some, y'know, other reason.

Therapist: Do you think all these things may be because we think there's something more serious. . . .

7.   *Mrs. A:* Well, I would, but I can't see how . . . um, well . . . I mean I would ordinarily but I don't think I'm that bad . . . I don't think there's anything seriously wrong. . . .

Therapist: Well, if that's the case, if you feel you aren't that bad, then why is it these things bother you?

8.   *Mrs. A:* Well, it's just the idea that . . . I'm coming . . . well, I don't know, I just think I'm not that bad, and I wondered why I was getting treated differently. . . .

Another thing that bothers me is what that couch is for. . . . Do you have to lay down there and talk? They said that down here you just talk, that they do it a different way than a private psychiatrist would. Private psychiatrists have you lie down on a couch and talk, I don't know what about, and so I was kind of at ease, and then I came in and that couch was over there . . . (*laughs a little*) . . .

Therapist: Well, we'll answer that in just a moment, but tell me a little bit more about what comes in your mind in connection with seeing that sofa—why does that make you uneasy?

9.   *Mrs. A:* Well, uh, what do they do when they make you lie down on the sofa, is it . . . uh . . . do you talk the same way as you do now? Or are you asleep, or what?

Therapist: Tell me more about what's on your mind—why do you ask these questions?

10.   *Mrs. A:* Well, it's just, uh . . . well, I was just wondering what they do do—how do they, uh, like talk to you . . . uh . . . is it all this way, or do they have another way of, uh . . . this whole, uh, this whole treatment is very interesting. I can't figure out how, uh, like a medical doctor and all that, it's much different and I can't figure out how they can, uh, how they can cure you. You probably don't know what I mean, but, uh, just by talking to you, I can't figure out how they can really cure you by just that, and I just wondered if this is just what they do do.

What time, uh, how long am I to be here? I mean, how long is the appointment?

Therapist: Fifty minutes as usual.

11.   *Mrs. A:* Fifteen minutes.

(*long pause*)

Therapist: I might mention, too, that twice a week is usual. It's the custom, at least for many of us. It sort of depends on the personal preference of the doctor. This is a common thing.

Now, I'm wondering whether you have been talking about these things for some reason. It's almost as though you came in here and I asked you to say whatever is on your mind, and then, uh, possibly there may have been certain things in the back of your mind which you preferred not to talk about, and so you've been asking me questions and making me talk about the methods and our procedure. This is a possibility—that you found it easier, instead of doing as I asked you, you found ways to make me do a lot more talking than I intended to. I'm just wondering about that—whether there is anything else in the back of your mind now that we should be talking about.

12.   *Mrs. A:* Well, uh, could I ask one thing? If there is anything in the back of my mind, is it impossible for me not to know about it or would I know? I mean, if there was something in the back of my mind, uh, is it, does it stick right out, or is it something maybe I won't be aware of?

Therapist: These are usually things you aren't aware of. But now what is this you are talking about?

13.   *Mrs. A:* What do you mean?

Therapist: It's almost as if you have something special in mind that you think may be in the back of your mind, as you say, that you want to talk about. So you keep finding ways to ask me questions and make me talk.

(*long pause*)

14.   *Mrs. A:* Well, uh . . . only I shouldn't ask a question (*little laugh*). When, uh, will I be coming again?

Therapist: Can we talk about that at the end of the hour?

15.   *Mrs. A:* Well, haven't I been here long enough? You said fifteen minutes.

Therapist: I said fifty.

16.   *Mrs. A:* Oh, fifty!

Therapist: Apparently you find it fairly uncomfortable here. This may be the way that I've been behaving, or it may be something else which makes you uncomfortable today.

17.   *Mrs. A:* Well, there is something else on my mind. (*Pauses and begins to cry.*) It's probably the whole thing.

Therapist: And it's hard to talk about.

18.   *Mrs. A:* (*crying*) Well, it's silly, because my husband . . . and I guess that's what matters. I can't see why I'm so . . . why it's so hard to talk about it. It's nothing that I'm hiding, y'know, at least from the main person that matters. No one else. . . . Well (*sobs*) my husband and I . . . is this normal to be . . . for someone to not want to tell you something? Well, I came down here with the attitude that I wasn't going to tell you . . . that I really know what . . . that I can't . . . that there's no point in coming . . . really that's all. . . all that I can think of is that . . . that's all that's on my mind because I know that's probably what you're trying to dig out. Well, anyway, my husband and I weren't getting along. . . .

(*Here followed a long account.*)

That's why I didn't want to tell you, because I'm so ashamed of myself and I even know that you're here to help me, but I never told anybody, and that's why it made it so hard . . . and now I've got it all off my chest. . . .

Therapist: I'm glad you did, because I think there's a lot we can do now.

19.   *Mrs. A:* Well, I know I wasn't getting any better, and the thing was . . . well, I came down here with the attitude I could hide that . . . and I just knew that when I sat down and you told me what I had to do that I just couldn't hide it. When you kept saying think of something, that automatically came because I was hiding that. And it automatically came to my mind. . . . It didn't take long, but I feel a lot better.

Therapist: Yes, I think we have a good basis for getting started, and seeing what we can . . . seeing if we can't. . . .

20.   *Mrs. A:* I'm not afraid to come here anymore. . . . That, on top of the earlier trouble I had, it's just, well, it's just more or less pulling me apart. And I really think that if I hadn't done something about it, that I was really headed for a breakdown, because I was feeling terrible.

Therapist: Well, there is a chance now. . . . I think that

you can think through some of these problems. There are still certain things which you have to think through for yourself.
21.   *Mrs. A:* Yes.
Therapist: And there's every chance that, I think you agree, too, that these things can be settled in your own mind and that you can come out of this.
22.   *Mrs. A:* Well, what do you mean? Without coming here?
Therapist: No, I didn't mean that.
23.   *Mrs. A:* You mean, with your help, too. With the help I get here. I know now that I can overcome it. At one time I thought I'd never get over it, but that was before I came down here. And even when just this past week I thought, well, I'm wasting my time and I'm wasting his time. I don't intend to tell him what really is the matter. . . . I'm too ashamed to. But I thought that he's not going to. . . . I just felt that there was that lapse in my story . . . there was a basic reason for my being upset and nervous earlier on and the only thing I could keep saying was that my husband and I weren't getting along. Now I guess I more or less got over that . . . well, I don't think I really got over it, but more or less got used to living with that earlier trouble and that I didn't get along with my mother and all that. I was just about getting over all that when this came up, and of course, well, this affected me twice as much as the other. . . .
      Well, I gotta admit that you're pretty good because you got it out of me all quick and nice and I never thought anybody would. You hit the nail right on the head when you said that I kept trying to think of things to ask you.
Therapist: Now I will answer your question about the next time. As I recall you said that you can't get a babysitter until three?
24.   *Mrs. A:* Well, no, my husband has decided that we won't get a babysitter anyway, because twice a week it's going to mount up. So he can easily take off work, especially if it's nearer this time, and it's much better for me . . . but, uh, is three a good time?
Therapist: On Thursday four o'clock is a good time, I think.

      Mrs. A shows amazing ingenuity in devising forms of resistance. In a third of an hour, she employs perhaps a dozen strategems to avoid filling the role of the patient as she had accepted it. As she indicates at the end of the hour, the conflict was peculiarly intense because partly conscious. But the same devices of resistance are shown by persons even without any conscious awareness of the conflicts they feel or how they are meeting them. In contrast to the cooperative, fluent, intelligent, and insightful person she showed herself to be in the first hour, and again at the end of this second hour, she showed herself, in the interval, remarkably stubborn and stupid, irrelevant, and rambling. She is, for twenty minutes, a failure at, for her, the crucial task of being a therapy patient, and she is agonizingly aware that she is a failure despite her strong and genuine motivations to be a successful patient. Conflicts, impulses, and defenses have surged up, in spite of herself, to get in her own way. That these are the same conflicts, defenses, and impulses which have surged and disrupted her life to the point of bringing her to therapy we shall show later.

The analysis of Mrs. A's resistance will be at three levels: First a descriptive summary; second, as careful an analysis as possible of the "dynamics" of the resistance, in the light of all available information about Mrs. A (i.e., why she resisted, how this resistance was related with the rest of her life); and third, an account of how the therapist viewed and handled the resistance.

The appearance of the resistance

Mrs. A's first response to the free association rule, after consenting to it at 1, is to show at 2, 3, and 4 an uncharacteristic kind of stupidity and naïveté coupled with a dutiful obedience. She repeatedly asks for clarification of the instructions and for a confirmation of her own understanding of them. She would seem to be trying hard to fill her role, but she is trying too hard. As was clear from her behavior before and after this period of resistance, this is definitely resistance, evoked by we don't know yet what disrupting emotions. She is not "really" this stupid or dutiful.

Her next effort, through most of 5, is a long, rambling recital of the events and feelings immediately preceding this therapy hour. In being diffuse and without clear point, it is again uncharacteristic of this woman's normal behavior. This also makes it partake of the mode of innocence and what is here called a degree of stupidity. It also shares the tenor of dutiful obedience in that she can claim—as she in fact does, toward the end of this recital—that she has told everything presently on her mind. The laugh accompanying this claim betrays her own, probably unconscious recognition of its hollowness. Indeed, she has touched on real problems in her life—she hasn't invented them—but not the seriously disrupting problems for which she sought therapy and which now occasion the resistance.

In the second paragraph of speech 5, she asserts more explicitly her claim that she wants to and is cooperating to the best of her ability; it is just that she is helpless.

At the end of speech 5, she adopts another common pattern of resistance. She discusses the administrative details of the therapy. As in her previous resistances (and in all resistances) there is, of course, some basis for the remarks. People don't invent materials for resistance; they use materials which the situation of therapy provides. There are certain facts of interest, and she does have some feelings about them, even mildly upsetting feelings. She has some apprehensions that the recommended frequency of therapy represents a serious diagnosis, and some apprehensions about the use of the couch. But these, though real, appear to be mild and incidental concerns. As she indicates in quoting her husband and in response to the therapist's inquiry, she is not seriously worried or fearful or upset by these things. It tends to be a façade discussion, substituting for and distracting from discussion of more genuinely troubling feelings. This is still offered in the guise of helplessness, but also introduces a mild assaultive mood. She is very mildly challenging the therapist.

It may also be seen, in the subsequent speeches, as a bit manipulative. She has, perhaps catching her second wind, chosen a topic more clearly likely to attract the therapist's interest. In this she was apparently successful in part. The therapist will at least make some effort to check out the nature and degree of concern which lies behind the discussion, in order to establish to their common satisfaction that this discussion is primarily in the service of resistance, and not a basic anxiety. She continues this discussion of the arrangements through speech 11.

By the end of 10, her challenge to the therapist, although still couched in the guise of helpless feminine innocence, is much more overt. Her lure—presumably trying to extend this discussion by mildly baiting the therapist—is partly successful. He does, after her speech 11, retort with a mild assertion of his competence and author-ity. But he does not permit the discussion to be extended.

Her misunderstanding at 11, although it is not caught by the therapist until 15, is compelling evidence that she has lapsed into uncharacteristic but defensive ignorance. In the preceding hour and in discussion with the admitting staff she was fully informed of the usual length of therapy. This was part of the discussion of fees. Anyhow, anyone with the curiosity and the knowledge she has already evidenced concerning psychiatric procedures knows full well that the "fifty-minute hour" is customary in therapy.

After the therapist intervenes to call her attention to the resistance, she is apparently driven in a kind of desperation to persist at 12 on the problem itself.

At 13 she adopts an almost desperate pose of helplessness—perhaps more obvious from listening to the tape than from reading the tran-script. Her pleading this time is successful insofar as the therapist does succumb to her temptation to adopt the helpful, masterful role and to explain to her, at some length, things she already well under-stands.

This apparently emboldens her to more aggressive wiles at 14 and 15. The therapist cuts off this line of retreat abruptly.

Instead of pointing out again that she is employing resistance, the therapist now ventures, at 16, to suggest an interpretation of one pos-sible basis for the resistance, some of the motivation which may be prompting it. He moves to what we shall call in Chapter V a "second level" of depth.

The resistance dissipates gradually at the beginning of 18 as she timidly and gingerly approaches the anxiety-provoking material, the telling of which she has been resisting so ingeniously and steadfastly.

The major portion of speech 18, which is deleted, is a long recital of a traumatic sexual experience.

From a more distant perspective, even this recital of the difficult sexual experience can be regarded as resistance or "cover story." [10] The sexual expisode itself was not so much a major precipitating cause of her difficulties as a symptom of them. Later in therapy, she discovered still "deeper" and fundamentally more anxiety-provoking bases. Relative to them, this sexual episode was easier to face and therefore could provide distraction and buffering from these still more severe stresses.

The meaning of resistance

Before commenting analytically on Mrs. A's resistance, it might be appropriate first of all to point out that the therapist experienced genuine frustration in her resistance and a temptation to take more direct action to overcome it. He experienced some temptation to remind her of the free-association rule, of the authority and sanctions behind it, and of her agreement to it, and to impose this rule with more vigor and authority. He wanted to urge her to try harder to abide by it and to speak more freely of more significant matters. He might have reminded her that therapy could be successful only if she would follow this procedure—a procedure found necessary and effective by experts through long experience. He might have scolded her repeated instances of resistance and succumbed, even more than he did at 15, to engaging in arguments that she was resisting. (Any similarity here with some ministers' remarks to or about their congregations is not coincidental.) Instead he supposed that her resistance must have some meaning along the lines to be discussed below, even though he did not then understand what that meaning might be. The last section of this chapter and the end of Chapter V will discuss some of the clues that the therapist might have followed to lead him to suspect that the resistance had meaning.

We have attempted in the previous section to describe both the

[10] Cf. John Dollard, Frank Auld, Alice White, *Steps in Psychotherapy* (New York: Macmillan, 1953).

manifest, objective behavioral aspects and the more subjective, intuited flavor of several instances of Mrs. A's resistance. Now we can turn to a demonstration of how both the fact and the form of the resistance is peculiarly revealing of internal conflicts and their disruptive consequences in the nontherapy experience of Mrs. A. The resistance is the ice floe on the surface betraying the presence and contours of a dangerous underlying ice mass.

The link between the resistance and the underlying dynamics can be charted in two ways, one related to the fact and one to the form of the resistance. In the first place, the *fact* of the resistance, regardless for the moment of its particular nature or content, coming at a particular time and in a particular context in the therapy, indicates that some underlying, highly conflictful material is related to that particular time and context. Second, the nature and *form* of the resistance betrays, along with the context and timing, some of the particular characteristics of the underlying dynamics. These were the two characteristics which were discussed, the latter more than the former, with Miss N. From the fact and context, we can learn something of *what* is bothering the person and disrupting his life. From the form of the resistance, we can learn this and also something of *how* he characteristically copes, presumably less than effectively, with this disturbance—how his coping reactions cause further disruption.

INFERENCES FROM FACT AND CONTEXT. The fact of the resistance indicates that the client's talk or other matters in therapy have moved to a point that put him on the verge of some significant and troublesome matters. The resistance means that therapy is touching or almost touching something which he cannot quite handle, something which is anxiety-provoking and cannot be admitted to its place in the discussion without serious distortion or curtailment. It cannot be handled in the therapy conversation, just as it cannot be handled appropriately and satisfactorily in any other situation.

In the case of Mrs. A, particular sexual experiences were so guilt-laden and anxiety-provoking that she was unable to face them, in therapy or outside of it. It was precisely her difficulty in facing these experiences which was unconsciously influencing and damaging certain sectors of her life. She could not bring herself to think about them or try to bring herself to pray about them. Even though she had once discussed the incident with her husband, the anxiety was still expressed in her own sexual unresponsiveness to him and in the general disruption in her relations with him.

The circumstances which brought her to the anxiety-provoking verge of telling these experiences in therapy may have been various, each of them potentially indicating something of her responsiveness to particular situations. Her recital of her problems and her interpretations of them in the previous hour may have exhausted most of her conscious thoughts about her problems. At the same time, the recital may have provided enough relief and reassurance that she began to feel some confidence about moving toward a deeper and more troublesome level of thinking about herself. The fairly abrupt explicit imposition of the free association rule may have enhanced this tendency and perhaps, in effect, may have pushed her too fast and too hard for her to follow easily.

More specific to the underlying dynamics, in the previous hour she had established a warm relationship with the male therapist. This, we may suppose, aroused some mildly sexual feelings toward him; they were not great enough, however, to arouse anxiety or be unmanageable. The second hour, begun by his own announcement of a lifting of restraints, may have made her unconsciously feel less control and hence more anxiety over her own impulses in the therapy hour. Her concern about the possible use of the couch may be related to this, as may her other concerns about the physical arrangements for the therapy which seemed to her to isolate her with the therapist from the main area of the clinic.

This supposition is partly supported by the fact that the interpretation of the therapist which finally precipitated her breakthrough of the resistance was a reference to himself and to their relationship. The exact function of this interpretation is not clear. If, as has just been suggested, she had been made anxious by the unconscious arousal of the prospect of sexual activity with the therapist, this interpretation may have sufficiently brought this problem to her conscious attention and allowed her to recognize that internal and external safeguards were too great to permit such an event. Or the mildly apologetic, solicitous tone of the therapist may have reassured her unconsciously that he had only a professional, not an exploitative, interest in her.

Also more specifically, the recital of her problems in the previous hour had begun to focus more on the sexual relation with her husband as a critical area of her life, more so than she had previously conceived it. This may also have led her to the verge of recalling the difficult experiences. The general point here, which may also apply to the church, is that resistance has meaning as the response of a particular person to particular circumstances.

INFERENCES FROM FORM AND CONTENT. In nature and content, the resistance reproduces in miniature the underlying conflict which is re-enacted in daily life in countless symptomatic forms. The resistance is another one of these re-enactments, but in a particularly accessible situation. It displays the type of characteristic defensive strategy and maneuver the patient is likely to be accustomed to employing—a defensive maneuver which is likely to be a less than ideally adaptive one and to be part of the occasion for difficulties in daily life. In the case of Mrs. A, she demonstrated a kind of manipulative, controlling reaction under a guise of helplessness and cooperation. In the face of a threatening situation, she did not remain merely aloof and passive, but undertook to try to dominate and control it so as to distract from and control again the threatening circumstances. This undoubtedly represented a characteristic way in which she would, for example, behave toward her husband in late evening or in other sexually suggestive situations which might arouse her anxiety. She might be "willing" but just "unable" or "busy."

But along with demonstrating the defense, the resistance—like any symptomatic behavior—betrays, although in distorted form, the underlying wishes. Any symptom, including resistance in psychotherapy, is the compromise resultant of conflict between the expression and the restriction of some impulse or wish. In the case of Mrs. A's resistance, her behavior represented a kind of exaggerated helplessness and naïveté, along with a certain coquettishness which was mildly seductive in character.

Mrs. A, then, found her life beset and disrupted, if our reconstruction is accurate—and subsequent data during the therapy seem to confirm it—by unconscious conflict she experienced over her own sexual impulses. On the one hand, she experienced lively sexual interests—perhaps all the more strongly for never having brought them under conscious and mature supervision and control. On the other hand, the arousal of such interest in herself made her anxious and prompted various maneuvers to avoid sexual opportunity and to deny sexuality. For example, her fear of walking with her children in the street was later traced to just this anxiety, that walking with her children seemed to her unconsciously to be acknowledging her own past sexual behavior which had produced them. Indeed, children are evidence of sexuality, but this was exaggerated in her unconscious representation; she leaned overboard to avoid any such acknowledgment.

This was precisely the conflict involved in her difficulty in speaking freely in therapy. At one level, to speak freely represented psychologically a move toward sexual involvement with the therapist; to speak to him of sexually intimate thoughts and past indiscretions would seem especially inviting and seductive. At another level, to speak of the material which was logically and psychologically on the tip of her tongue was to recall the anxiety-provoking past sexual experiences; to recall them would be to admit undeniably such impulses within herself.

Response to resistance

But the above analysis is all retrospective. In the light of much subsequent information about Mrs. A and much leisurely reflection, it is possible to perceive and to assert the relevance of her resistance, to show the underlying but intimate links between her resistive responses to the therapy situation and the more fundamental "problems" of her life. But none of this is what the therapist could perceive or hardly even guess at the time. Let's return to the situation as the therapist first encountered it.

Mrs. A's remarks during the first twenty minutes of this (the second) hour seem largely irrelevant to the important themes and problems of her life. In the first hour she had recited with a fair amount of torment, an array of serious phobic and compulsive difficulties and bitterly hostile episodes with her husband. Now, when she is asked to continue talking even more freely, instead of pursuing these areas of difficulty and digging into them more deeply, she presents a variety of relatively casual concerns. These are real concerns, real problems. That a person doesn't invent issues and instances to throw up as resistance is too important not to be repeated. Anyone is beset with enough fears and dilemmas of life not to have plenty to talk about if a situation suggests itself. In this case, Mrs. A recites such things as her excessive concern for promptness and for her baby's health, her irritation over her husband's "little petty things," some of the general anxieties she may feel over her own mental health, her genuine curiosity and apprehension over the techniques of therapy, the status of the therapist.

To pursue any of these concerns on her own terms would be to touch real and important issues in her life and perhaps would lead to still more real and important issues. Some psychotherapists would do just this, especially those without a major psychoanalytic orientation and those, such as Carl Rogers, who would put a dominant emphasis on the tactical advantage of invariably dealing with the patient's accounts on his own terms. Ministers in churches may often pursue, with some effectiveness, the resistance on its own terms; that is, respond to the degree of truth and genuineness which is in the rationalization, rather than to the fact that it is a rationalization. For example, the person who says he stays away from worship because "he doesn't know anybody" may thereby enlist the minister's help for some supervised sociability. Or the usher who counts attendance during the pastoral prayer because he "gets a good view of the sanctuary" at that time or, alternatively, because he doesn't "really understand much of the theology of this prayer business" may receive from the minister some administrative help in choosing another time or location for getting a good count, or he may receive from the minister a lecture or a book discussing the theology of prayer. All such responses leave completely untouched any of the possible underlying meanings which such behavior may have—such as anxieties that may be involved in approaching prayer or group life. But they may touch something of importance and may establish a rapport, an avenue.

If these concerns, in the case of Mrs. A, are real and genuine dilemmas, they also have characteristics that stamp them undeniably as resistance. They are meandering and without a discernible focus that would suggest critical importance. They are not accompanied by signs of emotional torment, neither agony nor control against agony. There is not a helplessness and despair about these "problems." On some of the questions, the therapist has explored the issues a bit precisely to discover whether his tapping elicits a genuine emotional ring. It appears that they are real problems, but they are problems which she has essentially handled. They have, rather, a strong characteristic of being "something to say" to meet the situational demands. The fact that they are to some degree rationalizations seems more impressive than the truth which is in the rationalization. The dominant event—not necessarily the exclusive and not necessarily the conscious theme—in Mrs. A's emotional life at the moment is the dilemma which she is experiencing over the conflict of speaking candidly, the predicament she is feeling in wanting to be a good patient and to work hard in the requested ways, but not being able to do so.

This is as much as the therapist could know: there was resistance betraying some conflict over fulfilling the patient's role, especially in speaking spontaneously and candidly. Besides this, all he had was his general conviction that such resistance and such conflict must be intimately relevant to the important and troublesome themes of this person's life, whatever they might be. He didn't see then what these might be, nor did he need to. His only tools, really, were first, his ability to sense what was going on most immediately in the patient's emotional life in response to the immediate situation in which she found herself, and second, his willingness to regard her response to the immediate situation as potentially of genuine and major importance and urgency. Her difficulties in being a therapy patient were not regarded as incidental procedural questions to be sloughed over or waived away or otherwise summarily disposed of in order to return to more significant "substantive" questions pertaining to her "real-life" situations. The therapist did not abandon his role. He maintained the same attitude toward this immediate problem as toward any of her problems—characterized in his case by a kind of accepting yet probing curiosity. He did not forsake, in order to hurdle this procedural problem of therapy, the type of response which he believed most effective as a way of dealing with "substantive" problems in her life—in his case a strategy of reflective clarification. The "procedural" difficulties did not evoke a barrage of special responses, the most tempting of which might have been exhortation. Instead, the full energies and resources of the therapist were brought to bear on this troublesome "procedural" problem just as though it had been a problem wearing all the badges of crucial significance in the life of the patient. And, similarly, the full attention and not inconsiderable resources of the patient were invited to the same problem.

In this case, the therapist responded to the feelings and behavior of the woman as she demonstrated them in response to the therapy situation precisely as he would have to feelings and behavior she might be describing in some problematic "real-life" situation. He *reflected* the nature of the problem, especially at 11 and 13, trying to clarify and define it as crisply as he could, to hold it in front of the patient. He demonstrated, especially in 17, his *understanding* of the psychological discomfort she felt, hence making it more possible for her to face this. He ventured, at 16, a tentative and general *interpretation* as to a possible source of the uncomfortable feelings which were provoking the resistance. Throughout, he demonstrated a kind of calm *acceptance* of the problem, indicating his conviction that it was a discussable and manageable problem, not impossible for him to face even though it involved frustration of his own objectives, and not beyond her own coping with it. His unwillingness to get trapped in the resistance and his determination to focus on, not avoid, this immediately troubling problem, "his" problem in a sense, must have enhanced her own inclination to face and master her own problems.

By calling attention to the resistance, the therapist made it a problem for her to solve and also helped her to solve it. By focusing her attention upon it, he invoked the various resources she already had available, especially by calling attention to it within the context of a threat-free atmosphere already established. She could bring to bear on this problem, even though not entirely consciously, her significant ego resources. The forces underlying the resistance were hardly known consciously to the patient, any more than to the therapist at this point. But the intervention of the therapist, although he was blind to these underlying dynamics, held the problem before Mrs. A's consciousness enough for her to solve it. She could sense what her sexual fears may have been; she could sense that these fears were not realistic, that there was not great likelihood of sexual arousal which she and the therapist could not control; she could decide effectively that it was unnecessary to allow these fears to dominate and disrupt her behavior. These remedies she herself was capable of providing and did provide, even though the therapist could not understand the basis of the problem or its resolution. His task was to identify the problem in a context which made it possible for her to address it and resolve it. She discovered that she could respond effectively and directly without disguise to such a situation at the same time that she discovered more about how disruptive her previous defensive behavior could be.

The various patterns of reaction which have been characterized above had substantially self-defeating and disruptive consequences in the usual situations in which she employed them. These were the "problems" which brought her to therapy. This time, in therapy, they had completely disrupting consequences; they did not work at all (or almost not at all; the therapist did fall victim once or twice). As an experimental psychologist might say, these problematic modes of reaction suffered an extinction trial, at the same time that more adaptive self-confrontation and solution of the problem received reinforcement. The greatest therapeutic work of the hour went on in the few minutes of silence—and most of this was probably unconscious—in which she decided to speak. The confidence gained in making this decision and in carrying it out represented no small gain in her maturity.

One can confidently expect the "centrifugal" generalization from this gain to the other similar and related problems in her life. The recognition of unrealistic fears and of their disrupting influence and of her ability to overcome them—all of these gains in this therapy encounter are now part of her. They will be exercised in subsequent encounters in nontherapy situations. Given enough such resistances and a successful overcoming of them, that is all that therapy need do to ensure a person capable of facing effectively the major problems which have brought him to therapy. Even though these latter have not been explicitly discussed, their equivalents will have been actually acted out and resolved in the therapy encounter. Indeed, Mrs. A's therapy did proceed substantially along these lines from resistance to resistance, and indeed, she did show marked improvement in her ability to deal with the original dilemmas of her life.

The church, like its Master, is fully human and fully in the world; and an analysis of the circumstances of psychotherapy may have helped to define how this is so. But is there not more to be said, at least about the church? As much as the church may be in the world, is it not also different and set apart from the world? Must we leave psychotherapy at this point, or can psychotherapy also provide some model for understanding how the church can be "in, but not of the world"? Are not both of these institutions called "out of the world," in an important sense, in order to provide a norm and a remedy for the world? If these are to be agencies of healing, does not one have a right to expect more health within them? One measure of the strength of such expectations is the anger and disappointment that new patients, new church members, novelists, journalists, and other social commentators, express when they come face to face with the fact that either the church or therapy is fully "in the world."

The next chapter proposes that psychotherapy, and especially the handling of resistance, can continue to be a helpful model for understanding how the church is created and called to be separate from the world.

Freedom from the World

Of the many images by which the Christian church has understood itself and its mission, none is more central or more persistent than the metaphor of the church as the body of Christ. Among other implications of this daring claim, the church means to express its conviction—dazzling as it may seem—that it shares and perpetuates at least two exalted characteristics which the Christian faith attributes to the role of Christ: uniqueness and a redemptive efficacy. If Christ represents a unique and redemptive divine intrusion into human affairs, so does His body, the church, remain a very special, divinely commissioned instrument of God's healing and reconciling purposes among men. Human institution though it be, no other human institution is so particularly called into being or so magnificently sustained with the promises of participating—painfully, yet definitely and finally—in God's active purpose of healing the brokenness of men.

Such a self-understanding, it must be remembered, is held as part of the same faith that stoutly insists on the stubborn intransigence, even depravity of men, whether they are in or out of the church. In any sensitive or sophisticated thought about the church, there is no chance of confusing it with the Promised Land or Paradise, nor of confusing its membership with mankind in a redeemed state. The conviction of its unique and efficacious redemptive role is not a faith in the men who comprise it but in the underlying and continuing structures by which the church has been created.

Such assertion of a power and quality in the "structures of the church" apart from the characteristics of its individual members often seems like theological word-play, vague and unconvincing. As one reader of the above paragraphs noted at this point, "I agree in theory, but I don't see how it works in practice. It seems to me that the unique quality of the church situation which makes 'therapy' possible is due to . . . the minister and parishioners as *individuals* and not to some transcendant power of the church as an entity." This is precisely the vagueness and implausibility to which this chapter addresses itself. The claim is that an understanding of the "structures" of psychotherapy can help us understand how the church *can* be a healing force as an "entity" apart from the lives "in the world" of the individuals who comprise it.

Psychotherapists share a similar faith about their own enterprise and its unique and redemptive possibilities, feeling that it transcends the fallibilities and the foibles of the particular individuals who participate in it, either as patients or as therapists. No one, not even Christian preachers most insisting on human sinfulness, was more sensitively aware than Freud of the ambiguities of human enterprise, whether individual or collective. Freud saw that the mental health of an individual, in or out of therapy, relies precariously on the same feeble though insistent "ego" which can also skillfully sabotage his mental health. Defensiveness, neurosis, resistance are all "achievements" of the ego, no less than health and maturity. Freud saw even more clearly that the same social institutions which mark the progress of civilization necessarily cramp, distort, and pervert the human nature whose accomplishments they also gloriously celebrate. Yet, even with such hard-headed realism, Freud and psychotherapists since have permitted themselves substantial confidence that the particular circumstances of the enterprise of psychotherapy provide a radically effective opportunity for remedy and healing. Therapy, to be sure, is one more fallible and ambiguous structure "in the world," but it also, perhaps uniquely, insinuates healing elements not "of the world."

Chapter II insisted that psychotherapy, like the church, is a slice of real life, evoking, even enhancing, personal deficiencies. We now need to consider the crucial differences between psychotherapy (and presumably the church) and experiences in the world. When a wife, an employer, a parent, or anyone else in other "slices of life" says, "You're not behaving as you ought to," a person may get angry, or anxious, or depressed, or defensive. He is hardly likely to show improvement or to remedy the defects. But when the therapist, and perhaps the minister or fellow churchman, tells a person this, there is some prospect that he will mend his ways. Why? What context does therapy provide for its "slice of life" so as to make the encounters and self-encounters within it remedial? How are therapy and the church in but not of the world?

The key answer to this question seems to be the freedom in therapy and the church from constricting pressures with which the world shapes our behavior into distortions. This chapter will discuss a half dozen sources of this freedom. In each instance, the contention is that freedom emerges out of the very structures by which therapy, and by analogy the church, is constituted. The first of these, "acceptance," is most familiar because of discussion in the last two decades of acceptance in pastoral counseling. Because of this familiarity, rather than in spite of it, acceptance will be discussed at length. A fresh statement in this context may suggest interpretations and applications to the church other than those implied in pastoral counseling. We want to demonstrate especially that acceptance can be the result not of benign personal characteristics of the therapist, but rather of the given structures of psychotherapy itself.

FREEDOM IN TRUST AND ACCEPTANCE

The nature of acceptance and its effects

Therapy and presumably the church proceed in a context of what has been called "unconditional acceptance," in which persons may feel a relative freedom from threats and demands. The nature of this acceptance, how it is communicated, and how it produces its effects will be discussed here at some length. The next section will argue that the acceptance depends less than is usually supposed on the benign personality characteristics of the therapist or the clergyman, and more on the particular structures of the therapy or the church; in therapy and in the church are forces tending to result in an atmosphere of acceptance independent of whoever happens to be therapist or clergyman. The reader to whom the material of the present section is familiar or the reader who is impatient to see the applications to the church may want to turn immediately to the next section, called "Acceptance is built in, not a personal achievement" (see p. 100).

An atmosphere of acceptance—although fundamental to and assumed by all schools of psychotherapy—has been particularly linked in the United States with so-called "nondirective" therapy. And for good reason. An important characteristic of life "in the world" to which therapy provides contrast and relief, is the siege of constant nagging "directiveness" by other persons. To get through life, each of us faces a never-ending barrage of demands, big and small ("Do this; be this . . ."), most of them backed by an important "or else." The chief sanction children face is the withdrawal of parents' love and support; parental love is made conditional on proper performance of parental demands. But this experience is not left behind in childhood; one continues to meet demands backed by the manipulation of important psychic satisfactions.

To maneuver amidst these threats, each person devises a repertory of psychic coping devices. Most of the time these strategies of the ego's devising work well; they comprise an appropriate or adaptive, we may even say "healthy," personality. But sometimes, especially when circumstances change—and especially when the person is expected to make the transition from childhood to adult roles—these defensive strategies fail to balance effectively among the many demands and sanctions, or they produce their own new difficulties. Then the mask or the armor becomes a crippling impediment, and the person may find himself in therapy, or in church. Life closes in and he seeks relief, a "new life."

To a person in such a plight, the therapist holds and communicates an attitude something like this: "I have a fundamental and unshakable confidence and trust in your ability to discover, develop, and use the valuable resources available to you. (These resources include your own ego abilities to analyze and reflect and learn; they include the many varieties of support and wisdom available to you from other individuals; and they include awareness of divine intervention in your life, in judgment or forgiveness or direction.) I have confidence in your ability to make your own decisions, large and small, in guiding your life. You may not "heal" yourself and you may not be soon living a life which either I or you would regard as ideal. But given the choice between me or you deciding what you should do and how you should live, the chances are much greater that you have available the intuitive wisdom about yourself and about your circumstances—and also, have the basic God-given responsibility—to do a better job than I can. If you have not done too well lately, the chances are great that it is because you have had to devote so much energy to coping with the demands of other persons, past and present, as to how you should live. Here there are no such demands; you can begin to withdraw energies from the defensive struggle, peek out from behind the masks, and venture to move without the armor."

As applied to *past* behavior and experience, such an attitude takes the form of not judging or scolding or criticizing the person for doing what and as he has done. The therapist believes and says, directly or indirectly, that in the same circumstances he, the therapist, is hardly likely to have made any better decisions. "There but for the grace of God go I." As applied to the *future*, it consists of an unwillingness—because of a genuinely believed inability—to tell the person what he should do about making practical decisions for himself, or to prescribe for the person what his style of living or pattern of personality should be. As applied to the immediately *present* circumstances of the psychotherapy, especially the resistance that develops, the trust is expressed in both of these ways, as an absence of scolding and as an unwillingness, again because of inability, to prescribe how this resistance shall be overcome.

Such an attitude of trust in the person is to be distinguished from other attitudes with which it is sometimes confused. It is not the same thing as the more superficial sentiment of "liking" in the sense that one finds personalities compatible and one would enjoy developing social relations. Nor is such trust the same thing as approving his behavior, in either past or present, in the sense that one would sanction or recommend it as a social or ethical norm.

It hardly requires elaborate or abstract theory to understand how such an attitude of trust and regard experienced by the patient, perhaps for the first time in his life, can serve gradually to free him from past defenses, habits, and postures. As he slowly comes to believe that this trust is genuinely available to him regardless of what posture he presents to the therapist, he gradually peeks from behind the masks, flexes some muscles without protective armor, and tries something new—"being himself." In such freedom a person may venture to make new use of old resources or to discover new resources, including those within himself, within his social environment, and within his religious faith. He can come more nearly to being "that self he truly is." [1]

It is the conviction, both of the church and of the therapist, not only that the accepting, trusting atmosphere they provide for a person is uniquely redemptive but also that it is in some sense more fundamentally real and true than the demanding, buffeting encounters a person may have otherwise experienced. The assumption—or faith—in each case is that the buffets and threats of life which have produced the defensive and protective distortions are in some sense perversions and distortions—"a fall"—from the more essential and truer state of affairs. The therapist can convey acceptance not just because it works pragmatically to bring about personality changes, but only as he is genuinely convinced that such a view of the person is a fundamentally more valid appraisal of him than the guarded and demanding appraisal more often experienced "in the world." Religious language is rich with images asserting this faith that fundamentally man lives, or is intended to live, in a harmonious state of affairs in which he is trusted and therefore free and responsive. The images often are couched in terms of a remote time or space (Eden, heaven, end of the world). Accordingly, both the church and therapy

---

[1] A phrase from Carl Rogers, *On Becoming a Person* (Boston: Houghton Mifflin Co., 1961).

are sometimes accused of representing a false and illusory world. Both are accused of providing a simple refuge from the buffetings of world, by those who would regard the latter as the more fundamental reality, and of failing to equip people to return to the "real world." Church and therapy alike accept the role of making their faith in underlying support and trust more plausible by making it less remote.

ACCEPTANCE OF RESISTANCE. Of the diverse ways in which the therapist communicates this acceptance and trust which he feels for the patient, we are particularly interested here in how he expresses this with respect to the resistance that the patient shows within therapy. For here—in the patient's own performance as patient—is where the therapist is prospectively most likely to be making demands. Here, as the patient faces the task as he sees it of being a "good patient," here in the most immediate and most unavoidable aspects of the encounter between patient and therapist, here is where the impact of demands or of trust has most effect. A therapist might be quite able to accept a patient with respect to his past indiscretions, his present anxieties, and his future indecisiveness, but still find it difficult to tolerate, much less accept, the patient's difficulties in speaking candidly in the therapy hour. It is very possible that a patient might find himself accepted and trusted with respect to those parts of his life outside therapy which he reported upon, but might find himself urged, or instructed, or even commanded with respect to his behavior in therapy as patient: "Try to speak more freely and express your emotions more candidly." "I think it is more important for you to be talking about these things rather than those things." "Here is what you should be understanding about yourself."

A church member might find his fellow churchmen and his minister thoroughly understanding, accepting, and trusting of him with respect to his blunders and difficulties and even outright misdeeds in his family relations or work life but feel earnest pressure to conform to particular cultic practices within the church: attend services, support the men's club, don't have unkind thoughts about your fellow church members. (Such demands for "perfection" in the church, combined with toleration of imperfection outside, illustrate the misunderstanding of the church as deriving its unique "difference" from the world from the redeemed or sinless or faithful character of its members, rather than from the underlying nature by which it has been called or founded.)

COMMUNICATING ACCEPTANCE. The therapist conveys his acceptance of the patient's imperfections in general and of his resistance in therapy in particular sometimes by directly expressing it in so many words, but more often by behavior which implies it. The therapist's attitude toward resistance is one of curiosity and sadness and confidence that it is neither fundamental nor permanent for the patient. The therapist does not feel anger or frustration or fear or despair or other such moods with which other persons have responded to the patient's imperfections in the "old" world. Because the therapist's attitudes are different, he reacts differently from the way other people have reacted to the patient. The therapist's expression of his "accepting" attitude toward the resistance, then, needs to be understood in constant contrast with the patient's more common nontherapeutic experiences.

Essentially, the therapist accepts resistance by talking about it *calmly* and matter-of-factly. In the past—perhaps in many actual church experiences—the patient has been able to detect his misdeeds and other's displeasure by the embarrassed pause, the averted gaze, the quickly changed subject, or by the overjovial laughter and backslap. The therapist simply talks about the resistances with no more and no less emotion than about anything else. He is not angry or anxious or embarrassed about the patient's "failures" to meet "expectations" because he is not threatened or disturbed by them. The patient's resistance to the therapy is simply objective behavior in which the therapist is seriously interested because he is concerned about the patient, but not because it frustrates or disturbs him. The patient doesn't have the experience that conversation is suddenly shifted to the casual "cocktail party" tone as a signal that things are getting too intimate or too stressful to be handled comfortably.

But neither does the therapist so insistently dwell on the matter of resistance with a kind of exaggerated persistence and concern which others also often use to betray their own anxiety or anger. One of the ways in which our psychologically sophisticated generation has learned to cope with uncomfortable situations is to skewer them with analytic probes. Pinning problems with heavily intellectual labels and insisting on holding them fixedly in full gaze is a way of finding assurance that they will not get out of hand emotionally. Thus, the essentially defensive nature of much of the popular "group dynamics" and other use of intellectually analytic techniques to cope with stressful emotions. We easily learn the recited formulae by which others may signal that something is making them uncomfortable: "I sense that his remark makes you feel angry" or "You seem tense." Perhaps the most serious rejection experienced in this psychologically sophisticated age is the coldly pronounced, "You need help." Such insistent analysis is often a thin veneer for anger and anxiety, and is readily recognized as such, especially by those sensitive persons who finally appear in therapy. The therapist speaks of matters calmly, but not with compulsive persistence. If the topic is dropped, the therapist is not afraid of that either.

Beyond his calm recognition of resistance, the therapist conveys his acceptance of it by his expressed *understanding* of it as a conflict in the patient's experience. He understands resistance in the same way and with the same effects as he understands other emotional affairs in the life of the patient. By making his understanding more explicit, he communicates at least two of his convictions: that the emotional life of the patient is important and acceptable enough to examine, and that the person is capable of facing and handling such "difficulties." The therapist, in mentioning the resistance, implicitly reminds the patient of the "norm": his confidence that the patient can live in a more open and free way and participate more fully in the therapy. But he does not urge or cajole or command him to change.

SAME LANGUAGE WITH DIFFERENT IMPACT. The "new reality" in church or therapy may be expressed in language identical to that used by parents or wives or employers or others representing the "fallen" reality. Both, for example, may say something like, "Why don't you behave yourself?" or "Why can't you do better?" From others this "question" has really been a protest against the offender's basic incorrigibility. This language from the therapist, the patient gradually comes to learn and to believe, means quite literally and naïvely to pose a question of curiosity, mingled perhaps with a sadness.

The therapist does focus upon the patient's difficulties, especially difficulties in performing satisfactorily in therapy. He does puncture cover stories. ("All that anger at your wife doesn't seem to be consistent with the simple fact that she let the car run out of gas.") He does call attention to the patient's deficiencies as a patient. ("You are rambling today and not saying anything significant.") In this, he might sound very much like wives or parents or other people who also jump on the patient. They are also motivated and skillful at puncturing cover stories and pointing out deficiencies. (A wife, too, is likely to have said something like, "Why do you get so upset at a little thing like that?" or "Why can't you stick to the point?")

But there is one important difference. The wife has punctured the cover story in order to communicate her anger and resentment, to attack her husband, to communicate her mistrust of him "down deep"; she stands over and against him. "If your anger is greater than objectively justified, there must be something wrong with you." The therapist stands on the same side as the patient, and they are looking together at his behavior. The therapist punctures the cover story in order to communicate his understanding of what is going on in the life of the patient, to express his concern and his curiosity, to show his trust that there must be something more important going on in the life of the man than is showing at the moment. "If your anger is greater than seems objectively justified, it must be produced by something we can't see yet," or, "If you can't speak freely in therapy, let's find out why not." He may feel and express a kind of sadness that the patient is momentarily deceiving himself with a cover story or finding so much difficulty in candidly expressing important things about himself. But the sadness is mingled with a confidence that the patient doesn't have to be this way, that he can be different. The deficiency does not represent a rotten "core," as the wife would have it; there is a solid "core" which can be counted on and trusted to make things better and different. One measure of the therapist's trust is precisely that he calls attention to these deficiencies forthrightly, "man to man," in a manner which discloses his confidence that the patient can do something about them.

Perhaps the agents both of the old reality and of the new reality express themselves in a loose syllogism in which they would perfectly agree on the second premise concerning the patient: his present behavior is deficient. But their different conclusions betray their highly divergent major premises about him. The wife's "conclusion" is of the need for correction and is expressed in nagging or scolding. This betrays—and betrays it to no one so clearly as to the person getting the correction—her major premise that he himself is basically bad, hopeless, and untrustworthy. The deficient behavior reflects a person "rotten at the core."

The therapist's conclusion is expressed more like this: "There must be something curious deflecting your behavior, something relatively incidental, transient, external, definitely something different from the basic 'you.' " This conclusion implies—and again to no one with so much impact as the person experiencing it—that the therapist is working from a major premise that the person is fundamentally and centrally good or healthy and to be trusted as able to conduct himself relatively wisely and well, once he is freed from crippling impediments.[2]

[2] This discussion is with reference to the psychological *experience* of a person, not his status from the perspective and criteria of theological considerations. We are discussing here the relative difference in the psychological effect of being badgered or trusted *by other people*. Other persons provide a *relative* index by which a person feels more or less regard, more or less threatened, more or less defensive. We are not necessarily discussing the impact or the process of feeling oneself measured by *ultimate* criteria, such as "in the eyes of God." The parent, or the wife, or the therapist feels the person to be trustworthy or not in comparison with themselves, the parent, or wife, or therapist. These persons communicate their opinion that the person is to be trusted to make better decisions without their intervention, or else he is not. The "old reality" makes a person feel judged lower on a scale than those who are judging. The "new reality" does not. But it is perfectly conceivable for a therapist to hold such a trusting view of a person with respect to these standards and to communicate such a sense of trust to him at the same time that he is willing to judge by more absolute standards that the person is not "fundamentally" good. In simplest language, the therapist may believe that the person may be trusted to get along without his (the therapist's) manipulations but may still need God.

The psychological experience of feeling oneself judged by other people is what

When the therapist places a high value on spontaneous free expression, symbolized in some forms of therapy by the expectation of free association, he runs the risk that it will sometimes seem to the patient that he is saying, "You *must* be spontaneous!" But ideally, the therapist's "expectation" in this respect is just literally that, a hopeful prediction, an expectation, that the patient *can* express himself spontaneously and undefensively. It is not the demand that, for example, teachers or parents have betrayed when they have said, "I expect you to. . . ." The therapist's emphasis on free expression or free association is his expression of trust that the patient is capable of conducting himself within therapy according to his own inner promptings and self-determination, and that such self-generated behavior can be efficacious and good, better than behavior responsive to other people's pushing. The therapist's explicit emphasis on free expression becomes a baseline by which both patient and therapist can detect defensiveness and distortion. It becomes a "norm" in this original sense of a descriptive standard of measurement, not as a demand. Since the "norm" has as much reference to the patient's own inclinations as the therapist's, any gap or discrepancy between the patient's performance and this norm then becomes a matter of mutual curiosity for both of them. It is not a matter for condemnation because one person has failed to meet the wishes of another, more powerful, person. When resistance appears, as when the patient finds himself unable to express or face important matters in his life openly, it is clearly a difficulty within himself; it is not the resistance one person is offering to the will of another.

BENEFITS OF ACCEPTANCE: FREEDOM. This accepting, trusting attitude by the therapist, especially as it becomes most believable by being focused on the immediate resistance, gradually induces a psychological freedom with at least three important benefits. First, the patient becomes able more easily and candidly to display the resistance and hence to *gain access* to the troublesome spots in his life

makes one feel defensive, crippled, and unfree. The psychological effect of being judged unworthy by God ought not to be so, unless God has been so anthropomorphized as to seem like one's own father. For the judgement of God is tempered with mercy, not backed up by slaps and derision.

and their potential resolution. When a patient begins to show, by tardiness or other resistive behavior, that some things confronting him anger or hurt him, then there is some basis for therapy. But there is no basis if the patient is dutifully following schedules and procedures to meet what he feels to be the therapist's demands and to avoid his immediate criticisms. Then all we can see is his tendency to obey demands of authority figures, a more or less normal, more or less universal tendency, which would mask characteristics of more fundamental and individual importance. (If the patient still shows patterns of dutiful obedience, even in the context of acceptance and absence of real demands, then he is showing particularly strong characteristics, generated from past encounters, which probably are, in this case, of importance to him and to his therapy. But this anticipates the points to be made near the end of the chapter about therapy providing a minimum reality base as another way of being not "of the world.")

When a minister presses people to attend worship, to support parish activities, to be attentive to the sermon, to feel reverence during prayers or gratitude during the communion, he may achieve some compliance. But, among all the other effects he garners by representing the "old reality" of personal demands, he destroys the possibility of his parishioner recognizing and examining precisely the points at which confrontation with the word and sacraments of God are most troublesome. Hence, he reduces the likelihood of the parishioner better preparing himself for deeper encounter. Persuasive demands can lead a parishioner to attend and even to be attentive, at least for short periods, but they cannot make him drink deeply so long as his thirst is a deeper thirst.

The second benefit of the acceptance-induced psychological freedom is, of course, the opportunity for more creative, more energetic, more concerted attention to the problems disclosed by the resistance. Without the need of putting on a false front or good appearance before the therapist, there is more opportunity for the riskier procedures of *trying out new ways* of thinking and feeling and responding. By a more or less frankly trial-and-error procedure, a person may experiment with alternative ways of approaching the difficult parts of his life—so far as they find focused representation within the therapy encounter. He can even risk being, in a sense, playful about his difficulties and possible solutions—for creativeness is at its best a playfulness. He can experiment, with the confidence that "failures" in his trial-and-error effort will not bring disasters; there is no pressure from the therapist to be "successful." Energies can be released from the task of providing defensive masks and can be concentrated on the demanding task of finding more permanent and fundamental resolutions to the real issues.

Third, above all, the patient can discover from this acceptance and trust that he is not necessarily compelled to adopt new resolutions which are essentially defensive. He can be *open and free.* He himself can trust. The trust of the therapist gives him the incentive to discover that life, even outside therapy, may not be so full of demands and threats as it once was (when he was an infant), or as he may blindly have feared it still to be. Defensive postures and traits which may once have been appropriate, as, say, for a small boy before his parents, may hardly be appropriate for him in his maturity. But in the midst of his habitual reliance on these defensive strategies, he is not likely to discover this without some radical, intruding experience such as the therapist's acceptance of his resistance to the therapeutic process.

Acceptance is built in, not a personal achievement

Acceptance, especially when made a norm for pastoral counseling or other personal relationships within the church, is often misinterpreted individualistically and sentimentally. Discussion, as in the preceding pages, of providing a "threat-free atmosphere" may seem to be making heavy demands on the personal skill and temperament of a counselor, on his mental health and emotional stability, and even on his state of grace. A counselor, reading such discussion as the foregoing, may feel that the effectiveness of counseling and the mental health of the client depend critically on his own ability to exude an overwhelming personal charm and warmth with an unruffled equanimity. When such discussion becomes a model for church life, a minister may sometimes feel that the salvation of souls in his care depends on his own personal ability to supply for all persons a kind of unending, unconditional, embracing, enfolding love, which a Christian believes only God is capable of. Some pastors can be observed who labor under such a stressful vocational obligation to love. Such love tends to become a cheerless, trivial sentiment, defined primarily by an inhibition of anger, however great the provocation, and by a pretense of liking the unlikeable.

To be sure, a certain fundamental health and control over their own emotional lives is important for therapists and counselors and probably also for clergymen. When therapist or clergyman finds that the patient's situation raises strong anxieties or impulses in himself, triggering defensive reactions, he is distracted from giving full attention to the patient's affairs. To preclude this, personal therapy is often recommended as part of a therapist's training and perhaps would be similarly useful for a clergyman. But this is simply to provide a kind of minimal level of freedom from distortion in the therapist's or clergyman's functioning. This is not to suppose that a personal therapy can build him into a paragon of grace and incarnate love, or that he needs to be one.

To suppose that the success of therapy, or of a church, depends on the ability of the therapist, or pastor, to sustain a particular emotional tone is to trivialize therapy and to misunderstand the nature of acceptance. This is to treat as a sentiment what is a much more fundamental characteristic. It is to substitute the personal, more or less accidental and temperamental characteristics of an individual for the more essential characteristics of the given situation. It provides a poor model for the church, for it seems to suggest what is patently not possible, that minister and people should all be exemplars of saintly grace and incarnate love for each other. This becomes a new version of the Donatist error in supposing that the efficacy of the institution depends on the particular characteristics of those who happen to be filling positions or roles in it.

For "acceptance"—as one of the conditions of therapy, or of the church—is "built into" therapy, or into the church, as part of the very structures by which this institution is "called into being." The acceptance which the therapist shows to the patient depends in great measure on the particular situation in which therapist and patient find themselves, not on the particular and individual characteristics of the therapist himself. Whatever the personality of the therapist or his past history, and however he might react outside therapy, the "structures" of therapy tend to make more likely for him the calm trust of the patient which is acceptance.

NOT MERELY AN EMOTION. For one thing, the acceptance is not mediated as a kind of personal loving or compatibility. It may not have any of the overt emotional gestures by which one person typically shows affection or friendship for another. It is the much starker experience of being fully known and trusted and shared with. In emotional tone, it may be more like the relationship at the end of fifty years of a good marriage, rather than that at its beginning. Or it may be more like the comradeship of soldiers, their relationship seasoned and tested in battle, fighting alongside each other in mutual trust. Almost regardless of what individuals may be involved, the trust in therapy, as in the marriage or in the battalion, comes as a consequence of having exposed oneself to the searching gaze of another, amidst stress, and still finding the other standing and laboring alongside.

First-century Christians in Rome did not have to have "acceptance" generated artifically by being asked to shake hands with their neighbors after services. And perhaps the modern church most provides a therapeutically accepting group membership when it is least preoccupied with its own "fellowship" and most strenuously losing its life in its tasks of mission in the world. Probably the therapist is most accepting who is least concerned with generating the proper emotional mood, who, heedless of himself and how he may or may not display emotions, bends every energy to the task of following and comprehending the patient's own account of his life, no matter how stressful or tortuous this may be.

The validity of a religious experience is not guaranteed by its emotional tone. In fact, an intense overt emotion-filled display may be grounds, as Jonathan Edwards among others has insisted, for suspicion. Rather, one looks for evidence deeper than emotional display of the experience of a person standing naked, naked of emotions as well as of everything else, before a God who fully perceives and still stands by and trusts.

THERAPIST FREED FROM RISK. As keenly and intensively as therapy reproduces personal relationships and other segments of life "in the world," it is so arranged that it is "out of the world" in one very important and very clear way which produces the possibility of the experience of acceptance. Without this, the therapist would, indeed, have to be a saint to provide the kind of acceptance we have discussed. He would have to generate from within himself, out of his personal transcendence of the stresses of life, the accepting attitude. But with this characteristic, even persons who may be quite demanding and nonaccepting with family, colleagues, and others, may as therapists provide an accepting atmosphere for a patient.

This characteristic, most simply put, is that the therapist has nothing to lose. He himself is not under the pressure of having something important at stake in the therapy relationship. There is nothing the patient can do, in or out of therapy, which realistically makes any important difference to the life of the therapist. His important personal and professional satisfactions and rewards are not dependent on whether the patient does or does not treat his wife fairly, or on whether a patient does or does not come on time to therapy, or even on whether a patient does or does not get well. These conditions of therapy provide a unique experience in the midst of a life otherwise beset by tangled webs of personal interdependency. The therapist can afford to be genuinely disinterested and objective at the same time that he is most keenly interested. In this sense, he does enjoy a kind of Godlike unassailable aloofness from life, which permits a kind of Godlike acceptance. From the structures of the situation, the psychotherapist gains a psychological freedom to accept others in the same way that, in another realm, academic freedom of professors is guaranteed by the institutional arrangement of tenure.

For what is it which disrupts mutually accepting personal relations "in the world" outside therapy? Why is it that parents and employers and spouses, including the therapist as parent, employer, or spouse, do make arbitrary and punitive demands and fail to express a sense of trust? It is hardly that they are personally so depraved or malicious or innately sinful and unmoving, any more than that the therapist as therapist can be accepting because he personally is so saintly or God-like. It is that they themselves are under pressures from others past and present.

I scold and punish and threaten my child for essentially harmless noise when I feel that someone else—a neighbor, a grandparent, my wife—will otherwise be annoyed with me; or I scold and punish and threaten my child for noise when this disturbs a project such as the writing of this book on which I may be desperately intent for reasons of strong personal or professional pressures; or I may scold and punish and threaten my child for noise when this violates a pattern of behavior vigorously and fixedly lodged in me by the punishment and threats of my own parents. To the degree that these pressures can be off me—as happens to a relative degree on vacation—I can be more accepting of my child's noise. This does not necessarily mean that I approve of it or do not sometimes correct it to meet the requirements of realistic social responsibility, but the correction is in the context of acceptance and not in the mood of anger and threat which produces defensive distortions and only superficial obedience.

If the psychologist can provide any model with which to help specify the theological understanding of the transmission of sin, it must be at this point. Here is the suggestion of the process by which persons inherently not "sinful" or mistrustful or rupturing of relationships, come under a kind of transmitted influence of mistrust and ruptured relations which make them so.

Children may sometimes wonder why parents seem so inconsistent in what they expect, for example, in table manners. "Natural" table manners are sometimes sanctioned, but suddenly at times many rules of etiquette and decorum are insisted upon. The children gradually learn to discriminate that the latter come in the presence of other persons, especially of those whose opinion means most to the parents. So, ministers, for example, or grandparents, when guests in a home, must often suffer, through no fault of their own, the painful experience of finding themselves indirectly provoking harsh discipline and a punitiveness which exactly contradicts the mood they would most like to convey to the home.

A Sunday school teacher observed this happening in herself. She had an excellent relation with her class of nine-year-olds most of each hour, while students and teacher were probing study materials and undertaking craft activities with a kind of loose order, genuine sense of companionship, and adventure. But the teacher found herself literally tightening up inside toward the end of every hour and becoming irritated and scolding signs of disorder and inattention which she hadn't even noticed for most of the hour. She thought at first that she was simply becoming tired, or that the children were, in fact, becoming increasingly unruly during each hour. But then she realized that at the end of each hour she began to anticipate the parents' return for their children and began to see things through their eyes. The result was that she tried to make over the class and the classroom into something she felt would be more acceptable to them.

Therapy is purposely arranged to be "out of the world" in this sense. This is one of the reasons that a therapist normally does not accept friends or relatives as patients and refrains from accepting any relation outside of therapy with a person so long as he is a patient. This is to preserve the disinterest of the therapist and his immunity from feeling particular motives within himself concerning the patient and his behavior. This is one of the important reasons why therapy traditionally goes on in the neutral ground of a therapist's office, rather than, for example, in the home of either therapist or patient, or in some place that would be haunted by the ghosts of other associations. This is a justification for psychotherapists being relatively secure financially and professionally and a justification for the patient's fee being substantial enough to compensate the therapist fairly and genuinely for his time. So long as he is getting satisfactory money rewards for his time (and so long as this money is not contingent upon any behavior of the patient, such as his promptness in attending sessions) the therapist is less likely to be tempted to try to derive other rewards and satisfactions from the therapy relation by making demands on the patient.

These structural arrangements help to provide relief from one of the motivations which the therapist may be most tempted to feel with respect to his patient—a determination to be successful: The patient *must* get better, and evidence to the contrary will not be tolerated. This obviously disrupting pressure which would make it difficult for a therapist to trust his patient through episodes of resistance, has important parallels in the case of the church. It is handled in the case of the therapist partly by previous analytic extirpation of primitive pressures or anxieties which would lead to undue concern for success, and partly by these structural relationships, which guarantee minimum personal satisfaction, regardless of overt signs of "success."

UNENCUMBERED RELATIONS IN THE CHURCH TOO? So far the general implication for the church from this analysis of therapy is that clergy and laymen are more likely to provide a sense of acceptance for fellow church members to the degree that their relationship is similarly "out of the world," to the degree that church relationships are separate from other important relationships and do not carry important and fundamental personal rewards. This, for example, may be one argument for a pluralism of churches and of church activities within a single parish. Also, it would seem desirable if the major power and role relations, as between employer and employee, and even between husband and wife, and parent and child, were not reproduced within the church. Nor should the economic or other pressures on a minister be linked to other aspects of his relations with parishioners. There will, of course, be power and role relationships within the church, between those having more and less authority, those controlling, in some sense, rewards for others. But these will be removed, "out of the world." They will not have the same relatively desperate urgency which these relationships have outside the church. When a church parish, as in a rural or small industrial town, simply reproduces within itself the entire social structure—with the mill owner serving as chief deacon, or with the women effectively running things from behind the scenes—there is no opportunity for the majority to feel a freedom and a distance from the "world" to venture newer and perhaps more successful patterns to their lives. Then the church is too much contained by the world.

FREEDOM IN MORATORIUM

The preceding section has emphasized that the *therapist* in therapy is removed from the major risks and threats of life, giving him the freedom—at least in therapy—to express a trust and acceptance of the patient. This same relative remoteness of therapy from the risks and threats "of the world" also has an important direct effect on the patient. The *patient* is freed from undue anxiety and preoccupation with the question of how "well" he is doing, how "good" he is. This is not only because of the therapist's acceptance, but because of the absence and the impossibility of other persons imposing their controls and demands on him. For this one hour of the week or of the day he is quite literally removed from the world. He can experience a moratorium from his usual concern with what the important people in his life, past and present, think of him and his performance. He is, to be sure, engaged in an important and demanding task and in establishing a close personal relationship. But, perhaps for the first time in his life, he can do it his way, without needing constantly to adjust to those who are looking over his shoulder, and—for reasons of their own—wanting to shape him to fit their own conscious or unconscious needs, rewarding success and obedient conformity, punishing noncompliance.

The therapist guards well the privileged nature of the therapy hour, not only from legal investigation but also from prying curiosity of friends and relatives. This is true even when others have some degree of legitimate interest, as, for example, genuinely concerned parents who are paying heavy bills for their child's therapy, or a minister whose collaboration might aid the therapy. The therapist must run the risk of sacrificing rights and potential values in such instances for the critically important sake of the freedom which the patient must feel in this, his hour "out of the world." He strongly supports a patient's freedom from having to discuss this hour with

persons outside therapy. When the therapist records interviews—as
he sometimes does for research or teaching or record-keeping purposes, or to give him opportunity to reflect in more leisure on the
proceedings of the hour—he candidly explains it to the patient and
also makes clear to him that the recording can in no way affect his
life or his therapy. If the patient is not fully reassured about this, the
therapist is likely not to record. The patient's essentially groundless
fear, thus disclosed as "resistance," is itself, however, something to be
worked through; it may later be dissipated and the recording re-
sumed.

From this isolation therapy acquires, as from the therapist's
acceptance, a freedom from past ruts, a freedom to make mistakes,
and a freedom to correct mistakes in new and creative ways. This
applies especially to the immediate task of working out one's role as a
patient and working out the relationship with the therapist. There is
a freedom to resist the role of the patient and to resist the therapist
and there is a freedom to face this resistance. Therapy assumes a
playful mood, perhaps even a kind of dreamy, wonderland, "as if"
atmosphere. It may be like the play of preschool children, and perhaps it serves many of the same purposes. For with their dolls and
toys and each other, children try to reproduce in their play much of
the real world. They experiment with taking different roles and filling
them in different ways. All of this is free of any important immediate
consequences for their lives. At any point they can—and it is crucial
that they realize this—whenever their assumed roles and reactions are
not working well, snap their fingers and break the spell. They can
pick up their dolls and go back to the real world or try some new
playful pattern another day.

The patient does not often literally pick up his dolls and go home.
But he comes to have the feeling that he can, and that he is free to
try out any kind of relationship, without fear of being subtly coerced
or punished by therapist or by anybody else. He can try being aggressive or submissive, compulsive or irresponsible, intellectually controlled or emotionally free, or any other combination of moods in his
approach to therapy and the therapist. The therapist will help him
look at these reaction patterns, especially when they are objectively

impeding the patient's own best course (to be distinguished from annoying or threatening the therapist). But the therapist is recognized as having a trusting curiosity about these, not an interest in punishing or reshaping them. And there is no one else around to be concerned!

Church as moratorium—I

It is possible that members of a church can experience this same kind of healing freedom when their activities within the church life are not linked with the administration of important rewards and punishments in life outside the church. People ought to feel a moratorium, a playful freedom from their otherwise constant preoccupation with meeting expectations and pleasing others. The church ought to provide as much of this relaxed freedom as an evening at the bar, or a night at the lodge, or an afternoon's absorption at a football game. But it also ought to provide the important difference that within the church (as in therapy and children's play but not usually in bar, lodge, or stadium) there is also the opportunity within this freedom constructively to work out behavior patterns in important relationships. This is why it is good and necessary—and this, of course, is the more fundamental theme of this book—for churches to have in their parish life struggle and stress, even demands and pressures, a true slice of life as it is lived outside. But the suggestion being made here is that these pressures and stresses not be accompanied by the desperate, sometimes almost life-and-death sanctions which they have outside.

More of the implications of the church as moratorium, including several examples, will be suggested after discussion of the next freedom, closely related to this one.

FREEDOM FROM PRESSURE TO PRODUCE

There is a leisure about therapy. If there is a relative freedom from demands to produce particular kinds of behavior, as just discussed, there is also a relative freedom from pressures to produce any behavior, to make any decisions, to adopt any personality characteristics. Therapist and patient generally agree at the outset of therapy on a moratorium from the patient's making decisions or taking any important new action in his life, at least until late stages of therapy. The more important the potential decision or action, as in matters concerning vocation and marriage, the more explicit and decisive is this ban. Therapy is not oriented toward solving immediate pressing practical problems, personal or social. It is, rather, a consolidation and maturation of resources so that the practical problems may be freshly tackled with new vigor and new wisdom and presumably greater success. The practical problems are not permitted to loom as demanding monsters. The patient is supported in the temporary postponement, even denial, of pressures and problems. As always, some important values may be sacrificed for the sake of the therapeutic benefit. Here there is the risk of some irresponsibility, but it is believed necessary for the sake of eventually attacking the responsibilities with greater effectiveness. It is a deliberate withdrawal from the front lines for the sake of re-grouping forces before new assault.

The same freedom from pressure toward solution accompanies the problems the patient finds with therapy, that is, the resistances. When things do not go right in therapy, when resistances develop, there is no pressure and no deadline for doing something about it. There is a confidence that eventually things will get better, and indeed considerable effort may be spent in attacking the problem. But meanwhile, the difficulty or the resistance is simply accepted and lived with as long as it exists. This is one reason why therapy must take a long time and why the end can never be clearly foreseen. Again, this is obviously regrettable from many points of view, but is necessary for the sake of the unique leisure.

Obviously, time itself does not heal and solutions do not come simply from procrastination. But the leisure provides an important opportunity for assessment of fundamental issues and resources and responsibilities not possible in impulsive or hasty decisions or under pressure. Even more important than simply providing time, however, the leisure releases energies. It is as elementary as the difference between a person (or a committee) fretting about not getting a problem solved or an agenda met and the same person (or committee) spending the same time and energy in actually addressing the problem. More creative solutions to problems come, mobilizing more resources of the person, when a deadline is not threatening and hovering —whether it be a deadline for choosing a college, the deadline a wife may feel for correcting neurotic symptoms to meet a husband's ultimatum, or the threat a person feels by an approaching twenty-fifth birthday without being married or an approaching fortieth birthday without having realized vocational dreams.

Such leisure may be especially important in the context of American culture in which many persons are made to feel a pressure to do something and to be somebody, no matter what, so long as it is achieved decisively and promptly. Even infants and the elderly are hardly permitted to be themselves by a society which applauds machines that teach three-year-olds to read and which celebrates the retired man who keeps constantly busy. Persons are not permitted to be themselves, if such self-direction implies a leisure or a playful or a reflective or a passive state of approaching life; they must be constantly chalking up points on society's scoreboard (or ticker tape). A minister's study time is viewed with suspicion by parishioners, and so is the writing of this book by neighbors who happen to have little conception of intellectual life. The minister—or the writer of this book—feels real pressures to defend himself by relegating the study and writing to early morning hours and proving productivity in other ways during the day, or else by a large educational campaign to show that reading and writing can be accepted as productive.

A most vivid example of American emphasis on the values of accomplishment comes just at the moment of writing. The 1965 "reform" in immigration laws does indeed do away with old prejudices for and against particular national origins. But it substitutes for these the modern prejudices in favor of notable achievement and productivity. Welcomed to the United States now are those with demonstrable ability and potential productivity in technical and professional fields. (These, it happens, are those persons most needed by the countries they leave.) Near the famed inscription on the Statue of Liberty, which invites "your tired, your poor, your huddled masses,"

President Lyndon B. Johnson signed a bill which more clearly excludes these than ever before.

Illustration of still another kind comes as an editorial reader insists that the above paragraph should be a footnote. Apparently, by the going codes, such casual observations intrude unacceptably into the more conventional and formal presentation. A leisurely, passing reflection based on a newspaper account must go to the bottom of the page in smaller type. It does not have the same status as the more abstract, carefully prepared, and "scholarly" words that are supposed to make a book. (This paragraph, even more unconventional and playful, is probably even less acceptable.)

Therapy provides an island of relief from such pressures in which it is enough just to be, without the need to be something or to do something. It seems not at all impossible that the therapist's view of the person—seeing his worth as in himself and not in his accomplishments—must be closer to God's view of the person than is the American culture's view.

Church as moratorium—II

It does not seem wrong to suppose that the church, like therapy, is intended to be out of the world in some similar sense. The church, too, represents, and ought to communicate, a view of persons who are created and are redeemed in terms of more intrinsic values as persons and not in terms of their success in accommodating to culture by achieving within its terms or by solving the problems which living in it poses.

To be sure, it may be a corollary conviction of the Christian that the person experiencing the forces of personal redemption will consequently assume a responsible, even vigorous and productive role in society—just as the therapist anticipates that the person healed in therapy is more likely to take important, responsible, and effective action than when his behavior is constricted or compelled by defensive needs. But the priority is on the affirmation of the person without pressure to do or to be or to achieve anything in particular. When responsible return to the world follows, this is welcomed, even anticipated, but it is not made a condition of the personal affirmation.

The recommendations for the church which seem to follow from the above considerations may seem at first both absurd and reactionary—especially to ears that have been tuned to the idealizing, if not the idolizing, of the values of success and achievement. For it is going to be suggested that it may not be such a bad thing if church machinery, committee meetings, and all the other business grinds away without issuing many products, if the church organization and structure remains frustratingly impotent in solving its own problems and in addressing those of the world about it. This must be within certain limits, of course, and must assume that other conditions are met, such as those proposed in this book, for deriving fruitful benefits from even the impotent grinding.

It is not easy in our culture to want the church to be anything but an active, vigorous, effective agent within the culture. The pressures for achievement and productivity are powerful. Those who identify with the church naturally want their church to display these values, just as we so keenly want them for our children and our retired parents. Any suggestion that the church is *other* than an efficient and active agent for working change in the culture may seem a treasonable suggestion that the church ought to be less than the best. But the church, as the body of Christ whom culture crucified, bears a relationship between God and man which transcends the immediate concerns and time schedules of any cultural considerations. Of the dimensions of eternity which men ought to find at least hinted at in the church, certainly not least must be a kind of timelessness in which leisurely delving into the fundamentals of life is more important than solving any problems or developing any program or meeting any schedule. This is true even in the face of the urgency of the problems in the culture and of the responsible relation of church members to them and even in the face of what often seem the still more urgent problems of the organization of the church itself.

WHICH ARE ROOTS AND WHICH ARE BRANCHES? The problem is related to a value choice which is made between what are often called the public and the private spheres of life. One may choose to believe that the fundamental realities of life lie in such spheres as the social and economic and political structures and institutions, rather than to suppose that these are something more like convenient abstractions for social scientists to study. Then one is, of course, likely to regard the activity of men outside of these spheres as missing the point. If you see men in personal, home, or church life not directly engaging these entities, it may seem as though they are in regrettable evasion of the basic realities. This is a bias underlying much friendly and unfriendly critique of the church within the last decade.

Alternatively, one might suppose that the private sphere, meaning a person's involvement, for example, in therapy, in his family or in the parish church, may be at least equally fundamental. A person may find in this so-called private sphere a direction and a perspective and a personal integrity and identity which in effect emboldens him and prepares him for encounter in the public. Without this firm rooting in "home base" he may be buffeted about by these elements of the public sphere without purpose, direction, integrity, or effectiveness.

Analogies suggest themselves. Although it may well be true that "man does not live by bread alone," it also seems to be true that hungry people are not readily brought to higher levels of religious commitment, ethical responsibility, aesthetic appreciation, or political acumen until they have something in their stomachs. Indeed, ethical and religious men may lose the higher values they have, when sufficiently hungry.[3] The suggestion is that there are some realms of life, important as they are, into which men do not readily or effec-

---

[3] This has never been illustrated more dramatically than in Josephus' account (Book V of the *Jewish War*) of the reactions of the Jewish community to famine under the Roman siege (an account cited happily by Eusebius [Book III of the *History of the Church*] almost as though Christians would be immune to such deterioration): "All human feelings, alas, yield to hunger, of which decency is always the first victim; for when hunger reigns, restraint is abandoned. Thus it was that wives robbed their husbands, children their fathers, and—most horrible of all—mothers their babes, snatching the food out of their very mouths; and when their dearest ones were dying in their arms, they did not hesitate to deprive them of the morsels that might have kept them alive. This way of satisfying their hunger did not go unnoticed: everywhere the partisans were ready to swoop even on such pickings. Wherever they saw a locked door, they concluded that those within were having a meal, and instantly bursting the door open, they rushed in and hardly stopped short of squeezing their throats to force out the morsels of food. They beat old men who held on to their crusts, and tore the hair of women who hid what was in their hands. They showed no pity for grey hairs or helpless babyhood, but picked up the children as they clung to their pre-

tively move until prior concerns are satisfactorily handled. Hunger may be one of these prior concerns, and, at another level, the opportunity which the private sphere provides for developing direction and resources and identity may be another. At least two psychological theorists—Abraham Maslow[4] and Erik Erikson[5]—have developed systematic psychologies based on this principle of a hierarchy or pyramid of concerns, and their epigenetic relationship.

THEOLOGICAL BASES FOR A NORM OF LEISURE. Therapy has evolved its conditions, including leisure from pressure for accomplishment, largely on pragmatic and strategic grounds; these are conditions found empirically to be effective for the process of healing and the accomplishment of therapy's aims. Beyond the pragmatism is only the most implicit and vague assumption that these conditions accord more truly and harmoniously with the essential nature of man and that hence the therapeutic effect comes from a return to a condition more like the "pre-fall" state. However, the main grounds for recommending this leisure in therapy are, ironically, pragmatic: it brings results.

The church, on the other hand, has not only pragmatic grounds but also strong theological reasons for maintaining conditions of freedom from bondage to achievement. The church represents a doctrine that attributes an importance to man as a created child of God, quite apart from any particular abilities and accomplishments or the effectiveness of his adaptation to a particular society and his ability to make an impact on it, or to answer its demands. The church also holds principles which combine, on the one hand, concern for man's responsibility to confront the circumstances of his life with whatever energies and abilities he can muster, and on the other, a firm recognition of the likelihood that he will fail in any particular effort to improve decisively the circumstances of his life. The perceptions and the abilities of men are both sharply limited and

cious scraps and dashed them on the floor. If anyone anticipated their entry by gulping down what they hoped to seize, they felt themselves defrauded and retaliated with worse savagery still."

[4] Abraham Maslow, *Motivation and Personality* (New York: Harper & Row, 1954).

[5] Erik Erikson, *Identity and the Life Cycle*, Vol. I, No. 1 of the series *Psychological Issues* (New York: International Universities Press, 1959).

sharply distorted. In groups, these distortions are probably less often compensated and reduced than they are multiplied and enhanced by the particular conditions of group relations. It is consistent with Christian faith to expect that when a man or men set out to solve a problem, to accomplish a work, to guard against the contingencies of life, the chances are very good that they will not only fail in their objective but will create still new problems for themselves and others. The faith emphasizes that men are still responsible for making the effort, that life moves at this very imperfect hobbling gait, but that men should not expect these efforts to bring about their salvation, neither in a small sense of the solution of particular problems, nor in any larger, more ultimate sense. The Christian makes his finite and sinful struggles not in a desperate or frantic or defiant mood, such as that of the modern existentialist, but rather with the calm assurance that there are creative and redemptive forces in the world transcending his own puny efforts. Nor is there the desperate, crusading, urgent feeling that the fate of God and the Good depends, finally, on his own efforts, a view associated with many magical rites, with several non-Christian religions, and with some Christian heresies, such as Manichaeism, as well as with some tracts in our times.

If this faith provides an individual Christian with a sense of freedom, it should do so still more for the organized life of Christians in the church. Indeed, if an individual Christian is ever to feel this kind of faith as real, the chances are that it will have to be through an individual local church which displays this faith in its attitudes about its own life. Church life is not consistent with this faith when members feel, or are made to feel, a desperate life-and-death urgency about the activities of the church, when committees are made to feel that they must get through agendas and make decisions by deadlines, when women's groups and men's clubs are scolded for not "accomplishing anything," when Sunday school classes feel an obligation to cover a given amount of curriculum material, when church groups are made to feel that the solution of social problems depends exclusively on their own immediate political involvement or transformation into a local social welfare agency, when the fate of the world is made dependent on missionary contributions, or the fate of God's church on regular pledging. All such emphases put a premium and a pressure on the human activity which is inconsistent with the Christian faith, and unproductive of anything like a therapeutic or redemptive atmosphere for members. The world is indeed too much with us.

Church life as a divine joke

One would suppose that the Christian faith ought to suggest a kind of playfulness about the organizational affairs of the church. Members ought to share a secret but divine joke as they go about their busy-ness within the church—hopefully as a way to learn how to be similarly playful and loose in other busy-ness. The joke is just in this paradox, that they will all labor, struggle, even bicker, *as though* the issues and their efforts were of ultimate importance—but they will all secretly share the knowledge that they are not. If agendas and goals are not met, even if agendas and goals are not agreed upon, this is not the worst thing that can happen. The church should provide members with full opportunity and training to go through such life "in the world" as committee meetings and organizational struggles to formulate and meet goals. But these activities should be "not of the world" to the degree that they lack the final pressures and deadlines and ultimatums for accomplishment. It ought to be acceptable for decision and action to be delayed.

It could be emphasized, for the sake of those concerned with the church's impact on the world, that as a pragmatic fact, such leisure and its benefits do make more likely, rather than less likely, a vigorous and responsible return to the world. But to argue this is to pay apologetic homage to the norms of productivity and effectiveness, the sovereignty of which the church and this section of the book are both intended to deny. Leisure, like acceptance, may be efficacious. But that is not the reason for recommending them. Leisure, like acceptance, is to exist in the church because it presents a more faithful image than the world presents of what life is "really" like.

Several case instances follow.

THE CASE OF THE BUILDING PROJECT AS A FLOUNDERING ARK. Consider the case of the church board, which, for the best of reasons, let the concerns and pressures of the world flood in so that the church was swamped rather than remaining afloat as an ark of prospective renewal. The church program was so completely identified with the urgent worldly needs that it became indistinguishable from them. The board became concerned with the need for housing the elderly in its community and resolved to make use of available federal loan funds to initiate an apartment building near the church. The board was determined to develop this project successfully and at the earliest possible minute, which meant meeting a strict timetable for application procedures and construction. Their urgency came in part from the clear urgency of the need. Beyond this, however, the minister and some of the board members felt keenly criticism of the impotence of the church, which had some currency among church members and within the community as well as in the culture more generally.

They soon found themselves engaged in many of the ways of the world. Some of the frustrations produced anger, recriminations among each other, and bitterness toward governmental authorities. The frustrations, the work, and the time demanded made others, even some who had started with strong idealism, lose interest and withdraw from the project. In trying to acquire land they wanted, they followed some procedures of dubious ethics, alternately disguising and exploiting the fact that they were a church group, as it proved expedient.

The trouble was not that such worldly ways developed in the church, but that nothing happened to them in the church. In church projects as in any human programs one expects to find friction producing both heat and sluggishness. But the church is a place (like therapy) in which one also expects such defects in human affairs to be exposed, examined, reflected upon, and in some way transformed. In this case, any inclination the minister or others felt to hesitate, to reflect upon what they were doing and the way they were doing it or why—all such inclination was lost under the pressure to get the project successfully completed.

The net result of this project: The apartments were built, then quickly filled. A critical need for housing the elderly continued in the town; no one seemed to feel inspired by the church's example to do anything further. The church did not gain much general prestige for undertaking the project. The board members, rather than feeling a personal delight from having brought this about, instead felt a kind of dull distaste and discouragement from the difficult and bitter ordeal.

We can paraphrase Luther discussing good works: [6] It is good if the church does projects of this kind—social action, political action, church building programs, Bible study groups, stewardship campaigns—but not if there is a desperate urgency or needfulness about them. A church project or program may be good for the community, it may be good for the church itself, it may be good for individual participants. The apartment for the elderly was probably good on all three grounds, including the real possibility that individual board members were finding some sense of religious meaning in this mission. But the necessity and the urgency which the project had about it voided all these potential benefits. The needfulness of the program betrays a kind of exclusive, even idolatrous, reliance on the program to accomplish the goods and precludes the possibility of growth in Christian faith and responsibility as a consequence of the project.

Because the Christian recognizes a perspective which transcends the issues of success or failure, action or inaction, effectiveness or ineffectiveness, even urgent needs of the world sit on him loosely enough to permit him to pause to examine and explore other questions and other demands in his individual and corporate life, when these seem of even greater significance. In the example above, some significant issues in the Christian's life were encountered: problems of dedication and commitment, especially wavering under frustration; and ethical issues, especially the relation of ends and means. If such problems had been exposed and examined theologically and existentially as they occurred, the chances seem great that not only would the apartment project itself have finally been completed with more personal and community satisfaction all around, but also the men would have been significantly affected by it. They

---

[6] Martin Luther, *A Treatise on Christian Liberty* (Philadelphia: Muhlenberg Press, 1957).

would have been better prepared to detect further needs in their community and respond with sensitivity and involvement and candor. Such exposure and reflection would have required leisure and freedom from urgent demands for successful completion.

THE CASE OF THE DENOMINATIONAL QUOTA. Consider the case of the minister who received from his denominational offices the announcement of a quota which his church was expected to contribute to an urgent missionary appeal. The quota and all that it represented—for example, a project dear to denominational officials, the reputation of his church and of himself in the eyes of denominational officials, the genuine need of the missionary area—did not loom so important and urgent for the minister that he either conformed or rebelled. He neither pressured his church to meet the quota, nor put the letter at the bottom of the pile under projects he personally favored more. He simply confronted his board with the facts of the case as he saw them, that here was an appeal, made by the denominational offices which seemed to have much intrinsic merit but also had all the characteristics of a pet project of the national office. What would the board do with it? It was ten months before the board came to an answer—a period during which the denominational office became insistent, but a period of indecision which the minister and his own people tolerated well. They acknowledged this insistence of the denomination as one more "fact," which they considered. But they themselves neither shared the insistence nor rebelled against it.

In that interval they found themselves exploring many questions. The quick, patronizing sneer with which some of the board members greeted the first mention of missionary activity evoked a study of the preconceptions and biases they all held concerning worldwide dimensions of the church. This in turn produced a corrective study of the church's role in the contemporary world situation. Similarly, when some board members showed signs of supporting the quota simply because it was requested by the denominational headquarters, and other board members showed signs of resisting it for precisely the same reason, this was not sloughed over. It was carefully attended to by the minister and the board members themselves. It evoked considerable examination of their understanding and of the church's traditional understanding of church polity and authority. It also evoked, incidentally, some analysis of some individuals' characteristic reactions to authoritarian demands.

That the quota was eventually approved and surpassed is beside the point. The point here is that the men had a unique occasion to mature in their understanding of themselves, their commitments, their church, and their responsibilities in the world. They were far better prepared to meet—with less blindness and distortion, and with more enthusiasm, sensitivity and responsibility—future demands and opportunities that might come in the form of a letter or an outstretched hand, in or out of their corporate church life.

THE CASE OF THE ANNUAL FAIR. Consider two different styles by which a women's bazaar or fair may be conducted. In one case the driving ethos is hell-bent on an artistic and financial success. In a second case, members feel free to decline to participate, to gossip and become friendly while setting up booths, to quarrel with policies or customs of the fair, even to propose alternative projects to replace the fair itself. In the second case, morale may well be higher and the fair actually more successful. But again, this is not the point. The point is that in the second case, the women have a chance to have something happen to them. While going through all the motions of planning and working on a common project—perhaps almost a constant mode of life for suburban American women—they have in the church fair one opportunity to knock off the intense schedule and pay attention to personal and interpersonal difficulties as they appear.

THE CASE OF THE MINISTER'S SALARY. Take the situation of a board considering the minister's salary at budget-making time. In some organizations salary-budgeting is often an embarrasssing situation or else one elaborately safeguarded by delicate procedures. In a church, too, a minister may meet the occasion by excusing himself from the room during the discussion (something like grade school Girl Scouts keeping heads down and eyes covered during an election for troop scribe). But such a move is a confession of the extreme importance which the minister attaches to the salary and believes that others should also. It would seem more characteristic of the Christian norm for the minister to have made it convincingly clear to his board that the amount of the salary is not of unique and urgent significance, that it is just one more of many facts of life which they can share candidly and openly. The facing together is of a much greater value than some notion of justice or fairness or other prudential considerations in handling the salary. The pressure is off in this one situation and allows men to say to themselves and to each other—and then to reflect on what they have said—and then to reflect still further on their reflections—what they barely permit themselves to think under pressures "in the world."

NEW WINESKINS

Most of us live out our lives in startlingly narrow confines and with a rigid monotony of patterns. If physiologists are right that we use only a small proportion of our brain cells, then psychologists might tell us that each of us uses an even tinier percentage of the patterns of behavior potentially available to us. When we are hungry, of the rich variety of foods and dishes potentially available to us, each of us turns with monotonous regularity to the same few. Similarly, when we are angry, we take it out on the same old people or the same old viscera in the same old way. And when we feel gay or guilty or anxious or hurt, we show it with the same expressions and reactions that have become rigidly our own personal patterns during many years of usage. Across cultures, and even within a single culture, one finds an extraordinarily rich variety of reactions and expressions of anger, delight, anxiety, guilt, hurt. But for any particular individual, reactions are typically strictly confined to the few well-learned patterns which stamp his personality as distinctive.

Even when these patterns don't work perfectly—when they cause difficulty for others or between ourselves and others, or when they interfere with our own aspirations and ideals for ourselves—the patterns still persist as ours. Even when a person resorts to psychotherapy with determination to change patterns, he soon becomes agonizingly aware of the difficulty of doing so. His agony is like that of the repentant sinner unable to mend his ways. Patterns of behavior are too firmly entrenched in the myriads of repetitions since childhood not to resist even the most strongly desired change. They are entrenched in the degree of effectiveness and satisfaction which they do achieve and in a tangled network of involvements with other persons. In the face of this relentless momentum, geared tightly with the momentum of the others about us, how are we to devise and try out and perfect alternative behavior patterns?

Psychotherapy provides just such opportunity. It is out of the person's usual world. It is as though someone pulls the switch on the fast-moving, intricately entangling machinery about him to which his own behavior patterns are geared and chained. When one becomes hungry in a strange place without familiar food, then he tries something new. He may like it so well that he turns again to this food to supplement or replace his former diet—or he may not. But the situation forces a sampling of alternatives with the possibility that they may prove more satisfactory than former patterns. Therapy tends to be like that. It is enough "in the world" that it evokes quite genuine "worldlike" frustrations, anger, desires, fears and anxieties, and the rest of the full range of human emotions. But it is also, quite physically and literally, far enough "out" of the patient's usual world, that he cannot follow his usual patterns of reaction. When the insistent authority of the therapist angers the patient, this may replicate the way his employer angers him. But the patient cannot resort to the reactions of sharing gossip and gripes with fellow victims at coffee breaks nor can he become a petty tyrant in turn for those working under him. In therapy, there are no coffee breaks, no fellow victims, no scapegoat underlings. It is as elementary, and as important, as that. The patient will have to try to do something else about his frustration and anger. The alternatives he first attempts may be more satisfactory or less satisfactory than past ways. Hopefully, the other conditions of therapy, including the other freedoms discussed in this chapter, will tend to encourage more satisfactory alternatives.

This is why new life in a foreign culture is so exhausting, because so many routine patterns are disrupted. This is why sponsors of attitude and behavior change—as for example, Chinese Communist thought-control strategists, Western advertisers, "evangelistic" preachers, or hypnotists—try to provide either a highly deprived environment or a highly novel one, so as to disrupt past patterns.

Of the three types of "entrenchments" listed three paragraphs above—repetitions, satisfactions, and interpersonal entanglements— therapy most radically alters the third; it breaks the familiar social, personal, and physical environment which has supported, and in a sense even required, the forms of past reactions.

Therapy interrupts the fabric and context of life. Therapy also makes a less direct attack on the other two "entrenchments." The therapist tends to conduct himself so that the satisfactions that old patterns have brought in past repetitions are no longer possible. For example, in the case cited in Chapter II, Mrs. A's seductive pouting in the face of threat simply failed to win from the therapist the yielding and reassurance which she was accustomed to gain by it. As old patterns don't work, they gradually extinguish, even though here, the therapist like the preacher may be pitting his one hour a week against the patient's life "in the world" the rest of the week and all of the previous years.

Church as new wineskins

The church resembles psychotherapy in this characteristic to the degree that parish life is removed from the other life-involvements of its members. The church member tends to encounter different persons in his church relations or, equally significantly, to encounter the same persons but in different role relations.

The texture of personal relations within church life tends to be more casual, less intimate, less intense than the primary relationships which a person has in his family, among peers at work, in such social groups as a bowling team or a lodge, or among close friends. In the church, persons typically know each other less well. They feel correspondingly inhibited from more spontaneous expressions to which they may be accustomed. They may have "less in common" and have fewer of the "raw materials" of a relationship with which to build familiar patterns. Walters cannot retaliate to the slight by Anderson as he would if Anderson were his brother or worked at the next bench or lived next door, because he doesn't see Anderson that often and because he lacks enough involvement with Anderson to have any weapons to use against him. The social structure and organization of the church is not so intricate or so formal or so well-defined with role relationships which might provide persons with the fabric and the materials for impulsive reactions. One member of an ushers' team simply does not have opportunity to sabotage the work of another usher with whom he may feel rivalrous or to "tattle" on him to the head usher or the minister. The fabric of church activity *does* seem sufficient to *provoke* problems and problematic reactions; ushers in a church on occasion may feel genuinely rivalrous with each other—for position in the center aisle, for seating distinguished or attractive parishioners, for standing taller when they stand with the collection before the minister. But the church relations lack enough of the fabric of the world to prevent the person from responding to these reactions or dealing with the rivalry in the most familiar and practiced fashion. Members have to find new responses and new strategies; These responses may prove more satisfying, more adaptive, more Christian, more healthy. Conditions discussed elsewhere in this book may make new adaptive response somewhat more likely than new maladaptive responses. And perhaps once developed and practiced in the church, the improved responses may be tried outside.

To be sure, the unavailability or the unusability of well-practiced responses may also bring a kind of helpless despair and blind groping. Consider the complaint [7] that in sorting clothes for a church rummage sale some women unwittingly disparage the clothes brought by another: ". . . 'I wonder who brought this rag!' Naturally they are not aware that the person to whom they are making the remark could be the one who brought the article. This happened to me, Abby. I am sure it must have happened to others, so if you print this letter it might remind other thoughtless ladies to be more careful of what they say and to whom." Few women would be so without resources as not to be able to handle this kind of problem in most

[7] Quoted with permission from a letter in "Dear Abby" column, October 1965, the New York News-Chicago Tribune Syndicate.

relationships. In family, in neighborhood, at the office, they would quickly find ways to bring the offender to justice and to "teach her a lesson." But opportunity is so slight in a church that it produces the despairing helplessness expressed in the letter. In this case the "new response" tried was in the form of a letter to Abby, not highly effective, though mildly satisfying. But there is also opportunity in such a situation for experimentation with more satisfactory alternatives, such as a direct and candid but charitable and good-humored confrontation with the offenders; some of the other conditions being analyzed in this chapter would help encourage the possibility of such a response. "You are probably going to die when I tell you this, but I wore that for four years. Let me show you the spot on the back where my baby spit up just when my husband and I were going out to dinner last month. That was the last straw. That dress has had it. It is a rag by now."

It may be harder in the church to invoke rationalizations to help evade responsibility, because the realistic support which rationalizations require may be missing, either because of the sparseness of the social fabric or because of one's ignorance of it. One can't say, "Let George do it" so easily when he doesn't know George. One can't say, "It's their fault" so easily when he doesn't know enough about "their" circumstances to sustain a plausible alibi. Deprived of the more accustomed mode of rationalizing away responsibility, one might try something new, such as accepting responsibility. Having ventured this new mode once painlessly within the church, he might try it again, even "out in the world."

RISKS OF SUCCESS. The characteristic of "new wineskins" is, among other things, a fruit of the pluralism of American Protestantism. Members of the same neighborhood, of the same work group, even of the same family, attend different churches. This particular way of being "out of the world" has not characterized most of the church's history. It is jeopardized by the very success of the church in at least three ways. One is in becoming an established monopoly. Another is in becoming so large that bureaucracy and other social structures in the fashion of the world must be reproduced within the church. The third is in establishing intimate primary relationships among members, achieving too much success in establishing "community." The first two are dilemmas especially of more established churches; the last is a dilemma of sects. All of these developments provide, rather than deny, persons an opportunity to react in church as they do "in the world." The church resembles the world too closely.

THE FREEDOM OF STARK FOCUS

The "slice of life" which one experiences in therapy is a clean cut. Therapy forces a sharp focus on exposed personal realities. We have just suggested how therapy (and the church) tend to disrupt a familiar, not entirely satisfactory pattern by depriving a person of the means or channels for it. Other perhaps more attractive trees, if not the whole forest, can be seen when the favorite or familiar one is no longer there. Here we add the converse. In therapy, each tree is looked at for what it actually is, distinct from all the similar trees and cut loose from the entangling branches and undergrowth which normally obscure it. Normally, any troublesome aspect of life is screened and entangled in an intricate mesh of past and present involvements and ramifications. As this same trouble develops in therapy, it emerges as relatively isolated, definable, and manageable.

Miss N, in the last chapter, began to tell the counselor of writing a letter to the now dying mother of a former boyfriend. "In the world" she might very well have found herself telling this same information to someone for very much the same reasons as in therapy, to impress the hearer with her graciousness. But almost anyone to whom she might ordinarily tell this would already be involved in the episode in some way, in relations with the boy, the mother, or Miss N herself; it just wouldn't come up in conversation unless there were such a complicating context. But this context would then provide so many distracting (albeit important) lines of thought—the health of the mother, the present relationship with the boy, etc.—that Miss N would have no occasion to realize, as she did in therapy, something of the immediate meaning which this telling had for her, namely that it was an instance of trying to impress a man. Something similar must happen in the relative isolation and even sensory deprivation of a worship service or a confessional. In particular, "resistance" to the worship or confessional must claim attention, stark and undisguised. More specifically, the isolation and focus which therapy gives to behavior provides two special benefits. (1) It reduces the threat of complexity and vagueness. (2) It enhances the integrity and straightforwardness of self-confrontation by reducing the bases for rationalization and excuse. We shall consider each of these at some length.

FREEDOM FROM AMBIGUITY. Probably no small part of the superficiality and defensiveness with which persons normally armor themselves is due simply to the terror of confronting complexities and ambiguities of any kind. If in such relatively remote affairs as watching a play or confronting world politics we like to have specific programs and clearcut analyses, then we desire this more so in personal affairs. Complexities and ambiguities tend to raise threats which we subdue by programs and clearcut explanations—which generally are distortions and limitations. Entering a new group or a new situation, one fears uncertainty as to how to conduct himself, so he adopts a "role," which provides a pattern and reduces the fear, but also limits and cramps. A person feeling moved to try to meet some of his social responsibilities in his community faces a confusing welter of forces, institutions, and needs. To reduce this confusion, if for no other reason, he is likely to remain satisfied with a gift of money or another token gesture, or else to become intensely and exclusively involved with a single question or activity or a single institution. Difficulties one faces in family life or work relations are so enmeshed in intricate tangles of the past and present that in order to reduce this complexity, if for no other reason, one adopts simple coping strategies and interpretations, which are almost always too simple to be adequate.

In taking personal problems and issues out of some of the entanglements of the world, therapy tends to reduce such threats and to make a person feel that a question may be more manageable and can be fully faced. Because it is a fresh situation, things tend to come up one at a time and without confusing associations. Miss N's difficulty in telling the therapist a mildly self-glorifying account becomes a fairly well-defined, manageable problem and its ramifications come along gradually and fall into place. But precisely the same experience and the same difficulty "in the world" would immediately evoke a barrage of related, though secondary, questions: Why am I attracted to this man I'm trying to impress? Is he the kind of man I really want to marry? and so on. Too much to handle, with the resultant shutting off of examination, perhaps in the form of a resolution: I must be more guarded. The therapist is distinctly remote from the normal world of the patient—there is no realistic question of marriage or other confusing issues—so that the initial question remains of more manageable proportions.

FEWER BASES FOR RATIONALIZATION. The entangling contexts of our plights are likely enough, without any help, to provide a disguising and confusing screen. But frequently enough we help along the screening process ourselves. Whenever we are motivated—and this is not infrequent—to deceive ourselves and to make our understanding of ourselves a bit more palatable and comfortable, then it is easy enough to find some circumstances to clothe, or better, to cloak, the true character of our plight. In psychological terminology as well as in everyday speech, this is rationalization. The more significant or the more troublesome our affairs, the more likely we are to draw over them a disguising mantle of rationalization. The kind of fundamental or problematic matters of most concern in therapy or in religious reflection are most vulnerable to such blanketing.

Almost always, what we do in these rationalizations is to push responsibility as far away from us as possible and as far into the outer circumstances of life as our ingenuity can arrange. A woman sums up the dilemmas of her family life: "If only my mother-in-law wasn't living with us!" (But after two years of psychotherapy, after the mother-in-law has moved out, and after the woman has tried many other externalizing explanations, she faces something closer to the truth: "Now if I could only get rid of me.") "I don't give more to the United Fund because I don't like the kind of appeal and collection system they use." "I can't feel any sense of confession or reverence during the church prayers, because the minister has a distracting mannerism of speech." "I recognize in principle some responsibilities for the racial problem in my town, but the circumstances and the times just aren't suitable for me to get involved personally."

It is, of course, one of the purposes of the therapist, as well as of many preachers, to strip away, layer by outer layer, these protective covering rationalizations rooted in outer circumstances, until a person confronts the circumstances of his life and his own involvement in them in sharper, franker focus. This applies to the dilemmas and plights of "real life" outside therapy, where the natural complexities have provided plenty of material for cloaking rationalizations. But meanwhile, as difficulties and dilemmas arise within therapy, the patient finds available rationalizations disconcertingly sparse. Psychotherapy is enough "out of the world," barren enough of entangling circumstances, that one is left with little but the embarrassing plain truth of his personal responsibility for the fact that things are going badly.

Consider the minor but significant difficulty which Miss N had in telling of writing the note to the dying mother of her former boyfriend. This difficulty seemed mostly to represent her exaggerated fear of advancing herself and being too forward. As explained in Chapter II, this fear was not hard for her to detect and to acknowledge, and this acknowledgment led to important analytic and therapeutic gains. But suppose the therapist earlier, in an attempt to be sociable, had happened to tease her about having lost her boyfriend. Or suppose the therapist, again to be more normally sociable, had earlier mentioned a serious illness in his own family. Such greater "involvement" by the therapist would not be unkind or unaccepting and would meet the demand of many counselees and some theorists of counseling that the counselor be more of a complete person and less of a "hollow mask" or "dummy." But suppose the therapist had been more sociable and more personable in such ways as this. Then when the question arose as to Miss N's difficulty in telling about the letter, Miss N would have had many external circumstances to point to as rationalizations for her hesitation. Even though, in fact, the difficulty had arisen from long-smoldering and long-nurtured fears within herself, she would now have been far less likely to detect and to acknowledge this—so long as she could easily attribute the difficulty to something more superficial in the social fabric of the relationship with the therapist. If a counselor tries to create too full and real a role in therapy, tries to meet the patient's wishes that he be a more real and full-bodied person, then the therapy is deprived of one of its very important advantages of being "out of the world." Therapy is enough "out of the world," barren enough of the usual sociable furnishings of life, that a patient is compelled to face, starkly and unadorned by rationalization, what he is doing with his affairs. The counselor refrains from engaging the patient in most of the conventional social amenities which normally ease and smooth personal relations, but precisely because they blunt and dull some of the sharpness and the focus. In this context, we can easily understand patients' pleas for the therapist to be more "natural," "to share his personality." It would continue the easements and buffers "in the world." And we can understand why the therapist, perhaps regretfully, declines.

The total structure of the therapy situation is just enough "in the world" to guarantee that many of the person's typical and problematic reactions to the world will arise. But therapy is just enough "out of the world," meaning here mostly the attenuation of the "personality" of the therapist and of the total personal-social relation between therapist and patient, that the patient is deprived of most of the well-practiced bases for rationalizing the dilemmas and problems as they arise.

AN ADDENDUM ON "TRANSFERENCE." Many of the processes and characteristics of therapy discussed in this book under the label "resistance" are frequently discussed by psychotherapists and theorists of therapy under the label "transference." The two terms carry somewhat different implications as to the psychological significance and the therapeutic handling of the patient's behavior. But descriptively they may frequently be applied to the same behavior, calling attention to only slight differences in the characteristics of the behavior (see Chap. II, footnote 7). "Transference" especially calls attention to the characteristic being emphasized in this section, namely that a patient's behavior cannot be easily attributed to the immediate circumstances of the therapy, but rather to characteristics of the inner life of the patient, presumably lodged there during past experiences and now only "transferred" to the therapy situation. The resistances are "transferred" from "real life" and are not "earned" by the circumstances of the therapy in which they are evoked. (Other, nonresistive instances of "transference," such as the patient's faithful pursuit of the task of therapy or a warm emotional feeling for the therapist, may be welcomed as "bonus" aids to therapy, but they are left unanalyzed.)

Whether the therapist regards it as analyzing resistances or analyzing transferences, his strategy is the same. He is moving from the behavior on the surface back into the meaning and significance this behavior has in the internal and emotional life of the patient. The point here is that this movement from surface to meaning is hampered when the surface reflects many of the contemporary events going on within the therapy relationship. Then the patient can too easily make the "meaning" of his behavior seem to lie in the therapist's behavior. When the therapy relationship is relatively barren, the personal meaning can less easily be avoided.

Church as focus

Ministers are sometimes criticized, just as psychotherapists often are, for being personally cold or aloof or neutral or uninvolved. Patients often wish about their counselors and therapists that they would be more "human" and conduct themselves in a more social and sociable role, more as they would at a cocktail party. Patients sometimes express this wish by asking the therapist pointed personal questions or by trying to provoke emotional involvement or emotional response. Clergymen are not infrequently characterized as being socially aloof or awkward, inhibited or withdrawn, less warm or expansive or outgoing than might be thought appropriate for a profession working largely through interpersonal relationships. How much truth there may be to such characterizations will not be discussed here. It will be suggested that such a characteristic, if and when it exists in a minister, is far from inappropriate in the light of considerations advanced here.

Churches are often judged by members, visitors, or ministers according to the degree of social congeniality and cohesiveness present. Such social congeniality and warmth—often called "fellowship" by laymen and "community" by their more sophisticated ministers— may be looked for in the way strangers are greeted at the church door, in the pleasantness of coffee hour or narthex conversation or of worship, in deeper involvement of continuing small groups, or at other points in the life of the parish. Such concerns reflect the common and profound longing in our increasingly depersonalized culture for close personal relations. It also may reflect the tendency to look wishfully to religion and religious institutions to provide compensations for the deprivations and frustrations of life. It is hardly unacceptable for a church to meet such a human need and longing, any more than it is unacceptable for a church to provide food for the hungry or medicine for the ill. But neither can social pleasantnesses and friendship—doing better than "the world" at the moment may be doing in providing what ought to be one of the fares of the world—be identified with the fundamental calling or charter of the church. The solidity to which the church is called, as one of the implications of being of "the body," would seem to be a much more substantial standing together, more like that discussed earlier in this chapter in terms of "acceptance," in a commonness of trust, plight, hope, and companionship. This may or may not show itself on occasion as social affability and congeniality.

The minister who is something less than the perfectly personable mixer, and the church less than the very friendly and sociable club may, exactly in these "deficiencies," be thereby providing one of the more fundamental and important conditions for fulfilling its continuing redemptive mission. A kind of unworldly barrenness, even asceticism, has traditionally been regarded as better grounds for nourishing spiritual maturity.

FREEDOM FOR INTROSPECTION AND CONFESSION

There yet remains to mention the most obvious way in which therapy differs from "worldly" encounters. It is perhaps a summary of all that has gone before. It is in one sense a characteristic which the church least shares with psychotherapy. It is in another sense a characteristic which most emphasizes the ways in which the church is "out of the world." We refer simply to the fact that therapy implies a commitment and a purpose to scrutinize personal and intimate affairs.

There are those, at parties, in classrooms, and elsewhere, who insist on exporting this characteristic out of therapy and back "into the world." They would convert every personal relationship into one of personal analysis and psychodynamic interpretation. Psychological analysis becomes the remedy for all ills and the response to any situation. Most of us are properly suspicious of such excessive evangelism. We are properly reluctant to convert the relation between husband and wife, parent and child, friend and friend, teacher and student, or minister and parishioner, into the relation between therapist and patient. We are properly reluctant to replace all the important roles in life with that of the intently self-scrutinizing therapy patient. We are properly reluctant to analyze motives and scrutinize emotions for every act. A healthy dose of repression is necessary for personal functioning. A larger dose of repression is necessary for the sake of social relations and the development of civilization.

We are particularly reluctant to have the intense analysis of therapy imported as such into the church. The relation of minister and member or the relations among members should not be that between therapist and patient. The calling of a person into the church is not an assignment to engage in intense introspection of the kind demanded from a therapy patient. This entire book necessarily moves along the brink of such a mistake and may even inadvertently at times slip over the precipice, but the intention is to avoid it.

On the other hand, this analytic commitment to therapy may remind us of a similar commitment of the church, a characteristic which separates the church from the world as much as the analytic posture separates therapy from the world. For it is an appropriate, indeed a constitutive, function and aim of the church to encourage and enable men to stand candidly and openly before their Maker, Redeemer, and Judge. If it is an error to generalize analysis from

therapy to "the world," it is just as much an error to let our reluctance generalize back from "the world" into therapy or to obscure the
radical degree of stark self-confrontation to which the Christian is
called. Adam's disobedience led him to compound the distortion and
separation with garments and with refuge behind a bush. So it is with
all of us in the world. The remedial work of the church is coaxing
and prodding us from behind the bushes, to the point at which we
dare expose ourselves as we are without pretense or excuse.

The church is called to foster the freedom that permits men to
dare the double terror of facing what they are and what they are
meant to be and to venture risky, faltering steps of change.

Resistance:
A Sign of Vitality

Then the eyes of both were opened, and they knew they were naked; and they sewed fig leaves together and made themselves aprons. And they heard the sound of the Lord God walking in the garden in the cool of the day, and the man and his wife hid themselves from the presence of the Lord God among the trees of the garden. But the Lord God called to the man, and said to him, "Where are you?" And he said, "I heard the sound of thee in the garden, and I was afraid, because I was naked; and I hid myself." He said, "Who told you that you were naked? Have you eaten of the tree which I commanded you not to eat?"

(Genesis 3:7–11)

At the risk of slighting the central meaning of this account, one can imagine many a minister feeling himself in the same plight as the "Lord God walking in the garden in the cool of the day." A minister has lavished his energies in providing setting, occasion, and guidance for his people to prosper in faith and mission. But when he goes forth to encounter them, they are not there. Either they are simply not present or they are not making good use of what he has provided for them. Adam and Eve were not enjoying the garden provided for them, nor were they open to face its creator. They were hiding

Worse, they were hiding behind the same leaves and bushes of the garden they were supposed to be enjoying. Still worse, they claimed that they hid from God because of their honor and reverence for Him. Laymen too may clothe their own neglect or repudiation of the church's ministry in the most religious of postures. In the narthex after the service, in the neighborhood Bible study groups, in the deacon's letter on integrated schools to the editor of the local paper, in the embarrassed dusting of the Bible when the minister calls, in a Sunday school teacher's mechanical proof-text quoting, in the table conversation at the church dinner, in the way the trustees conduct their meeting and apportion expenditures, in overfilled pews—the people have the garments and postures of their religious heritage, but they misuse the forms to obscure that heritage. The forms of the church, like those of the garden, are intended to put people in touch with their Creator and their fellow creation and to nurture their own growth. But they become the means for evading encounter and for stunting growth. "The Lord God called to the man and said to him, 'Where are you?'" and ministers echo this cry plaintively, desperately, or angrily.

One can imagine the minister, in his annoyance and frustration, wanting to say to his Adams and Eves, "Come on out from behind the bushes and take off those silly fig leaves. Let's be about our business." In this he might be echoed by the professional critics of the church, who would speak of the "bush captivity of the progenitors" and of their misuse of the "forms" of the garden only to cower behind in irresponsible retreat and comfortable sanctuary. This misappropriation of fig leaves and bushes to provide an illusion of haven, a buffer between themselves and the stark actualities of creation and Creator—all this would be taken as evidence of their irresponsibility, their refusal to get involved seriously with the realities of creation. From the minister's point of view the resistance shows the people to be unresponsive, insensitive, and uncommitted.

But there is a larger point of view. The fig leaves and bushes are, in fact, evidence of encounter far more fierce than the minister and the critic may vaguely suspect. Adam and Eve hide because they apprehend much too keenly for comfort the significance of the elements in the garden, because they have assumed a responsibility much too dreadful to bear. Taken at face value from the minister's perspective, the hiding of Adam and Eve is an annoying nuisance to be surmounted. But there is more than face value. The words of God go straight to the point. "Have you eaten of the tree . . . ?" This is not placidity, but a trembling vitality. This is not aloofness and isolation, but the reflection of fierce involvement. This is not insensitivity and irresponsibility, but a sensitivity honed too keen and a responsibility felt too massively.

The preceding chapters have asserted the *relevance* of the seeming irrelevant annoyance. The disruption is related to that which it disrupts. The trivial distortion of the fig leaves and bushes in their use as clothing and cover, so easily seen as a petty nuisance hindering more serious encounter, is actually the very sign of encounter. It is part of a more fundamental disruption, which *is* the serious business. But here we assert something more than relevance. The act of hiding, of covering up, of resisting may often imply *vitality*, resources, strength not possessed by persons not found hiding.

Resistance is an active, vigorous response by a sensitive person to significant confrontation. Further, it reveals a commitment to remain inside the given situation however conflictful and problematic, and to address it in its own terms. Resistance does not accidentally or passively just happen. It is actively prompted, and behind this prompting is a vital sensitivity and responsiveness. Adam and Eve ventured out of childlike innocence into some assumption of responsibility, decision, selfhood. Their adventure turned out, to say the least, ambiguously, as apparently such human venturesomeness is inevitably fated to do, but the point is that their resistance was occasioned by just such risk-filled exercise of human freedom and responsibility, daring steps toward fuller selfhood. In Eden, the birds of the air and the beasts of the field have no occasion to cover up and hide. Nor do infants. Nor do those who aspire not to venture significantly beyond the safe innocence of childhood and of the lower creatures. In the drama of the biblical narrative, Adam and Eve first emerge as recognizable persons and they first meet their Lord only in the moment of hiding. This is their first conversation with God.

In their search for effective, meaningful ministry, ministers and theological students often find themselves attracted to special groups of people—college students, hospital patients, study groups in the church, artists, emerging social groups, and others who seem to be facing the essential issues of their lives far more openly and far more resourcefully than typical suburban laymen. Such ministers were chided in the first chapter for seeking isolated sanctuary, in the company of such special groups, from the undramatic ambiguity of life that most of us have to plow through: the existential intensity of such groups, as rewarding as it might be to the minister on other grounds, might provide only an illusion of relevance. Here further warning may be raised. The minister may be attracted to such groups not only for the seeming relevance of their concerns to the important questions of our life and times, but also for the apparent resourcefulness and vitality with which they face these questions. But here, too, the seeming advantage these groups have over their more plodding, plain, and placid suburban brothers may be more apparent than real. Persons in crisis, personal or social, and those in transition, personal or social, often display a resilience, a sensitivity, a resourcefulness that astounds and delights a minister. In the hospital, in adolescence, in other times of stress or transition, they are able to identify, express, and respond to important dimensions of their experience in a manner that a minister does not usually see among his "average laymen." But these less exciting "average laymen" may also be showing, *in their own way*, some of the same vitality and resourcefulness. It is our purpose here to suggest how these less obvious signs of vitality may be discerned.

Resistance is effort

In an old joke, which one can still hear almost weekly on television, the buffoon is asked, "How can you be so stupid?" His reply is some version of "I work at it full-time," or "It takes talent." Perhaps the joke is so dear to such clowns as Red Skelton because it does, in fact, cost them so much effort and ingenuity to play convincingly the role of a lazy dullard. The psychological armor and masks that all of us defensively create to protect ourselves, but which also distort our selves, require real effort and talent; the more successful and elaborate and impregnable the defensive covering, the more talent has gone into its making. This includes the defensive strategies of evasion and resistance.

In his frustrations over resistance the minister may often sigh to himself, "It would be so much easier for them just to follow along." A straightforward, positive response would seem so much easier and simpler for his parishioners than the kinds of resistive operations they pursue. "How can they think of so many things to talk about—in the deacons' meeting, after the sermon, in the study—other than the planned topic?" Or, "Why do they go to all that trouble just to organize a campaign of opposition against a simple plan to exchange choirs with a Negro church? Why can't they just come and enjoy it or stay away that day?" Or, "How can they be so placidly noncommittal and unresponsive to the provocative things I say in the pulpit or even in their living rooms?" Or, "How can they always misunderstand what I'm trying to say?"

Distortion, blunting, inappropriateness of response—resistance—is never automatic or accidental. The minister is likely to be right in his intuitive sigh. It would take less psychic energy and talent for the people to move with him. To avoid or to evade takes a vigilance and resourcefulness which is regrettable, among other reasons, precisely because it is a drain on energies that might be more constructively and less defensively used. We are proposing here that the minister's better strategy, like the psychotherapist's, is to think of his task as welcoming, garnering, and rechanneling these energies and resources revealed by the resistance, rather than in wishing, arguing, cajoling, or blasting them or the resistance—or the resisters—out of existence. The more inappropriate, the more excessive, the more intense, the more rigidly persistent, the more stubbornly repetitious, and above all, the more miserably frustrating for the minister are these resistances, the more, we make bold to suggest, he may look to them for hopeful signs that persons are in fact gripped or touched, that they are sensitive and responsive, that they feel themselves committed within a context that makes them feel it necessary to grapple, even so obstinately.

The emphasis in the first chapter ran the risk of seeming merely a Pollyannalike hopefulness for opportunity and resolution in the face of adversity. Here the risk is that the statement will seem little more than a general apocalyptic affirmation that things have to get worse before they can get better. Here as there, of course, a somewhat more precisely analyzed assertion is intended; more is intended, too, than the cliché of actors and others that a bad notice is better than no notice, although probably this is true and generally accepted. The main point here is that many responses which seem to be "no notice" are in fact actively and energetically "bad notices."

Resistance is motivated

To claim that resistance may be vital, positive response seems a prime instance in which the psychologist is saying that things are the opposite of the way they appear. The present chapter may seem to top even such familiar psychologists' inversions as the claim that people who seem to like you the most may thereby be only covering up their dislike, or that the person who seems most self-confident is only betraying his inferiority feelings. For we are suggesting that instances in which a minister feels that his words or his dreams or his programs are being most neglected may be the times that they are most heeded. The vigorous signs of neglect or rejection are active response. Something must be hitting the target or he wouldn't be provoking what he experiences as neglect. It was only around the most sacred and holy of their possessions, the Ark of the Covenant, that the people of Israel built such a stronghold of psychological distance and taboo. And so are the most vital and significant events and objects of all times the subjects of restriction and taboo. When the minister finds that his sermon has provoked the most unhappy variety of inane picking at his illustrations or his posture or his voice, it is perhaps on these occasions that he has most effectively touched sensitive ears. The bland "I enjoyed your sermon" or "You made some fine points today, Reverend" may be the clues suggesting that he has missed the target—or they may be still more subtle resistance.

Resistance is an instance—a vivid instance—of "intrapsychic conflict," the fact of surging, competing forces *within* a person. Indeed, it was in the stubborn resistance of patients to his earnest therapeutic ministrations that Freud first discovered the fact of repression and its key to the conflicts within human personality, which have provided the foundation for "dynamic" psychology ever since. For, no matter how much an episode may seem to be a battle drawn between minister and layman, we are concerned here with the large proportion of instances in which the significant battle is within the layman. If a member is "fighting" what the minister wants, he also may well be fighting what he himself wants—or, to put it another way, he may actually be wanting what he seems to be fighting. A conflict has two sides, or two forces. If one side appears prominently in vigorous strength we have reason to suspect that the opposite side may also be present, and in strength, even though not visible. For example, an exaggerated show of affection may be elicited not by the object of the affection, but by the internal need to vanquish the dislike or hatred for that object; if there were less dislike or hatred, there would be less prominent and insistent "affection." Resistance, seemingly opposed to the purposes of God, as the minister would foster them, may in fact signal resources within the resister which are strongly allied with these purposes.

It is in the overwhelming nature of the Christian message that the understandable response should be one of awe and struggle. It is traditional in our folklore that the resistive holdout to an evangelist's preaching is a better bet for meaningful and permanent conversion than the easy convert. It was Saul's most vigorous, even violent "resistance" to the Christians and their gospel which gave evidence of an encounter with this gospel that was eventually to propel a ministry throughout the Mediterranean and to lay enduring theological foundations.

It is this possibility, that resistance signifies a promising vitality and encounter—as well as the relevance discussed in the earlier chapters —that we shall now try to make a plausible proposal and not just a psychologist's trick. We shall look first at the resources disclosed by the resistance shown by Mrs. A and Miss N, described in Chapter II. Then we shall consider more generally how important affirmative reactions seem inevitably to be mixed with and masked by negative reactions. Above all, before the end of the chapter, we need to consider the vexing question of distinguishing between behavior that is an active, energetic, prompted resistance, which we have been describing, and behavior that may superficially look like resistance but really be a casual, bland neglect. How to distinguish Adam and Eve's actively hiding because they have something to hide from and are overkeenly sensitive to themselves and their responsibilities—how to distinguish this Adam and Eve from other Adams and Eves who happen to be wandering around in the corner of the garden back of the trees because they actually are insensitive to the opportunities and responsibilities in the creation in which they have been set?

RESISTANCE IN PSYCHOTHERAPY: RESOURCES REVEALED

In their resistance, Mrs. A and Miss N displayed at least three valuable resources. (1) They were skillful at thinking and talking about psychologically important matters. (2) They were sensitive to psychological "dangers," and alertly adept at coping with them effectively or avoiding them in time. (3) They showed a sophistication about psychotherapy and a commitment to this enterprise and its methods. Because they possessed these resources, they were eventually, after they had "worked through" their resistances, able to make excellent use of psychotherapy and to achieve in good measure a substantial resolution of the torments which had brought them to therapy. But also because they possessed these resources, they were very "good" at resistance. Their resistance was, as the therapist might well have said, "good and annoying." It was successful and effective in its unconscious purpose of impeding the progress of their psychotherapy.

We propose that what can be demonstrated about these patients in psychotherapy may often be true in the church: the same skills and energies which make some people so good at blunting and frustrating the purposes of the church and the minister are also the promises that these same people can be most effective in realizing these same purposes. Both psychotherapy and the church have incisive aims, which can be realized only if they cut in enough to hurt and if people are able to yell, "Ouch!" or at least to rush for salve and bandage to cover the wound. No ouch and no salve—no healing. What the minister experiences as resistance may be their way of yelling "ouch" and of finding a bandage. If there is no such response to the cut it may be (1) because people lack the courage to cry out or the simple resourcefulness to look for salve and bandage, or (2) because people are too numbed to feel the pain, or (3) because people lack experience in cutting and healing or lack confidence that anyone will heed if they cry out, or that first-aid measures do any good. These are the three resources which the presence of resistance does suggest and which are about to be discussed: skill, sensitivity, commitment and familiarity. (However, the analogy also suggests the possibility that there may be no response because there has been no cut deep enough. This is the "reality basis" for seeming resistance— that neglect *is* neglect because there has been no genuine arousal; blandness is the response to blandness. This problem will be discussed at the end of the chapter.)

Skill

Out of context, Mrs. A's account of the annoyances and anxieties she experiences in the hour just preceding therapy seems to be an emotion-filled account of genuine torment, highly relevant to her therapy, told with good memory for details, with intelligence, fluency, self-insight, even a touch of humor, and with candor and directness. Out of context, her implied fears of mental illness, aroused by a seemingly "special" treatment in the clinic, seem to be a candid, courageous, and insightful disclosure of anxieties and concerns highly important to her therapy. In context, and by her own testimony, these discussions were "made up," using the vestiges and remnants of real but not very serious concerns to mask more important concerns and to obstruct the proper progress of her therapy.

Out of context and taken by itself, Miss N's discussion of the problems she felt in writing a sympathy note to a dying woman, especially the mother of a former boyfriend, might seem laden with intense emotional involvement relevant to her counseling; and her ability to recognize and face these problems might seem a tremendous step forward. In context, this episode is understood primarily as an intrusive and obstructive moment of resistance.

Taken out of context and by itself, any act of resistance in the church may seem to display a high degree of sophistication, energy, and motivation toward the church. Only in the context of the intended purposes is the act seen as disruptive and resistive, though usually, of course, unconsciously so.

When the Bible study group pursues at length and in detail the significance of a single verse or two, they seem to be displaying a highly promising biblical sophistication, imagination, and energy—until one realizes that they are dodging the questions the minister or the study guide posed at the outset about the meaning of the passage as a whole.

The polite greeting to the minister after church, the shielding of the minister by the trustees from close involvement in budget-making and fund-raising, may seem like appropriate respect for the minister—until one realizes the biting impact he wanted his sermon to have, or the vigorous conception he has of his own proper involvement and the relevance of his gospel in "worldly" affairs.

The time, energy, and ingenuity which the women devote to their fund-raising fair seem a commendable dedication, even sacrifice, to the church—until one remembers the minister's hope, at least at the beginning of his ministry, that the gospel could help to make far more genuinely meaningful their lives of relatively undramatic drudgery and neglect, or his hope that their energies could be mobilized more widely in direct ministry to the neglected residents of the convalescent home three blocks away, or the patients at the mental hospital outside of town, or the social needs of the new arrivals from the south farther in town, or the political issues, local to worldwide, which surround them on every side.

The intense discussion at the business meeting of the church over the most suitable hour for one or more morning worship services seems a praiseworthy involvement and acceptance of responsibility by church members—until one realizes that the purpose of the discussion on the time of service is to find ways more effectively to reach those groups of persons recently moved into the neighborhool around the church. And so it goes with all examples of resistance. Even the boy who is a "discipline problem" in the Sunday school is a "likeable, imaginative, energetic little lad" apart from the context of the teacher's purpose to hold the class's attention to certain planned material for a certain time.

SYMMETRICAL ERRORS OF SEEING RESISTANCE PARTIALLY. It is possible to make the error of seeing such behavior exclusively out of context, of being drawn *into* and caught *in* the resistance. The therapist may pounce on and encourage the patient's facile discussion of these little problems and concerns. The minister—forgetting or never feeling quite sure of his initial purposes—may feel gratified at the biblical sophistication his study group shows or the respect people show his role, and he may welcome the energetic commitment the women show to the church. Recognizing and endorsing that part of the reality which is used in the rationalization, he thereby participates in the resistance. In so doing, he overlooks the resistive, difficult elements of the behavior, which are usually more unconscious. He thinks positively, perhaps even sentimentally. Most criticism of the church today is addressed to those who participate thus in the resistance. They need to be reminded that the superficial support may be a profound denial of the church's ministry.

But it is also an error of partial blindness—and perhaps of the blind partialness of excessive "negative thinking"—to focus only on the problematic, on the fact that in the context of purposes and intentions, the behavior is a blunting impediment. This book happens to be addressed especially to those who make this error, who feel themselves victims of an unquenchable, smothering fog of resistance in the name of religion which settles suffocatingly and blindingly around their every move. It is written for those who feel caught behind a kind of stucco and lace, stained-glass curtain of respectable religiosity which clatters down to obstruct their every step forward. To those with feelings like this about resistance, the book suggests that as profound as the disruption may be, still more careful scrutiny may show positive promise, as well as discouraging disruption, in such behavior.

Resistance can hardly be successful unless it does make skillful use of some fragment of reality. It must deal with matters that seem more than superficially relevant and pertinent to the purposes it is intended to blunt. And it must deal with these partially pertinent matters with a skill and energy great enough for the exercise to be taken seriously and plausibly by all concerned. These are the requirements of effective resistance, unconsciously perceived and met by those who pursue it. One cannot be too clumsy or obvious about forcing a detour of intentions or it will not fool him or anybody else—and it is the purpose of resistance to do both. The detour must look plausibly like a main road. Viewed most abstractly, the effective resistance is an admirable work of art. The effective resister must have the talent to find plausible detours almost on instant demand and the skill to provide instant maintenance of such byways in order to keep up their plausibility. If the obstruction of intentions is too crude and clumsy to look like a pursuit of these intentions, no one is fooled into following them, and the resistance is not effective. Too abrupt a change of topic, a stony or stormy refusal to participate, a tearful or fearful withdrawal—these are "resistances" of a kind, but so obvious that they can be addressed directly. They do not hold the same frustration for the therapist or the minister, or the likelihood of productive "working through."

MRS. A AND MISS N. The circumstances of Mrs. A's therapy hour brought out her talents clearly. It happened that the "free-association rule" was introduced at the beginning of this hour. It also happened that to follow this rule was particularly threatening to her because seriously anxiety-provoking material was very close to conscious verbalization. Even while still reeling from this surprise threat, she had a pattern of response ready (at 1, 2, 3, and 4), docilely asserting her compliance and repeating the instructions. Without missing a step, she rolled with the punch. After catching her breath in this brief flurry, she launched an account at 5 in which, hardly stopping for breath, she recited with insight and candor details of irritations in her relations with her husband and boy, her compulsiveness over promptness, and her baby's health. It took her only a slight interval more to come up with her implied concerns over more serious diagnosis (at the end of 5). And so she remained, fluent, agile, imaginative, producing plausible and tempting detours for the therapist to follow. Only when she was made more desperate and fearful by the therapist's challenge did her talents forsake her, and she resorted (as at 14 and 15) to cruder escape strategy.

In the case of Miss N, the threat did not come from a sudden move by the therapist but rather from her own unconscious perception of where her talking was taking her, toward an account no less anxiety-provoking than what Mrs. A had in mind, even though the looming material was perceived only unconsciously. But this threat was no sooner perceived, apparently, than Miss N had a plausible detour all ready.

Churchmen cannot so nimbly deflect a minister's intentions or his attentions unless they have a good repertory of information, interest, attitudes, and energies pertinent to their relations with church and minister, as well as skill at employing these. These resources employed in devising and developing resistance are the allies of the therapist or the minister, and of the person's own constructive striving for health and salvation. They are the same skills; it is not even correct to speak of them as needing to be rechanneled or used in different ways. The person *is* doing in the resistance exactly what he will do in his more productive development, and doing it in the same way. The metaphor is not that these are weapons being used by the enemy, to be captured and used by us. These skills in the resistance are truly allies. The metaphor is perhaps that they are now being squandered in small defensive and futile skirmishes. The person may eventually come to battle with more meaningful enemies of his own choosing, rather than being fatigued by defensive skirmishes.

From the perspective of each patient's own inner dynamics, she *is* "solving" her most immediately pressing problem when she distracts herself and her counselor from the prospective anxiety-provoking theme. When she no longer has to face and solve this problem—as, for example, when the same themes seem more manageable and less anxiety-provoking—then she will employ the same resources in solving more substantive problems. Instead of being used to devise attractive distractions and covers, the same alertness and insight, and knowledge and skills, may go into the problem of discovering why the material made her so anxious; such a use can only lead to more constructive and productive ends. The same energies which go into a man's flaunting and disguising the objectives of the gospel—when the presentation of the gospel poses such a threat to him that his problem is to blunt its impact—may go toward the fulfillment of those objectives, when he is freed to make *that* his "problem." The major task of psychotherapy is to detect the circumstances which seem to require the person to resist, and to change these circumstances so that resistance is no longer necessary and the resources can be released. A similar strategy would seem appropriate for the church.

Sensitivity

Adam and Eve's "resistive" hiding represented an awareness, a knowing. "The eyes of both were opened and they knew." They possessed a self-consciousness. They knew what they had done and they understood its implications. They knew full well the criteria and standards by which to judge their behavior and themselves. Without such "knowledge" they had no need for cover. From their cover could be inferred their "knowledge."

MISS N. If Miss N had not been burdened/blessed with a keen sensitivity, she would not have had to resist. Her sensitivity, first of all, made the past experience anxiety-provoking for her. It made her able to recognize easily such characteristics of her behavior as her "forwardness." It made her aware of the evidence in the past that this "forward" behavior had produced difficulty for herself and for others, while other persons with less sensitivity would have been blithely unaware of such consequences. It helped her discover, perhaps half-consciously, those cues in her immediate behavior with the therapist that she was being "forward," and that this was "bad" behavior; others, again, would have been blithely unaware.

But beyond making her feel anxiety and torment over such behavior in the past with a boyfriend or in the present with the therapist, her sensitivity also made her anticipate, from considerable distance, the approach of this account in her conversation, in plenty of time to take clear evasive action. Other persons would have, and do, wander into difficult and even anxiety-provoking situations "before they know what's happening" and too late to take any resistive action. The torment then just has to be endured. Miss N's sensitivity led her to see far in advance, unconsciously, that her conversation was moving toward an anxiety-provoking account. This sensitivity permitted her to develop strong resistance, where others would have blundered and suffered anguish.

The same sensitivity also led Miss N to some very important solutions and remedies in the course of her counseling, where less sensitive persons would have remained unhelped. For example, her sensitivity enabled her to learn to discriminate between objectively threatening situations (e.g., instances in which her "pushiness" might actually injure or antagonize another person) and those situations which were actually "safe" but which bore superficial resemblance to the others (e.g., instances of natural vivacity). She also came to discriminate signs of real self-deficiency from those cues which made her *feel* self-critical, but which did not really justify such an appraisal. Further, to bring undesirable behavioral reactions under her control, she needed to be aware of when they were happening. She needed to be able, as it were, to say to herself, even though more or less unconsciously, "There! I'm doing *that* again." Or, "There, I'm *about* to do *that* again." This ability to recognize and identify—her sensitivity—was a great aid in her maturation.

EVADING PRAYER LIFE AND GROWING IN PRAYER LIFE. May not sensitivity work similarly in a person's religious confrontation, both to enhance resistance and to enhance growth? Consider a man whom we may describe, to simplify a bit, as resisting prayer. He smothers the minister's sermon references to personal prayer in a barrage of discussion afterwards on other things. He may even be sensitively alert enough to detect in announced texts and titles likely emphasis on prayer so as to volunteer to help in the simultaneous church school those Sundays. When the minister calls, Mr. X is able to steer the conversation smoothly away from any prospect of prayer. If the minister stays for a meal, he maneuvers the beginning of the meal in a busy flurry of serving and passing so that grace is overlooked, or else he suggests a "Quaker-style grace," for which he may even have an elaborate theological rationalization supporting this type of table prayer. Or he may ask the children to sing "that cute grace you learned in Sunday school." He senses, from a long way off, whenever the minister's conversation may be moving toward the subject of a small devotional group.

We may suppose that such a reaction could derive from a number of factors, many of them enhanced by the man's sensitivity. Perhaps he is rebelling passively against what seemed to him as a child as arbitrary, authoritarian, hypocritical, and magical attitudes associated with prayer in adults who forced him to engage in it and who put on sanctimonious displays themselves. Perhaps, especially since surges of independence during adolescence, it has been difficult for him to assume the dependent, submissive posture he sees prayer as requiring. Perhaps—and perhaps not unrelated to the above feelings—some kinds of feelings of unworthiness or guilt or disobedience make it seem unbearable for him to approach God in prayer.

Whenever his resistance (and its underlying roots) is directly identified and challenged and "worked through," we can expect his sensitivity to be of great benefit in dissipating these vestigial difficulties and in advancing his religious maturaton. For example, we can, as with Miss N, count on his ability to make important distinctions. He may be able to see past the superficial similarities to discover that the occasions for prayer proposed by the minister are not arbitrary demands which "put him on the spot" as he felt he was in childhood; that there is a genuine spontaneity possible; that he is not required to participate as a believer in magic, or to surrender passively the vigorous, responsible grappling with personal and social problems with which he feels identified. He may learn to distinguish the difference, as a less sensitive person cannot, between the feelings of truculently surrendering automony to arbitrary or parentlike authorities, and calmly acknowledging one's finite limitations, his dependence as creature on Creator, and as redeemable on Redeemer. His sensitivity may help him detect signs of grace and forgiveness, or feelings of unworthiness, once these are exposed. He may be helped to isolate the essentially infantile and petty feelings of guilt and disobedience which he has pushed to the background of his attention because they are not too oppressingly great, but which still torment him at points, as when he contemplates prayer. He can distinguish these from the genuine and basic demands of God and from the full-blooded, earnest ways he does feel that he and his society are in trouble. He can distinguish the remnants of Sunday school toying with petty piety and mawkish morality—against which he feels rebellious and disobedient—from a kind of vigorous, manly wrestling with the genuine problems of his existence in the presence of the ground of his being. Such distinctions are not always easy to perceive, especially when the infantile and the mature are so closely mingled in most practices of prayer which a man may encounter in church; it takes all his sensitive powers of discimination to participate in that portion he can, without rejecting it all because it carries elements and language of the infantile.

Put another way, such a man may come to distinguish between false and genuine grounds for guilt feelings. He may sometimes feel guilty (with such resulting inhibitions as his resistance to prayer) for trivial or infantile reasons. Sensitivity can help him to recognize these as unworthy grounds for genuine guilt. On the other hand, false guilt feelings may intrude to dilute one's recognition of legitimate and compelling bases for guilt. Sensitivity can straighten these out when directed to the problem. Put still more simply, a sensitive person may come more easily than others to discover the difference between his own self-judgments and God's judgments of him.

PENETRATING PREJUDICES. One could probably analyze most instances of resistance in the church along these lines, to show that persons' sensitivity enhances resistance but also helps in the solution of the problems the resistance betrays. Consider the case mentioned earlier of the church business meeting, which is vigorously discussing innumerable pros and cons of different hours for Sunday services. As interpreted above, this is a resistance to facing the question of the church's ministry to different ethnic groups newly moved into the neighborhood. The more sensitive among the members are more likely to see the far-reaching implications of considering ministry to and closer involvement with the different ethnic groups. This sensitivity to fearful implications fosters resistance. But the same sensitivity by which they can identify long-run fearful implications also enables them to make distinctions that reduce the fearful aspects of the implications, when the resistance and its grounds are frankly faced. They can see through stereotypes and prejudices and be sensitive to the facts which refute them. ("Housing values don't always decline.") They are potentially sensitive to individual qualities and characteristics which permit more genuine relationships, potentially less blinded by gross ethnic characteristics, such as skin color. They can more readily distinguish different roles and types of relationships which are possible and likely. Sensitivity, in other words, helps to cut through the gross generalizations produced by fearful judgments.

Sophisticated commitment

For a minister, perhaps the most agonizingly frustrating thing about resistance to his efforts to develop the church and to present the gospel is that resistance is offered in the very guise of loyalty to the church and fidelity to the gospel. Certainly this is what most annoys the writers in our decade who are most annoyed with the church. Preoccupation with the forms and furnishings of the church interferes with and substitutes for attention to its real mission and ministry. The most diabolical ideology is clothed, masked, and hence accepted, in the garments of the gospel. How can you fight opposition when it claims the same premises, principles, and purposes, and uses the same language as your own? "I'm doing this for your own good," the resister seems to be saying sweetly; or perhaps more often (and even less open to rejoinder), "Yes, I'm with you all the way." "See what good use we've made of the foliage you have given us," Adam and Eve might have beamed proudly from their hiding place. "See what pretty clothes we have made with your fig leaves!"

"See how dutifully I'm following your instructions," Mrs. A could—and indeed did—claim, smilingly and imploringly, as she flagrantly and deliberately flouted them. She didn't use just any kind of distracting, meaningless chatter to resist the free-association rule and its requirement for her to face herself. Instead she talked about the rule and her loyalty to it, demonstrated her understanding of it, and, in her long speech at 5, presented her therapist with a fine example of a chain of associations in seeming conformity with the rule. All this, as we know, was in the service of resistance.

In the impasse over her next appointment time, Miss N so smothered the situation with her professed eagerness to accommodate the counselor and to get to her next appointment that she almost successfully sabotaged the possibility of making any new appointment.

In the church people sometimes make a community of love impossible by smothering each other with sweetness and love. A man may respond to—and in effect reject—God's demands for responsible Christian living in our time by reciting how often he attends church and by urging "all men to support the city-wide laymen's dinner next week which our committee has been working so hard to plan; we'll see movies from the last football season at the University."

"Yes, we certainly must be more responsively attendant to the needs of the people moving into the neighborhood near our downtown church; let's try to get them all to come to church."

"I'm so glad, Reverend, that you include prayers for peace and racial justice every week; it makes me feel so much better."

One can focus on either side of the ambiguity. One can be most aware that elements of the church's mission and ministry are being used as *resistance to the church's mission and ministry*. Or one can be most aware that *elements of the church's mission and ministry are being used* as resistance to the church's mission and ministry. Which is more important? The commitment, though partial and ambiguous, or the fact that the commitment provides the tools and materials for resisting its implications?

ABOLISH THE OCCASIONS FOR RESISTANCE? Those who are most aware of the resistance are likely to be impatient with the forms that provide the vehicle for the resistance. If the forms cover the real spirit and impede our true objectives, then away with the forms! "Ban fig leaves from the garden," their placards might read, so long as fig leaves represent the distortions between man and his true nature and destiny. "Let's discard free association from psychotherapy, or fixed appointments from counseling procedures," an impatient therapist of Mrs. A or an irked counselor of Miss N might plead, "since these things are used by the patients and counselees to obstruct the true healing work we can do." As for the church, we hear them say, "Let's abolish the forms and structures and language and all other visible signs of the Christian faith, because these are used by people to disguise and distort the true meaning of the faith."

Such a point of view has the difficulty that it suggests a futile treatment of symptoms. Whatever people use for their—at least since Adam and Eve, inevitable—resistive purposes, this view would reply with a knife, to excise it. There is something literally reactionary about such a view, since its thrust is always a retort or counterthrust, urgently removing the symptom after it appears. Various types of experiments have been proposed and attempted in our time for developing community and ministry shorn of these offending forms and structures; it still too early in most instances to discover what vehicles for resistance people will develop in such circumstances, when deprived of the more conventional means. But we don't need to wait to be sure that persons will inevitably find within their new situations what they need for impeding and distorting their own purposes. Sometimes it begins to seem that the nearly ritualistic recital of this new creed of freedom and untrammeled participation in the secularism of our time may become a kind of idolatrous formula which, like other excessive ritualism, impedes any advancement of its own realization.

The data are oppressively clear for at least one instance of an analogous situation, that of a professor cut loose from the usual confining forms of his academic life into the idyllic freedom of a sabbatical year. He is now freed of the routines of committees and appointments and papers and lectures and phone calls—the means which are supposed to implement the purposes of the academic vocation, but so often seem to impede it. (These are things easily resented as externally imposed distractions but inwardly repented as welcomed and invited means of personal resistance to the harder demands of the vocation.) However, although the present paragraphs *are* being written amidst the delightful sabbatical freedom, it is in the midst of constant harrowing struggle against different and subtler forms of resistance and distraction. These are less easily definable and therefore less easily damnable vehicles of resistance, and therefore less easily quelled. When the house is swept clean and the new devils come in, they are less easy to evict or to control than the first crew, who were so familiar and visible. When the critics of another generation come to decry the deficiencies and resistances of the new "free" experimental forms of church and ministry, they will not have so easy a time in identifying and correcting their targets as the critics of the present-day conventional church. Nor will the participants find it so easy to apply correctives.

WELCOME THE FORMS OF RESISTANCE? But the use of church forms for resistive purposes has two sides. The critics emphasize that it is resistance. It is also possible to be impressed by the fact that persons in such a situation are in fact using the materials of religion and of the church. In so doing, do they disclose some degree of commitment and confidence which needs to be taken seriously and in fact relied upon?

Adam and Eve did remain within the garden. They hid *from* God, and answered Him when he called. To hide from, actively to avoid, implies recognition of a continuing relationship, perhaps distorted or inverted but still a relationship. One's behavior is still governed by an acknowledgment of the claims of the other. There is more relationship and grounds for building further relationship in active hiding and in active resistance than in a bland nominal acquiescence.

Even if they misused the materials of the creation, they still used these materials and didn't try to invent their own. One might even suppose that there is something intentionally represented in the story in the fact that the means of hiding were of the same elements of creation as those which provided the occasion for hiding, namely, trees. It is not said, as it might have been, and as indeed is sometimes pictorially represented, that they clothed themselves with animal skins and that they hid behind rocks.

Mrs. A could have evaded the free-association rule, and the anxiety-provoking account she saw it leading to, in innumerable ways easier and more convenient to her than the one she chose. Outright silence, a repetition of the difficulties recited in the previous hour, or many other possibilities were open by which she could simply have ignored this threatening rule. That she actually worked hard to do her best, given the particular psychological situation in which she found herself, to follow this rule must have a significance which is not diminished by the fact that this effort simultaneously, because of other forces within herself, produced a kind of resistance. We can only surmise in a general way that this significance had to do with the commitment and motivation she felt toward the enterprise of therapy and toward the therapist. Perhaps it was a confidence she felt in the authority of the therapist and his procedures, perhaps a more primitive desire simply to please him and win his plaudits. Perhaps it was something more like her determination to find remedies, combined with the earnestness with which she had committed herself to these particular means. Perhaps she had previously heard of or had some actual experience with the way remedy was to be achieved with this kind of procedure; if, in her previous experience, "talking things out" sometimes helped, this benefit would generalize to her motivation in the present situation.

In presenting the "cover stories" which they used to obstruct more genuine disclosure, both Mrs. A and Miss N presented emotionally significant, "dynamic" problematic material. In so doing, they intuitively acknowledged a commitment to the basic temper and tone of therapy and counseling.

Similarly, one cannot simply write off the fact that churchmen *are* using the elements of their faith, even in resistance. Impure as the commitment may be, vague or partial as the comprehension may be, there must be in such behavior some recognition and some trust that these things are "of God," however impurely and remotely. For either therapy patient or church member it is not an easy task to devise those forms of resistance which will simultaneously express and inhibit purposes. To be willing to invoke this much ingenuity implies an attraction of some intensity. A person is "hooked" or gripped by the reality in these forms to the point that he cannot simply abandon them but must struggle with them.

SOPHISTICATION ESCALATES RESISTANCE. The more sophisticated one is concerning the forms of church or therapy, the easier his task of resistance, and yet also the more difficult it is. It is easier because familiarity brings facility in use. It is more difficult because familiarity brings awareness of stringent limitations; the material can't be made to stretch far enough to cover so many rationalizations.

In the cases excerpted in Chapter II, we can see how resistance was both enhanced and restricted by the sophistication Mrs. A and Miss N had about the affairs of emotional life which were relevant to their therapy and counseling. From the end of speech 5 through speech 8, Mrs. A adeptly raised questions about the possibility of more serious diagnosis of her difficulties. She made use of her substantial amount of information concerning psychiatric procedures, she reasoned plausibly from her experiences in this clinic, and she displayed no small amount of the kind of emotional reaction appropriate to such a concern. Above all, her use of this material as resistive "bait" presupposed her awareness that such concerns were likely to be regarded by the therapist as significant. Yet this very same sophistication about emotional life and psychiatric affairs led her to recognize, even without being really pressed, what essentially feeble resistance this was. She recognized quite as well as the therapist did (and perhaps before he did) that she was not displaying emotion characteristic of genuine wholehearted fear of serious mental illness, and that the overwhelming evidence was against any such serious diagnosis. She readily "saw through" her own resistance. In the nature of the case, this made it useless as resistance, since resistance generally has far greater importance for deceiving oneself rather than for deceiving others.

Miss N was less self-conscious in this instance that she was resisting, but she was more sophisticated generally. She produced important, "dynamic," "meaningful" material, recounting her relations with Mrs. Hagan, her feelings about death, etc. But she also intuitively saw through these accounts that she was not displaying genuine enough or intense enough concern (as, for example, in her fear of death) really to sustain these accounts of resistance. Rather than smothering the discussion under a single effectively resistant account —as Mrs. A more nearly did—she was forced to escalate her resistance. She resorted to flitting and meandering. This irritating rambling itself was in part evidence of Miss N's sophistication and of her commitment to the very criteria by which the therapist judged her behavior as resistant. Had a less sophisticated person chanced on either Mrs. A's account or Miss N's account as a form of resistance, he would have been able to sustain the account as a plausible and convincing fulfillment of his responsibilities as patient or client. He would not have the same high understanding of his responsibilities and commitment to them which would escalate his resistance. When resistance is "good," plausible, difficult to identify and harder to dislodge (effectively leaving the situation blocked and the minister frustrated), then the minister may justifiably infer that the resistance has been pushed to such a nearly unassailable point by the person's own judgment of the implausibility of "lesser" resistance. Such judgment discloses a commitment to criteria that the minister must welcome as allies, that he may have even previously labored hard to lodge in just this person.

As an example in the church, let us consider first the simpler case of outright verbal rationalization before moving on to another example of "rationalization-in-action," which is what resistance is. Consider a minister who, in sermon, newsletter, discussion group, and private conversation, urges a more responsible "apostleship" in meeting the many needs of the community. This elicits in one deacon some of the common arguments against social responsibility, including the slogan, "The church and the minister should stick to religion," and a kind of exegesis of the text, "Seek ye first the kingdom of heaven. . . ." He cannot invoke such a rationalization-resistance without enough sophistication to develop the arguments with some degree of plausibility. This is the annoying factor, that some sophisticated understanding of the church and of the Bible is now used to oppose the mission of the former and the meaning of the latter. This is what might drive some of the impatient, ban-the-fig-leaves critics to want to do away with discussion of church and Bible—or perhaps even to do away with church and Bible—since these can be so readily turned to purposes of resistance. What we are suggesting here is that such sophistication about church and Bible may be regarded as only temporarily in the service of the opposition and still, essentially and in the long run, an ally. For such sophistication carries with it its own seeds of correction. The same knowledge that built the resistance is also potentially able to undo it. A deacon cannot discuss the mission of the church or the meaning of this particular text with a familiarity and facility to make them plausible arguments without also being aware, dimly or acutely, of the defects in his account. The Word, to put it another way, carries its own self-correcting vigor; the deacon cannot know the text well enough to use it for rationalization without knowing the fuller meanings which now begin to present themselves and to challenge within himself, perhaps still unconsciously, his own rationalizations.

As these challenges become increasingly apparent to the deacon, the rationalization becomes gradually untenable and is abandoned. He may move "up" to a still more sophisticated and less easily challenged form of rationalization. Or he may move "down" toward a more candid acknowledgment of his actual reasons for opposition (political conservatism, fear, economic insecurity, or whatever), now laid bare by the abandonment of the rationalization. Whether he moves "up" or "down" depends primarily upon considerations discussed in Chapter III. This has to do with whether he finds himself challenged and buffeted here as in any other controversy "in the world," or whether he finds that in displaying controversy and resistance within the church, he finds a freedom different from "the world."

We may say exactly the same thing about the more common situation of "rationalization in action," namely, resistance, as we have just said of sheer verbal rationalization. Suppose, for example, that the minister's plea for apostleship is met not by rationalized objection, as above, but rather by a smothering resistance. For example, a deacon or a board of deacons may go into elaborate discussion of architecture, or city planning, or transportation problems, or economics. These are in the guise of pursuing the minister's plea for apostleship, but are actually serving the (unconsciously intended) purpose of deflecting it. Again, the sophistication which feeds and sustains such resistance is annoying. One may feel the impulse to abolish all such knowledge because it is so diabolically useful.[1]

The sophistication necessary to mount such a resistance implies a sophistication necessary to puncture it. To be sensitive enough to the minister's call for apostleship and to know enough about city planning to offer the latter as resistance to the former implies also a sensitivity and a knowledge capable of recognizing the limited relevance of one to the other. If the discussion of city planning is not a totally adequate response to the minister's plea, and if the minister can recognize this, so in all probability must the men who are engaging in this discussion. Those who know enough about it to keep the discussion going must also know enough about it to recognize its logical limitations. This is not to deny that this (resisting) motive, the strong need to be involved in city planning rather than in apostleships, may not completely dominate the discussion and keep such recognition of limitations quite obscured. This is only to argue that one may assume with considerable confidence that the sensitivity to the plea for apostleship and the judgments against the resistance are already lodged somewhere within the resisters. If they are not acknowledged consciously, the reason is motivational, not informational.

ENFORCED SOPHISTICATION DOUBLY ESCALATES RESISTANCE. At this point we should acknowledge a minister's own natural inclination to provide challenges to resistance or to raise them immediately from unconscious apperceptions to unmistakable clarity. But it seems rather that the minister's role at the time of the resistance is to reflect, and enhance attention to, the challenges to the rationalizations as these challenges become apparent in the deacon. The minis-

[1] One may even succeed in such abolition, within his own career, by finding a ministry among the unsophisticated. Or one may welcome such sophistication, proudly recognizing that understanding of city planning is necessary for the most effective kind of apostleship if it can only be enlisted. Much debate about vocational specialization within the ministry goes on in these terms: ministry to the simple and needy and directly responsive, or ministry to the sophisticated who are the most effective resisters but who are also the potentially most effective builders of the Kingdom when they can be genuinely enlisted in its service. But this debate is only part of the point here.

ter's role on other occasions, hopefully in advance of such resistance, is by instruction and preaching to enhance the likelihood that such challenges will be available within the deacon's own thinking. Whether the deacon finds in the church the freedom to acknowledge challenge and abandon his resistance depends in great part on whether the minister feels obligated to force recognition of the defects in the rationalization and to carry on a debate on the merits of the deacon's exegesis and appraisal of the church's mission. This is the question, in other words, of whether or not the minister gets sucked into participating in the rationalization on its own terms, or whether he is able to recognize the larger meaning of this rationalization in the life of this deacon, and to communicate something of this understanding.

It is difficult but essential for the therapist or the minister to recognize that he is dealing with an internal conflict, within the patient or within the deacon. We are not speaking here of the more basic conflict which has provoked the resistances, the appeals vs. the fears of apostleship, or Mrs. A's desire vs. her fear to discuss a traumatic episode. We speak, rather, of the conflict described in this section as to whether or not the resistance is tenable. At any degree of sophistication a person is likely to generate a type of resistance for which he himself can perceive both the plausibility and the implausibility. Because the therapist or the minister is particularly aware of the implausibility of the resistance he may be inclined to enter into the debate, pitting his own awareness of the defects and implausibility against the patient's (or deacon's) awareness of the plausibility. This has the fatal disadvantage of converting the proceedings from a debate *within* the person, between plausibility and implausibility, to a debate *between* the patient and the therapist, in this case between the deacon and the minister. This is an almost irreversible transformation which changes the situation from one of potential spiritual growth to one of increased defensiveness and increased resistance. Freedom for growth is more likely when the minister conveys his larger understanding of the deacon's conflict between plausibility and implausibility, and his acceptance of the larger conflicts in which this resistance is embedded.

Yet the first instinct of the minister—to challenge—may be quite sound. It is part of his calling and his opportunity to enhance what we are here calling awareness of the implausibility of the resistance. He wants to and should share with his people the criteria, the commitments, the comprehension, the sensitivity, the insight, which will make it most difficult for them to use their sophistication in the service of resistance. The problem is the timing. In this, the minister has a great advantage over the therapist. The therapist meets his patient only at the moment of resistance and, unless he is going to enter into destructive debate, he must rely on whatever sensitivity to implausibility may already be lodged in him. At the moment of resistance, the minister is in the same situation as the therapist. But the minister has other occasions in dealing with his people, when defensiveness and resistive barriers are not provoked and when he has opportunity to foster instruction and inspiration. Through teaching and preaching, he may nourish just those tools of judgment and analysis on which he must then, in the resistive encounter, silently rely.

RESISTANCE AS AWE

So far in this chapter the emphasis has been on what may be called the positive characteristics invoked in the service of resistance. To achieve resistance, as to achieve anything else, a person must possess and exploit particular ability, sensitivity, and knowledge. Their appearance in resistance, especially in "good," effective resistance, is a promising omen that these same resources are potentially available for more constructive portions of the person's spiritual pilgrimage. We turn now to the still more startling possibility that the resistance itself, as a negative act and as an instance of opposition—quite apart from any positive skills which may be used to make it effective opposition—implies constructive, positive characteristics which may be legitimately welcomed by one whose aims and purposes are being resisted. This is to suggest that there are positive implications in the very fact of resistance, in whatever guise it might appear, whatever resources are used in its service, however effectively or ineffectively it may be executed. It is not merely negative obstructionism but a positively prompted and purposive response, and the promptings and the purposes are not necessarily alien to the minister's own. The therapist and the minister may actually be closer to realizing their purposes when these purposes are resisted than when they are not.

"Fascination" and "awe"—and the readily adopted Freudian term "ambivalence"—convey our recognition that positive and negative feelings are often not so easily distinguished. The same object or person or situation simultaneously attracts and repels. The same reaction simultaneously expresses attraction and avoidance. One hastily tears at the telegram but trembles so much as to have difficulty getting it open; ordinary letters open easily. The ambivalence-awe evoked within religion is well known; it is formalized in doctrine and represented in stylized acts such as bowing, which suggests both a positive respect and an aversion.

Playfulness must be a common and important example of the expression of mixed feelings or mixed desires: the cat with the mouse, the lovers, the young brothers, the minister wittily teasing the deacon. Informal lightness and playfulness of manner between persons is often taken, and properly so, as evidence of genuine confidence, respect, and affection. Informality and playfulness is also often taken, equally properly, as evidence of a naked hostility or disrespect.

Our language betrays other evidence of the psychological affinity of logical contradictions. Ask any person what word first comes to his mind after you say each of these: hot, good, sad, up, in, on, etc.

It is possible that resistance may be regarded as a form of awe which betrays simultaneously avoidance and attraction toward the enterprise and purposes of psychotherapy or of the church. If the expression of avoidance seems especially prominent and apparent when one's own plans have been disrupted, the component of attraction may still be there in the act, to be discerned on more leisurely reflection.

But if this kind of talk is not just so much illusory whistling in the dark, then it must mean something that can be stated more specifically and more carefully. To speak of ambivalence or the simultaneous expression of positive and negative attitudes in the same act might mean many different things. Some of these have been implied above. Two will be discussed at more length here.[2]

Resistance as Fidelity to Commitment

Resistance may be the reaction against unforeseen implications of a commitment—and hence acknowledgment of the commitment. When one makes a commitment, as to therapy or to the church, he cannot possibly recognize all the subsidiary commitments implied, all the demands and obligations which the future in this commitment will bring. When they appear, he fights against them. But he stays committed, and his resistance is within the framework of that commitment. When one promises to "love, for better or for worse," he does not always know how bad that "worse" can become. But as long as he grumbles and fusses or otherwise resists the "worse," he is faithfully honoring his commitment. Otherwise, the simpler thing to do is to walk out and forget it. Something similar is also true in the case of ordination commitments, and their unforeseen consequences. The resistance may be the thrashing that one resorts to when he finds himself in deeper water than he expected. But he *is* in the water. He wouldn't be thrashing unless he were. That the thrashing movements are also the rudiments of the swimming movements which will save him in deep water is what we have pointed out in the

[2] "Explanation" for maladaptive and self-destructive forces within a person is sometimes proposed with a label such as "death instinct": persons are innately and fundamentally attracted toward that which is destructive or diabolical, or, persons fundamentally abhor that which is most creative or healthy or otherwise good. Thus, the more rational tendencies to love the good and hate the bad are matched by the darker, contradictory psychological forces, resulting in the ambivalence. This kind of "explanation"—reifying and naming the tendency as though it were a fundamental force or "cause"—seems deficient. It may hold as a generalized description of what often, perhaps universally, happens—namely that persons *are* commonly attracted toward the destructive, and that they *do* avoid the good for some reason or other. As such a generalized *description*, concepts such as sinfulness, or even "death instinct," may be very important and valid. But as an explanation, they do not seem to go behind the phenomenon to suggest influences that might produce it. They simply offer the phenomenon as though it were its own explanation, its own "cause."

preceding discussion. Here we want to make the metaphor suggest that he does not really learn to swim until he is in deep water, and that the thrashing is the evidence that he is, in fact, learning.[3]

We posit for the present purposes that all important objects and events, such as those involved in therapy and in the church, arouse both positive and negative attitudes. We may also recognize [4] that the relative awareness of the negative over the positive becomes stronger the closer one is to the object or event. Defects—the thistles in the far pastures, one's aversion to them—are all overlooked from a distance. When one gets close, they become all too painfully clear, and one normally backs away again. But if one meanwhile has made a commitment, has locked the pasture gate behind him, then he must respond to the negative characteristics in some way other than mere retreat and avoidance. This coping is likely to be in the form of resistance. The appearance of resistance instead of mere retreat and withdrawal implies that some commitment or point of no return has been reached which makes it necessary to stand and fight rather than switch.

The nature of this commitment, this point of no retreat, may vary widely. It may be of a "high" order, and imply a high degree of individual ego involvement and freely reached personal decision. Or it may be of a relatively "low" order, based largely on external and arbitrary social constraint. The basis of the commitment, so long as it persists and is sustained, does not make too much difference for our present purposes, except insofar as "high" commitment is more likely to persist in the face of thistles, to be a genuine point of no retreat; external social constraints tend to develop loopholes and leaky commitments. The presence of resistance does not necessarily provide any immediate way for distinguishing the types of "commitment."

Mrs. A was in therapy because of some combination of the kind of

[3] It could also be said—if this were Chapter III—that the thrashing is *keeping* the person from learning, and that only when he gets out of the deep water and away from its threats can he feel free enough really to learn from his experience. The metaphor here would have to be that the church provides the deep water, without the fear of drowning.

[4] Here we are following too closely not to acknowledge specifically the "conflict" model developed by Neal Miller and reported, for example, in J. Dollard and N. E. Miller, *Personality and Psychotherapy* (New York: McGraw-Hill Book Co., 1950).

motives proposed at the beginning of Chapter II. Like most patients, she found the first steps difficult—overcoming inertia, overcoming fear of the unknown which therapy represented, and overcoming the stigma. But having got through this much, she now felt a commitment and considerable investment. She also, presumably, like most patients, felt a certain relaxation. She was over the hump, and the rest would be downhill. She soon found, however, as pointed out in Chapter II, that therapy is no haven but, rather, that the storms of the open sea also beset this "harbor," and are all the more intense for being so confined. But she was now "in it." Having ventured this far, having invested this much of herself, having made this much commitment, she had no viable choice except to continue. If this meant following the therapist's free association rule, if this meant being "trapped" into discussing things she intended not to discuss, then this was the path she had to face. If it happened that in facing it she also fought it, the fighting was the evidence that she was facing it.

The impact of unforeseen implications must be greater within the church than within therapy. The full challenge of the gospel, the full demands of the mission and ministry of the church, are so compelling and so comprehensive, and the circumstances under which one often makes his commitments to the gospel and to the church are likely to render him so naïve, that they are especially likely to leave one over-committed. In the church, perhaps one faces especially demanding implications of a commitment. The decisions which effectively "bind" one to the church are characteristically made at a young age, or during emotional stress, or under very limiting motivational influences, such as a search for tranquilizing relief from tension, or for certainties in the face of ambiguities. As essentially "valid" or "right" as such decisions may be, they do not prepare or forewarn a person of the implications that lie ahead. They only lead him to them. More than this, such circumstances, tending to have the effect of making the decision a strongly committing one, not only lead persons to the uncomfortable implications, but also tend to hold them there.[5]

[5] Debate can rage, of course, about the validity of such emotionally "binding" commitments made in the absence of full understanding of all their implica-

Social psychologists in recent years [6] have become aware of the power of motivation for consistency, the urge to make acts, attitudes, and even perceptions of facts consistent with commitments that one has entered into. This is especially true of commitments that are perceived as freely entered into and of commitments that have been strengthened by such events as a public declaration of them. When one can perceive that a commitment has been reached under some form of coercion or when it has not been spread publicly before others, the commitment is less demanding, less likely to require acts, attitudes, and perceptions to be consistent with it, perhaps more likely to be changed itself to correspond to newly acquired attitudes or perceptions. A man attending church services primarily and self-consciously at his wife's insistence, a woman attending a Bible study group primarily in response to the minister's plea for "a good turnout," the adolescent who recognizes that his involvement in church life is primarily in response to the hypnotic spell cast by a visiting evangelist—these persons' commitments, though they may seem strong and firm by other indications, are less likely to lead them into vigorous resistive battles with unwelcome implications.

Ambivalence as evidence of importance and attachment

Most, if not all, acts or objects or events or persons that are important enough to evoke strong attachments and attractions are also important enough to evoke antagonistic or resistive reactions. To say this, as this section will, does not necessarily permit one to reverse the equation and say that all, or even most, acts, objects, events, or persons that evoke negative resistive reactions, therefore, must have

tions. Arguments may range from those in which people are most impressed with the seeming violations of free choice (people are psychologically caught or trapped in a situation they might not have really chosen) to those in which they are most impressed by the "existential" importance of involvement and encounter as a positive and essential factor in personal growth (if you stay on the sidelines until you have all the facts, you'll never get involved in the game of life).

[6] The reference is to so-called "dissonance theory" as represented, for example, by Jack W. Brehm and Arthur R. Cohen, *Explorations in Cognitive Dissonance* (New York: John Wiley and Sons, 1962).

strong positive attachments or attractions. But it often seems to work this way.

There are probably many different psychological processes which cause ambivalence, which lead negative attitudes to creep into our feelings toward whatever we find highly attractive, whatever we value highly, whatever we offer strong affection and allegiance to. We shall try to suggest enough such processes here to make the general point plausible. The most frequently used illustration of ambivalence is in connection with other members of one's family—parents, siblings, spouse, children; for it is in the family that perhaps the most intense feelings are aroused. We shall also try to provide illustration in connection with therapy and the church.

INTIMACY AS A SOURCE OF AMBIVALENCE. Attraction and commitment bring proximity and intimacy. Proximity and intimacy inevitably bring occasions of frustration, which in turn bring anger, fear, or other "negative" attitudes. A man marries the woman of his choice, and the process of living together inevitably brings its frustrations in many guises. (1) Her personal habits may simply not gear in perfect harmony with his. (2) She, for reasons arising out of her own frustrations in the relationship, or for other reasons, may sometimes be motivated to needle and frustrate; the intimacy of the relationship born of the attraction provides both occasion and opportunity for this. (3) The intimacy, intensity, and prolongation of the relation means inevitably that many other emotions and needs than those first involved in the attraction come to be at stake. Most notoriously, for example, her cooking may or may not have been involved in the attraction, but the relation the attraction produced makes her cooking important, and a potential cause of frustration and discord. (4) It may be that the very motives which were part of the attraction are also particularly vulnerable within the intimacy of the relation. No one and no relationship can provide sustained satisfaction for all of the high and highly generalized hopes which a man brings to focus on the woman he marries.

HIGH HOPES AS A SOURCE OF AMBIVALENCE. Mrs. A was presumably attracted and committed to psychotherapy because of a number of characteristics which therapy and the therapist held. These probably included the therapist's authority and expertness in matters of mental health and mental illness, his objective remoteness from personal involvement in her life, and the promise that therapy would deal with the more intimate and emotional aspects of her life. But these were also the same characteristics which occasioned fear, mistrust, apprehension—and the resistance generated by these. In interaction with these characteristics, even details of time and place of therapy became occasions for resistance. If she had not perceived these characteristics so strongly as to attract her into therapy, then she would not have perceived them keenly enough to elicit so much resistance. In the same light, if the sexual episode around which the resistance in this excerpted hour revolved had not had the importance which made it come to mind so readily, and which made it essential to cope with at this stage of therapy, it would not have been so embroiled in her feelings as to make her fearfully resist telling it. Like most patients, Mrs. A probably had unrealistically high, even magical, expectations of the wonders which therapy would perform for her, hoping for a painless healing to deliver her from the turbulent distress she found herself in without therapy. When such dreams ran afoul of the hard demands which therapy placed on her, in many ways more turbulent and more distressing than life without therapy, resistance was occasioned. The grander the dreams, the greater the resistance.

DESPERATE SEARCHING AS EVIDENCE OF AMBIVALENCE. Psychotherapy and the church share a characteristic which sets them apart from almost any other enterprise. When persons turn to psychotherapy or religion with an earnest, self-conscious commitment and allegiance, with confident expectations and high hopes, this is likely to be an earnestness and allegiance born out of some kind of desperation —a desperation of searchings and yearnings unanswered, crises and problems unresolved. If "problems" are less severe, if solutions are more readily forthcoming in a person's ordinary experience, he is not likely to turn to therapy, counseling, or any earnest involvment with religion. It is precisely the vigor of persistent unresolved dilemmas in one's life that propels one into wrestling with these resources. It costs effort, struggle, personal drain, and social stigma to grapple for the blessing and healing promised by therapy or religion. One doesn't pursue this struggle persistently and insistently unless he is pushed by strong concerns seeking resolutions and pulled by that within therapy or religion which seems to promise relief, a promise to which he is ready to commit himself wholeheartedly. It is this cost which separates the earnest from the casual. "Talking things over" with one's friends, routine "conformist" participation in church forms and activities—these are casual, low-key, safe activities; they are most likely to be prompted by low-key motivations, maybe routine desires for sociability and social respectability, maybe minor internal restlessness of other kinds. To move beyond, into intense involvement and commitment, requires the impetus of turmoil reverberating more keenly and remaining resistant to more casual "treatment." Those who are compelled into more intense expectation of and reliance on the church must be those with the more "difficult" needs, the difficulty which will show up as resistance.

Why do such "persisting unresolved dilemmas" persist and remain unresolved? Why do some searching and crises yield to a person's normal unaided efforts, and why do some not? The most likely answer is the persistence of ambivalent feelings, contradictory and negative attitudes which have resisted easy solution outside church or therapy—and therefore also resist solution within church or therapy! On these grounds, we may suppose that precisely the same factors which lead a person to intense involvement with therapy or church are the factors which will occasion his resistance to the ministrations of either. Mrs. A's "difficulties with her husband," which drove her to therapy, remained unresolved partly because they were contaminated by lingering hates, fears, and guilts associated with the unhappy sexual episodes recounted in the second hour of her therapy. Although she had reported the events to her husband, she had never faced, with him or by herself, the powerful emotions connected with the events. These emotions, unfaced because too terrifying, persisted to disrupt the relations between husband and wife, making the difficulties for which she sought solution in therapy. The same emotions, still too terrifying to face, produced the resistance which we have noted in Chapter II. That this underlines the relevance of the therapy encounter to "real life" was emphasized in the first two chapters. The point here is to emphasize that the persistence and the intensity of the "difficulties with husband" produced both Mrs. A's resistance and also her genuine and strong motivation to benefit from psychotherapy, to commit herself to the enterprise and to follow faithfully its procedures and its leadings. The same powerful emotions resulted simultaneously in the earnestness of her commitment to therapy and also the stubbornness of her resistance to it. To this degree, the stubbornness of the resistance was an index of the earnestness of commitment. When the commitment was less obvious, the resistance could still be taken as a hint of it.

Similarly in the church, the yearnings and the strivings which propel people into vigorous involvement are so likely to be fraught with ambivalence that resistance is assured. In a Bible study group, for example, the searchings and hopes which lead people into vigorous engagement with the materials are compounded from sensitive emotions which throw up the resistive armors and masks just as soon as that material comes too close to the very emotions which lead them there.

A person's intense search for moral guidance and norms implies an uneasiness and turmoil of conflicting emotions and impulses and a resistance to previous attempts to control. When these do confront the direction which is sought, they will not be tamed or subside easily into order and control. They will resist. Less need for guidance or less clear guidance would result in less resistance, but it would also have occasioned less important attraction initially. So it is with whatever form of deliverance for which one turns to religion and the church. The more desperate the questions addressed to the church, the less readily and peaceably are they answered.

SYMBOLS AS FOCUS OF AMBIVALENCE. Just as therapy forces the transference of key ambivalent feelings onto the relationship with the therapist, religion brings to intense focus around a few critical symbols some of the most crucial, intense, and general of human aspirations. These are necessarily some of the points of greatest ambivalence, as, for example: relations to fatherlike authority, dependent feelings, conflicts between impulses and controls. Being ambivalent, these symbols are particularly likely to enhance attraction as well as resistance.

The woman who is chairman of three important committees and boards in the church, and a feverish, faithful worker on a half dozen more must be driven to such furious activity on behalf of the church by something. We do not mean to suggest here that the "something" is necessarily unhealthy or undesirable or in any way detracts from the genuineness of her commitment or the value of her activities. We simply mean to suggest that the something is likely to be compounded of some ambivalences. Her drive, or motivation, is likely to be elevated to such an intense pitch by some type of contradiction raging within her. Perhaps, for example, it is the genuinely religious and universal problem of wanting to find assurance of her value. Her efforts to demonstrate her "value" must be raised to this intense degree only by considerable, not easily assuaged, doubt about her "value." [7]

The busy woman leader would provide equally appropriate illustration if her motivation were construed in more conventional religious formulation. For example, one might find about such a woman that

[7] To speak of the "motives" for church participation not only is a presumptuously ambitious task in the psychology of religion, but also raises a number of difficult questions about the nature of such "motives." There is, for example, the potential debate as to whether such motives are more profitably analyzed in psychological categories of needs and motivations; in the more traditional categories of theology and piety, such as "repentance" and "need for God"; or in more existential, phenomenological terms, such as "search for meaning" or, as suggested in the example above, "seeking assurance of personal value." There is also prospective debate as to whether it is more profitable to give attention to the kinds of "problem-solving" behavior traditionally sanctioned by church doctrine, such as prayer and sacraments, or to other "problem-solving" behavior of a kind which doctrine frequently disapproves as "self-justifying" or "good works" but for which church activities frequently seem to provide abundant opportunity. The above example of the busy woman leader happens to imply "self-justifying" behavior of the latter kind.

Fortunately, the present point holds regardless of how such questions may be decided. The present discussion implies a more or less *quantitative* assessment of motivation. This general quantitative point would hold regardless of whether one emphasized psychological, theological, or existential categories of motivation, and regardless of whether one examined behavior which appeared as self-justifying or as more orthodoxly faithful.

her intense activity was prompted by her awareness of God's goodness and her desire to respond with appropriate gestures of thanksgiving and of service. In such a case, the prediction still is that we may expect some ambivalence and uncertainty implied by the intensity. For example, behind such intense drive for service we might suspect the woman to have some unconscious doubt as to whether her service is adequate or her sense of gratitude sufficient; this in turn might reflect some unconscious recognition of actual ambivalence toward God; if some sense of rebellion and of alienation suffuses the thanksgiving, it compels the expression of the latter to be all the more vigorous, in order to subdue the former.

Similarly, we might suppose that the same illustrative woman turns, for reason of one or another of these motivations, not to frantic, organizational "good works," but to more pious or sacramental means of assurance. The very scriptural or liturgical or homiletical words which come closest to assuring her of justification and value in the eyes of God also arouse resistance because they touch and raise the very questions she most fears to face. Her mind will wander during communion. She will discuss afterward the cleanliness of the glasses, or question the minister intently about the meaning of minute details of the communion service, just so long as they are not details close to her critical concerns. Or else she may cross examine him in an intellectualized or rapid-fire or meandering way, which the minister feels despairingly as resistance and which is in fact serving the resistive function of protecting the woman from just those elements that are most fascinating and yet most threatening. This is a kind of insidious sabotage of the genuine meaning of church activities which some may despair of and disparage as so much meaningless business which buries the heart of the church's mission and ministry. We here suggest, as elsewhere, that it is most meaningfully associated with an intense though often unconscious commitment to and perception of "the real heart of the church's mission and ministry."

We need to end this section on ambivalence as a kind of "awe" with the same precaution which began it, a warning about the direction in which one can make these inferences. It is being contended that strong, positive, attractive motives, as are involved in commitments to the church, are necessarily accompanied by those contradicting, negative motives which produce resistance. Strong attraction inevitably implies resistance, but resistance does not *necessarily* imply strong attraction. Resistance may sometimes result from a constellation of factors which does not include what we have here called commitment. We are therefore dealing with probabilities of some degree and not certainties. But it would still seem that considerations like those in the preceding paragraphs suggest an intimate enough association between commitment and resistance to make this an important instance in which resistance does hint important resources which are to be welcomed in the same moment that one feels frustrated by the resistance.

WHEN IS OBSTRUCTION REALLY OBSTRUCTION?

Despite all this discussion of meaning and vitality in resistance, suppose that the deacon's discussion, which seems to be meandering, really is just meandering and not an adroitly though unconsciously maneuvered resistance. Maybe the Bible study group, which seems to be missing the main point and picking at gnats, really is missing the main point and picking at gnats, and not evidencing their sensitivity to the central issue. Perhaps the fifth-grade boy disturbing the Sunday school class really is "just a difficult child" and is not displaying a meaningful response to the Sunday school session. It may be that the suburbanites who seem to be exploiting the church to rationalize their own evasion of social responsibility are doing just that. What if things really are as they seem, and not as an upside-down, turnabout psychologist might see them? Just perhaps, behavior which seems to be meaningless or irrelevant or a stubborn obstruction, may be exactly that, and not the evidence of meaningful, sensitive, purposive reaction. Maybe some Adams and Eves just happen to be wandering around exploring the garden behind the bushes and experimenting with fig leaves.

We do not claim that the kind of analysis suggested in this book applies to everything that happens in the church, or in therapy. We acknowledge that many frustrating obstructive episodes may be just what they seem and not meaningful reactions, capable of being exploited for the greater realization of objectives. We have tended to reserve the term "resistance" to cover the latter, but acknowledge that much disappointment and obstruction may not be due to "resistance" in this same sense. The emphasis of the book is warranted by the conviction that more of us err on the side of failing to find meaning which is there than on the side of inferring meaning where none exists. It must be that many more disappointing rebuffs are actually occasions of meaningful resistance than are recognized. But lest one get carried away in grand, intricate, and perhaps illusory analysis (and lest he even carry others with him), it is useful to acknowledge the equivalent of the boy calling out the stark fact, "The emperor has no clothes on!"

The question which ought to be clearly faced, even if it is not so clearly answerable, is: How can one look at an instance of behavior and judge whether or not there is purpose and meaning in it, in the sense we have been proposing? One cannot very often just ask the participants, because, virtually by definition, meaning or purpose is likely to be unconscious, or at least not ready for full verbal expression. Are there other clues within situations and the behavior within them which can help one to decide, never with certainty but with some probability, whether there is meaning and, to take the next step, what that meaning may be?

This question, of course, is the persistent question throughout the book. It has been alluded to and acknowledged previously, and all of the long Chapter V is devoted to struggling with it, in the form of asking how one can discover what the meaning may be. The present briefer discussion, concerned with the more general question of how to discover if there is any meaning, could well be regarded as an introduction to that chapter.

ONLY MEANING, NOT MEANINGLESSNESS, CAN BE SEARCHED FOR AND CLAIMED. In the nature of the case, the burden of proof, as well as the delights of discovery, belong to the one who would find meaning. The advance of knowledge and insight, whether of a civilization or of an individual, tends to consist of finding patterns and meaning in events that once seemed random, patternless, and meaningless. In events which were once thought meaningless, and which others may still regard as meaningless, one can discover and demonstrate, with varying degrees of credibility, patterns and relationships. But the reverse is not possible: one cannot argue for meaninglessness against the demonstration of some pattern or meaning. One can, of course, from more cynical philosophical premises, hold a position which acknowledges the demonstrated meaning but asserts this as relatively trivial and claims meaninglessness on some more "essential" grounds: "All is vanity," says the preacher of Ecclesiastes.

In science, for example, if one scientist demonstrates a pattern where none was previously seen in events, this may be disputed, but not on the grounds that the events are without pattern or meaning. Another scientist may claim that the relationship is based on more trivial factors than the discoverer believes, that the discoverer has "failed to control" for certain "artifacts." Or another scientist may prefer to understand the relationship in different theoretical terms from those employed by the discoverer. But one cannot argue for absence of meaning or pattern or relationship. There is no possible evidence for the argument of meaninglessness. One cannot "prove the null hypothesis," as the scientists say. When we, as a civilization or as individuals, fail to discern meaning, this may be because there is none there, or it may be because we cannot see meaning which is there. And there is no way to decide which may be the case. One can simply pursue the quest *for* meaning, and for the refinement and correction of meaning. That is the stance which this book recommends as a reasonable one for a minister.

Alternatives to meaning

What could it mean to assert that an instance was without meaning of the kind discussed here? Several things might be meant, and these possibilities can be understood within the scheme diagramed in the first chapter (see p. 26). There the distinction was made between events which were (*a*) primarily attributable to *situational* determinants, (*b*) primarily attributable to persistent *personal* factors, (c) primarily reflecting a *reaction* of a person to a situation. The kind of meaning proposed here is that found within the third of these possibilities, when we are inferring from an event the particular reaction which a particular person makes to a particular situation. As an alternative to finding meaning in this sense, one might suppose that an event simply reflects much broader, more general, and less interesting factors of the kind listed above as (a) or (b).

MEANING IN SITUATIONAL DETERMINANTS. A person's response might be a standard, common, and "normal" way of responding to particular circumstances. As such, it is fraught with no particular meaning. It simply represents "what everyone does" or "just what you would expect" under these circumstances. Adam and Eve might have been in the garden for no *special* reason, but simply because this was a standard, habitual, and customary way of responding when one heard God approaching: they were always afraid of God because He was a fearsome God, and—a criterion appropriate in any other case than for Adam and Eve—so was everyone else afraid. Or perhaps they just sought shelter and protection from the discomforts of the "cool of the evening."

One might judge behavior as being without any special meaning (1) if the behavior is essentially invariant and persistent for that person in such a situation; (2) if it appears, on some grounds, to be appropriately related to the objective circumstances; or (3) if it is a commonly shared reaction. When a narthex conversation after the service overlooks the intended thrust of the sermon and focuses on irrelevant details of an analogy or of voice, this might be regarded as meaningfully resistant behavior: refuge from the impact of the gospel is sought in trivials. But the present alternative might suggest that this behavior is simply situationally determined. The illustration may have been so vividly presented, or the style of delivery so compelling of attention, in comparison with the presentation of the "main thrust," that no other reaction can reasonably be expected, and this is, in fact, the standard reaction.

MEANING IN PERSONAL FACTORS. The events may disclose and be attributable to the characteristics and traits of the persons involved, but without any particular reference to the situation at hand. Adam and Eve might have made use of fig leaves just because they were curious and experimentally inclined, or they might have hidden behind the trees when they heard God coming just because they were generally timid and fearful. They might have hidden when they heard anyone coming. Their act might not have any particular reference to God or to the particular occasion or circumstances. This was "just the way they were." Similarly, the after-sermon comments on illustration or on style of delivery might simply reveal some general and not highly significant personality trait. For example, a man might be "just curious"; when a sermon illustration leaves some tangents undeveloped because irrelevant, he likes to pursue them. He would do the same for any public address, or anything he reads, if he had the chance. And in fact, he behaves this way in all conversations. Or perhaps a woman is just "aesthetically inclined" or "literary-minded," so that the niceties of voice and delivery are of dominating importance, again without exclusive reference to this particular minister or this particular sermon. One might even suppose that a person has persistent hostile feelings and a chip on his shoulder; he accordingly finds occasion in discussing the sermon to make critical remarks about the minister's voice—just as he finds some occasion with almost anyone to make critical remarks.

A minister may find important and legitimate interest both in such "situational characteristics" and in "personality characteristics" as these are suggested by persons' responses. They may be highly meaningful, even though not in the special sense here claimed for resistance. In the particular clarity and intensity of parishioners' relationships to him and his role, he may discover, if he can be objective enough, much about them which will illuminate his ministry to them. Taking their responses as an especially valuable mirror, he may discover things about the characteristics of his church and his ministry which he might never learn in any other way. In the next chapter, the reader will be advised to inquire very thoroughly into the possibility of "meaning" in one of these more general senses, especially for "situational determinants," before he begins to sleuth for more particular, focused, and deeper "meanings" of the kind with which this book is primarily concerned.

RANDOM MEANINGLESSNESS. There is still one other possible sense of claiming meaninglessness. That is to suppose that the event is without reference either to the situation or to personal characteristics, but happens out of response to some combination of many essentially trivial factors. It is random or chance. One cannot see it as related to any factors that are important and identifiable. Adam and Eve might have seemed aloof from God because some combination of whimsies and incentives led them to be "wandering around" behind the bushes and to be experimenting with using different products of the garden in different ways. The narthex commentator on the sermon might be just "making conversation" without any particular reason for doing so. He chances to choose this matter to mention for a constellation of reasons involving his own memory, interests, competence, what he had just heard the minister and someone else discussing, traffic noises or movements in the pew in front of him which distracted or enhanced his attention during the sermon. On other occasions these multiple trivial "causes" might lead him to chance upon some quite different topic.

Clues to meaning

In contrast to the above, we are considering here the special meaning to be found in those events which represent the *interaction* of personal and situational factors: how a particular person, with his particular individual characteristics and motives, reacts to a particular situation, with its demands and restrictions and opportunities. The fact that we are discussing an interaction suggests two important guidelines to meaning, two characteristics distinguishing behavior which is meaningful. (1) Such behavior should have a *directedness,* since it is "anchored" at both ends by person and by situation. (2) Because it is a resultant of the interaction of person and situation, the behavior may not quite fit either the person or the situation; there may be an *inappropriateness* about it when compared with expectations based on knowledge either of the person or of the situation.

DIRECTEDNESS. One clue, then, or rather, one cluster of clues, is the quality of behavior or events which suggests a *directedness.* It is the opposite of behavior that is casual, random, diffuse, accidental. It tends to be taut, controlled, unyielding behavior. Something specific is pushing or pulling it in particular directions. One does not need to detect what these pushes and pulls may be in order to recognize that the behavior itself is under their more or less tight control. If one comes upon a tautly stretched wire, he doesn't need to see the springs and hooks which are pulling it tight in order to recognize that it is being so pulled. He may never know just where these are, but he can tell from looking at the wire that something is pulling in both directions: it is straight, fixed, unyielding to the touch, and cannot be made to change its position or direction. A wire which is not so "directed" is slack, may be snakedly heading in all directions, can readily be moved into different positions and locations—and so may behavior which is not "directed." The analogy may even be pushed so far as to suggest that the slack wire may be both less dangerous to encounter but also less useful than the taut wire.

Or perhaps the analogy should be a flight of arrows, one after another, describing a smooth arc across a field. One does not need to see either the powerful bow of the archer or the target in order to infer that both are present, even though he may never know who the archer is or what his bow looks like, or exactly what the target may be. But if the arrows follow a wobbly or inconsistent or diffused pattern of flight, if their direction seems to alter in response to winds or shouts, then one is less confident about inferring a taut bow or a clear target.

We resort to analogy because it is more a quality of behavior which is involved, rather than easily defined specific characteristics. It is a quality of directedness which may show up in different concrete ways in different instances. Particularly important are the characteristics of intensity, persistence, resistance to change, a sense of narrow focus, a sense that the behavior is specifically prompted and controlled, that it is coming from somewhere and going somewhere. Some of these characteristics we will turn to again in Chapter V as essential clues to what the "direction," the "somewhere" may be. Here we simply emphasize the clues that behavior does have some direction.

Perhaps recourse to Adam and Eve may be helpful, still in the mood of fanciful analogy. One important and elementary fact is that their behavior in hiding was tied to a particular time and stimulus. They hid when "they heard the sound of the Lord God walking in the garden." We may even fantasy observing them over a period of time in which they consistently hid when they heard God approaching and not at other times. Such regularity does not necessarily or immediately tell us why they were hiding or what meaning this behavior may have, but it is strong evidence that we are in the presence of something meaningful. Further, we may fantasy that the hiding persisted in spite of contradictory influences tending to modify it. It might have been uncomfortably cool in the bushes, there may have been uncomfortable vegetation underfoot, there may even have been unfamiliar beasts sharing the bushes. If the behavior is chance wandering, or if it is determined only by situational or personal factors, such diverting influences as these are likely to alter it. If they do not, we have more basis for inferring that it is a "directed" reaction. Furthermore, the account in Genesis tells us that "the man and his wife hid themselves from the *presence* of the Lord God." We may fancy that they were careful to put the trees between themselves and God. We may imagine them standing rigidly tall and straight behind their shielding trees. As God moved about the garden, perhaps they shuffled about the trees to keep a tree between God and themselves. We may suppose that such decided directedness and intensity in their behavior is an important clue that there was meaning and purpose in it.

INAPPROPRIATENESS. The other general quality of behavior suggesting clues that it is purposive and meaningful is an element of surprise or *inappropriateness*. "That isn't what I expected them to do or what they usually do." Or, somehow the behavior "doesn't seem quite right under the circumstances." From what one knows about the person, or from what one knows about the situation, one finds he cannot predict exactly what does happen. There is a deflection of the behavior from what might be expected or what might be regarded as standard or "normal." Such deflection may suggest a purposive meaningful intrusion. It may raise a mystery which can be solved by understanding what reaction is producing it. The behavior remains, of

course, responsive to the situational factors, and it also reflects the
personal factors, and this relationship can be traced. But the result
differs from what exactly might be expected considering either of
these factors alone.

In the case of Adam and Eve, we might say, "It's not like them to
be hiding that way." In other words, the hiding does not reflect the
kinds of strictly personal or habitual characteristics which were spe-
culated in the preceding section. They did not otherwise appear to be
curious or shy. Or, similarly, there is nothing about the objective situation which seems to suggest hiding. That is, the temperature was
not more comfortable among the trees, and there is no evidence that
God normally and customarily aroused this kind of fear response.

Admittedly, this quality of surprise and inappropriateness, even
more than this quality of directedness, involves a precariousness and
an approximation of judgment. One can never know enough about a
person or about a situation to be able to say with perfect confidence
that some behavior is normal and expected, and some other behavior
is not. Furthermore, there is always the possibility that the deflection
or the surprise which is thought to be a meaningful one may in fact
be a chance variation in the sense discussed above. Here, of course,
repetition, regularity, and resistance to change would be important
supplemental clues.

CLUES IN PSYCHOTHERAPY. Let us see how the above scheme
might apply to Mrs. A. The behavior which we have reported in
Chapter II and characterized as resistance might not have been so. It
might have been the random rambling which it seemed to be (i.e.,
chance) and without the purpose which we inferred it to have. It
might have been just Mrs. A's style of conversation and of meeting
new situations (i.e., a personal factor). It might have been the kind
of wandering discussion which people typically interpret the free-
association rule as requiring (i.e., a situational factor). Indeed, her
behavior did reflect, in part, all of these. But it also had about it other
qualities which could not be adequately accounted for by just these
factors. There was a kind of intensity and directedness about it, and
also an element of mystery and inappropriateness, even bafflement.
The talk was too steady, too persistent, too relentless and without

pause; it did not suggest the ebb and flow, give and take, of really random conversation. It was more like the strained juggling to keep a tree between me and Thee. Questions were not asked to be answered. She did not seem responsive to or even heeding of the therapist's answers or his other interventions. Her behavior seemed more steadfastly "inner directed." Furthermore, it was not only directed, it was puzzling and "unexpected." During the resistive episode, this was not the insightful, intelligent, candid Mrs. A the therapist had become acquainted with and was to know again at the end of the hour. This was not the Mrs. A who could speak of her problems and disclose her feelings in a straightforward way. This was not the kind of use of the therapy hour which she had shown herself capable and desirous of making. When she intimated difficult feelings, as involved in rushing to the therapy, or inner fear of serious diagnosis, or her apprehensions about the couch, the discussion had a flaw about it; it did not seem genuine. She was not discussing these with the emotional components, including hesitations, and with the kind of open reflective pursuit which the therapist had learned to expect as appropriate for her, as for most patients.

CLUES IN THE CHURCH. So these would be the kinds of clues on which a minister might base his suspicion that in the midst of unwelcome obstructive behavior, he may be in the presence of welcome, meaningful reaction. When the irrelevant after-sermon comment on illustration or on style is *not* characteristic and habitual (i.e., not personal factors); when it is not supported by consensus of the congregation, or other evidence of the objective qualities of the sermon (i.e., not situational factors); when it is poured out in a rush, before the minister has a chance to say anything or to interrupt; when it does not respond to the minister's replies; when it shifts grounds, is always "away from"—staying in back of the tree—rather than following any more positive sequence or progression (i.e., directedness); when it just does not seem germane to the nature of the illustration or style (i.e., inappropriateness)—then one may suspect meaningful resistance. When the deacons' discussion rambles from point to point without understandable sequence, except that it is "away from," keeping the conversation between themselves and the intended topic;

when the boy in Sunday school class is not "always" such a discipline problem, only when the teacher is trying hardest to get her point across; when the trustees' arguments against plans for inner-city ministry display flagrant and uncharacteristic flaws of logic; when the emotional components of the discussion seem much greater, or much less, than one expected; when the woman picking at gnats of biblical exegesis does not seem ready to listen to answers to the questions she raises; when a man or woman in the suburban split-level monopolizes the conversation during the pastoral call with a stereotyped recital of the advantages of the church—all these depressing irritations are grounds for suspecting that one's message or presence is, after all, having an impact and arousing a response with meaning to be understood and to be ministered unto, among persons of sensitivity, responsibility, and ability. For more suggestion as to how to detect just what this meaning may be, we turn to another chapter.

Inferences: Not Timid but Tamed

"Wild analysis" was the vivid term Freud used to warn of perils in the misuse and overuse of his techniques and insights. But he could hardly have imagined just how wildly rampant his mode of appraising human nature would become. His concern was with the possibility of relatively overimaginative psychologizing by a relatively few psychiatrists. With the popularization of Freudian views and enhanced psychological sophistication of the last decades, psychological analysis has grown wild, even weedlike, far beyond its original confines. One never quite knows when he will face an impromptu analysis, generally searching, sometimes accurate, perhaps even helpful, usually unwanted. Over cocktails or cards, in the church kitchen or at Bible study, one may find psychological interpretation offered gratuitously and pointedly. Such informal analysis can usually be shrugged off harmlessly or, as an even better defense, returned in kind. More serious, because usually offered and taken more seriously, are psychological interpretations offered by professional persons, such as ministers.

So when this book proposes that even the most trivial and troublesome of events in the parish may have important meaning, and when it invites ministers to look for such meaning, it risks encouraging "wild analysis." It also risks alarming those who are properly appre-

186

hensive of such wildness and, for them, discouraging rather than encouraging psychological sensitivity.

More annoying and possibly more damaging than psychological insensitivity is psychological "hypersensitivity." This is the ability to discover other's motives easily, variously, universally; to explain any behavior with little if any regard for constraints of logic and evidence. The ingenuity of any one of us, our resourcefulness at inventing relationships and explanations, is great enough, and human personality and conduct provide such rich and varied raw material for analysis, that any one of us, if he wants to enough, can devise elaborate and plausible psychological explanations for anything. The risk is that the connections and meanings may be exclusively in the mind of the "analyst," rather than in the life of the subject. Some persons— though they are not likely to have come this far in this book—may suppose that any attempt at psychological sensitivity necessarily leads to such undisciplined "wild analysis." [1]

To both the "wild" and the cautious, and even those possessing some disciplined sensitivity, this chapter offers a miscellaneous set of methodological guidelines by which a person might appraise an incident of "resistance." Perhaps these guidelines may simultaneously encourage the insensitive, curtail the hypersensitive, and reassure the apprehensive. The guidelines may mark out a path at the same time that they establish some boundaries and limits. Wild analysis often resembles an adolescent exuberance with new-found powers. But the problems of adolescence are not best cured by abandoning the powers and regressing to childhood. Beyond the naïveté of insensitivity and beyond the adolescence of a buoyant, uninhibited psychologism may be a maturity of disciplined sensitivity.

[1] There are today two problems of "wildness"—popular diffusion of psychologizing and lack of discipline in making inferences—where Freud foresaw only one, the latter. But the two are correlated. Popularity in the use of ideas and tools tends to spread more easily than the discipline which accompanied their development and original use. Resistance to psychological sensitivity tends to feed equally on both these forms of wildness. We are offended and made suspicious of psychologizing as much by disregard for canons of taste and appropriateness as by disregard for criteria of logic and evidence.

Psychology—object of ambivalent awe

There is a more general way of putting the problem this chapter addresses. Psychologists find themselves in our times among those who through the centuries have been regarded in a priestly role— whether by their own claim or not. They are among those who have been assumed in possession of secret and powerful knowledge and skills, capable of working great good or great evil. Such a stigma, which is perhaps shared in our culture by all intellectuals and artists (along with magicians and witches of other cultures), evokes the awe compounded of intense respect and intense fear, popularity and antipathy. Such "priests" are sought out and shunned with equally enthusiastic trust and mistrust.

The services of psychologists are demanded by communities and individuals, and then ignored. A typical parent insists that his school system have "qualified and trained" (meaning properly initiated members of the mysterious priesthood) psychological counselors, and he also insists that his own children not go near them. Members of many professions, including the ministry, are strongly encouraged to partake of this special knowledge and, as soon as they start to demonstrate it, are roundly rebuffed for "getting too psychological" in their sermons and personal conversation.

The publisher or televison producer can be sure of successful response any time he offers an array of formulae for happier family life, job success, etc., so long as the recommendations come from an authority with degree and title proving membership among the initiated experts. Joyce Brothers, with all her many other assets, could hardly command the following achieved by Dr. Joyce Brothers. But the publisher and producer can be equally assured of the success of exposé and criticism of the role of psychologists in our culture. Rebellious attacks on the testing gnosis and therapeutic rituals of this mysterious, arrogant priesthood sell well.

One typical response to such secret wisdom and skills is the attempt to capture them and make them our own. If we can use this power, if we can control it ourselves, we enhance the grounds for our respect and reduce the grounds for our fear and mistrust. Perhaps this is how we may interpret the popular currency of psychological terms, attitudes, and procedures in our decades, especially that system of thought and technique which seems both mysterious and most powerful, "Freudianism."

Such is the context in which a book like this will be received, insofar as it is received at all. The reader can be expected to possess some blend, in different proportions in different persons, of welcome and of skepticism toward psychological excursions into the basis of church participation.

The purposes of this exercise seem modest and innocent enough. We are proposing, for example, that a minister understand as clearly as possible the personal meaning, significance, and background of behavior and events, especially those that are most involving and frustrating and evoking of personal reactions. This hardly seems a revolutionary proposal. It is part of the commitment which most ministers already honor and practice, whether self-consciously in terms like those used here, or in other ways. Furthermore, we are not proposing the technical knowledge and special practices of any particular cult of psychological priests. The starting point, indeed, does come from the analogy of one concept, resistance, in one theory of therapy. But beyond this, we are not engaged in promoting particular psychological theories requiring indoctrination, initiation, and subsequent faithful adherence to creed and ritual. We are not urging anyone to find *particular* "meanings" and interpretations in situations. Our exercise is not Psychological with a capital "P" in the sense that we would insist on interpretations of the particular perspectives and systems of anyone who presently wears a badge of "Psychologist." Our proposals are psychological in a much broader sense, and with a small "p," reflecting a more original and literal meaning of the term "knowledge of the inner life."

Yet, because the proposals are psychological even with a small "p," they will inevitably be viewed by some with considerable ambivalence of mingled enthusiasm and mistrust. The present chapter is an attempt to demonstrate just how modest, humble, and ordinary are the proposals of this book.

Psychotherapist or minister?

There is still another way to put the purpose of this chapter. This book is an exploration of the possibility that the conduct of a parish church might profitably imitate certain aspects of the conduct of psychotherapy. But the suspicion can very properly be raised about any such recommendation that it makes an unwarranted assumption of similarity between the two enterprises. It can be pointed out that as valid and valuable as psychotherapy may be, a church is something different, and what is appropriate or effective in the one may not be in the other.

Particularly, despite similarities noted in Chapters II and III, a number of conditions in psychotherapy do not apply in the church. These include first the particular talents, training, and experience of the psychotherapist which equip him to detect and respond appropriately to underlying psychological dimensions of a person's behavior and report. Second, psychotherapy provides a relationship far more intense and intimate than is likely to be found in any parish church relationship. During the lengthy hours the therapist spends with a patient, he comes to know far more about him, his inner life, and his history, than any minister is likely to know about one of his parishioners, even over many years. Therapist and patient may develop a relationship of candor and expressiveness which is unrealistic to expect within the limitations of even the most ideal relationships within a church. Third, and perhaps most important, the patient enters therapy with full expectation that his inner life will be analyzed and interpreted. This, to put it perhaps too mildly, is not an expectation most persons have of their role within a church.

The minister may feel that this book, like others before and undoubtedly others after it, is trying to make him become a psychotherapist when he is not a psychotherapist, does not have the training to be a psychotherapist, doesn't want to be a psychotherapist, isn't expected to be by his people, has purposes in his own vocation other than merely the psychological healing performed by a psychotherapist, and has bases of relationships with his parishioners other than those of an analyst to a patient.[2]

It is perfectly true that the model of the psychotherapist's handling of resistance fits only partially the situation of the church. Although the conditions of the two enterprises overlap considerably and considerable generalization is possible, it is also true that they do not coincide perfectly and that generalization has its limits. But very simply, it is suggested that churchmen can learn something from the psychotherapist, without being psychotherapists themselves. Particular elements of the psychotherapist's strategies can be adapted without imitating everything he does. To understand more clearly which elements *are* adaptable, considerable analysis needs to be made of just what a psychotherapist does when he faces resistance. In fact, for these purposes of *selective* adaptation, more careful and detailed analysis needs to be made than if we were simply recommending wholesale imitation of the psychotherapist. In limited ways, this chapter may be regarded as a glimpse into the processes by which a therapist's mind might work in appraising the significance of an instance of resistance.

BEFORE PROBING THE DEPTHS

First, the facts

In the headlong rush to display our psychological ingenuity, we are inclined to outdistance the facts. We are ready with an intricate explanation for why something has happened long before we are sure just what has happened. Explanations as to *why* are more fun, more challenging, and more reassuring, than descriptions as to *what*. Events hanging loose "out there" in objectivity may seem too alien until properly captured in our own net of explanations. We are too

---

[2] To be consistent with the distinction, to be developed in this chapter, between realistically oriented and personally based resistance, it should be acknowledged that the discussion here is with reference only to the degree of "reality" in the resistive argument just cited. To the degree that such resistance has a more personal "meaning," it is explored elsewhere.

accustomed to generalizing and abstracting and interpreting—particularly those of us who live by words in occupations that seem to demand a stream of insight—to find it comfortable to approach situations with anything like cold, raw objectivity. Particularly when we are participants, not just observers, we fit the events into categories relevant to our own participation. We can hardly see people and situations in their own terms when we have already approached them with our own terms, the categories and frames of reference in which so much of ourselves is invested. Even this book might easily seem just to encourage the substitution of one kind of interpretive judgment for another, the replacement of an angry "rejecting" judgment by a psychological "understanding" judgment. Ready psychologizing can be as glib a way as any other of disposing of a situation (and not necessarily without hostility) without paying serious attention to what it really is.

It would be useful illustration and discipline to attempt to record verbatim and objectively everything that happened in a simple conversation or a brief portion of a group meeting. What was said, by whom, in what sequence, in what manner, with what gestures? Who was present? How did they respond, in expression and gesture? It would be instructive to discover that it can be done. It would be more instructive to discover how difficult and wrenching it is, because it is so unlike our usual practice of stuffing events into the pigeonholes of our preconceptions and ignoring those which don't easily fit.

If proneness to interpret without observing is strong enough for other events, it must be especially strong for instances of resistance. Here personal feelings are most mobilized, and pressures against objectivity are the greatest. Massive emotional reaction—denial, anger, depression—is more natural and easier than close attention to the factual details of the context and content of the disruption.

CITING FACTS AS A RESPONSE TO RESISTANCE. Necessary prerequisite that it is, getting the facts straight is not very often sufficient as an appropriate response to the situation. There may even be times when recounting the facts is a defensive way of distancing oneself from the event and its meaning. But there are also some occasions when attention to the facts may be a useful and important response.

Maybe all a minister or a therapist has to do sometimes is point objectively to an event and its disruptive character. This is contribution enough. Let the others carry on from there. After all, parishioners and patients too are blinded by the narrow interpretive categories with which they necessarily have approached events. But they too have resources to transcend this blindness if given impetus.

Just to point out the simple, objective facts may serve two purposes. First, it may shake people loose from their preconceptions. A calm objective statement of the situation, set alongside their own judgments of it, may expose the inadequacy of the latter and trigger motives for more satisfactory understanding. If the story of the "Emperor's Clothes" is a bit extreme as analogy, it still may be appropriate. In the midst of a group feeling silent pride over their ingenuity in attacking the "interesting ramifications" of the initial problem, "You certainly are evading our original topic" is a stark fact that all can recognize, and perhaps begin to interpret once it is noted.

Second, pointing out the facts provides foundation and incentive for reflection and association. If it is true that the clues to the meaning are in the event, then the meaning can be traced from them only by consideration and reflection. Some might suppose this reflection to be the task of the minister or therapist. But the parishioner, or the patient, may be quite as motivated and quite as able to track down the significance once he is given the impetus of seeing the event objectively spelled out. Reflecting objectively a situation is sometimes all a therapist does to stimulate analysis and action by his patient. He may never even know fully what that analysis is. A minister need not be timid or apologetic about limiting his contribution just to this objective descriptive reflection. "I've noticed that this seems to be the case . . ." is a difficult enough contribution to be able to make, in the light of the problems above. And it is a valuable enough "springboard" contribution to pose the facts of the situation in a calm, accepting way that makes them suitable for consideration and generates further association and reflection. Reflecting the facts is hardly more than has been done in many of the examples already presented.

Discussion of responses to resistance is developed more systematically in Chapter VII, and the above paragraphs logically belong there.
But they are included here as a way of emphasizing the absolute
priority that attention to facts should have—even to the point of
becoming on occasion an adequate basis for response, without need
for further interpretation.

The "realistic" meaning of behavior

Even when facts are attended to, there is another step easily and
often overlooked in the rush for psychological interpretation. Perhaps
this is best introduced with a story, or legend, about Freud, which is
variously reported. It is said that at one time Freud began experiencing headaches at the end of long days at work in his office, seeing
patients and writing. I have found that when this much of the story
is told to students or ministers, they are quick with psychological
interpretations, usually ingenious, plausible, and theoretically sophisticated. As further details are recounted (e.g., the headaches were less
severe on Saturdays) these are readily assimilated to the interpretations. But the legend goes on to report that Freud ("of all people"
the students or ministers then say) reasoned that there must be some
toxic substance accumulating in the room during the day; as for
Saturdays, he worked not so late, and was therefore less exposed.
Following such reasoning, Freud had the stove checked and found that
it was, indeed, leaking carbon monoxide. When this was repaired,
the headaches ceased.

All behavior says something important and valid about the objective circumstances which elicit it, just as all behavior says something
important and valid about the person performing it. As diagramed
in Chapter I (see p. 26), behavior is always to some degree a realistic,
appropriate, and adaptive response to the immediate environment,
just as it is always to some degree a consequence of the inner life and
personal history of the individual, and his reaction to the circumstances. The relative proportions of the "realistic" and personal
aspects may vary from event to event, but each is present.[3]

[3] Psychologists commonly use terms like "reality" and "reality-oriented" to
refer to the objective environment of a person and to his perception and response

Our discussion of resistance emphasizes the personal reaction, but before a minister (or anyone else) moves too easily to inferences about the personal, he needs to give attention to the possible "realistic" meaning in the event. This is for two important reasons: (1) if the degree of "realistic" meaning is great, this is important for the minister to heed; (2) if it is slight, this is important for the parishioners to recognize, as an aid to moving beyond the reality-based rationalizations into the personal. We will discuss each in turn.

HEEDING THE REALITY. In the first place, one needs to "hear the message" about the circumstances, which is in the behavior of resistance. To some degree the resistance may be due to circumstances which can be and need to be modified if the resistance is to be dissipated and the goals more nearly realized.

Consider the psychologically tempting example of the usher who insists on "counting the house" during the pastoral prayer because he can get a more accurate count "when the tall ones have their heads down." Before pursuing an energetic psychological interpretation, as we shall do shortly, of what such disruptive and resistive behavior may reveal about the inner life of such a person and his reaction to

to it. They use them strictly as *descriptive* and *psychological* categories, to distinguish environmental stimuli and environmentally stimulated behavior, on the one hand, from, on the other, strictly internal subjective guides to behavior and behavior which is demonstrably controlled by such internal cues.

Perhaps the best known usage is in Freud's phrase "reality principle," which he paired with "pleasure principle." By the former, he meant to refer to responsiveness of persons to what they see in the environment surrounding them, to be distinguished from behavior generated from internal impulses.

In such usage, psychologists do not intend and do not need to become involved in other debates which have swirled around the word "reality," such as ontological questions about the nature of ultimate reality, or ethical questions about responsibility to the conditions of life, or philosophical questions about free will and determinism and the degree of a person's essential autonomy from environmental influences. They do not even need to raise clinical diagnostic questions concerning the normality or abnormality of behavior. The purely descriptive task of distinguishing the degree of environmental and internal factors immediately influencing any act is difficult enough, as will be acknowledged shortly, without becoming confounded with these other difficult questions. The results of the descriptive task do not even seem particularly relevant to these other considerations. Normal or abnormal, ethical or unethical, free or "determined" behavior—any one of these would be as likely to be found in behavior which is primarily responding to internal cues as in behavior which is primarily responding to external cues.

prayer, we need to stop first to ask what it may reveal about the circumstances in which this takes place. For example, is the usher subject to actual pressures, overt or implicit, from the minister or deacons or others to obtain a precisely accurate tally? Are these pressures so strong that he is driven to such desperate means to oblige? If so, the usher's behavior betrays something important about the attitudes of the church leadership, an objective fact with respect to the usher's behavior. Alternatively, may the usher's behavior reflect an actual irrelevance or other inadequacy of pastoral prayers, so that it is quite "realistic" and appropriate for him to use a pretext to avoid them? Perhaps his behavior does not represent any peculiar or personal or special internal prompting or "resistance." Perhaps all mature, rational persons would agree in the appropriateness of avoiding these particular pastoral prayers and would feel justified in using any means appropriate—in the usher's case, the opportunity to count persons—to assist such avoidance. Others in the congregation may discover other means.

Or consider the case of a congregation showing resistance in the form of obvious ambivalence toward the authority and role of their new, young, unmarried minister. Before pursuing an energetic quest of "their problem," the minister would be well advised to consider the "message from reality" which their response provides. Ordinarily, a younger man does have less wisdom and authority and ought to know it. Or, perhaps it is the fact that the church has had to employ a younger rather than an older man which disturbs people and occasions resistivelike behavior. Perhaps his employment and presence symbolizes for the parishioners the declining financial resources and status of their particular parish.

The deacons and study group may ramble, miss the main point, and fill up their time with trivial and irrelevant comments just because the main point has not been put to them clearly enough to be understood. They may act at sea and lost because that is the way they have been left.

We pose it here as though it were a simple question to answer: To what degree is the behavior an objective and appropriate response to the circumstances? But in practice of course the difficulties in making such an estimate are obvious and formidable. There is the problem of the inevitable interaction between the circumstances and the personal, so that it is more often a question of "both/and" rather than "either/or." There is the problem, discussed in the last chapter, of finding some baseline and criterion with which to assess the degree of "reality-orientation" of the behavior. There is the problem that a minister or anyone else may have his own perception of the relative appropriateness of behavior deflected by his personal motives. But despite all these difficulties, it is still possible to attempt some assessment of the relative degree to which any instance of behavior is responsive to the objective conditions and carries a "message" about them.

FINDING THE "REALITY GAPS." The second reason for needing to assess the degree of realistic, circumstantial, objective pressure on the behavior is to establish that it is limited in degree. Behavior may be appropriately responsive to objective influences and still be only partly accounted for by these. For the behavior may have a quality or characteristics not predictable from even a full understanding of the circumstances. This is the mystery or "inappropriateness" mentioned at the end of the last chapter. It can be established only by first attending to what *is* the "appropriate" response to the circumstances. As a discrepancy appears between the appropriate and expected behavior and the actual behavior, this provides both warrant and incentive to look beyond the "realistic" and ask what personal factors may be deflecting the behavior and producing the discrepancy. The intensity, the timing, the style, the emotional accompaniments, something may not "fit" and therefore may betray the influence of more internal and personal influences. Especially resistance may do so. Resistance, by definition, represents a less than maximum "fit" to the circumstances. Though it may be responsive to some elements of a situation, it is disruptive to others. To realize the limited degree of realistic appropriateness of the behavior is to discover and help to define the existence of more personal "meaning" in the behavior.

To find that "realistic" meaning may be limited may start a minister on the path toward discovering personal meaning. But it similarly may start a parishioner on the same path. It may be enough then for the minister to notice and mention the discrepancy, the limited appropriateness of the behavior, and let his parishioner carry on from there. To be sufficiently sensitive and responsive, a minister may have no need to go into "depth" speculation about the personal characteristics. The parishioner probably has better grounds for more accurate speculation and it may be the sufficient and unique contribution for the minister to goad him into using these resources by calling attention to the discrepancy. This is perhaps what he *can* see more accurately than the parishioner.

The difficult and special role to which the minister is called is not to probe with speculative forays into the personal bases for the resistance. Rather, his unique role is to note the resistance in a way that invites the necessary reflection by his parishioner. As discussed in Chapter III, to say, "Your behavior doesn't fit the circumstances" may arouse defensive apology for the behavior, an abortive attempt to prove that it *does* fit circumstances. The minister's role is to pose his query as a matter of genuine, well-intentioned curiosity which accepts the behavior and respects the behaver. If the acceptance is genuine, it will pervade and control the situation even though the minister must pose his observation as a mild challenge. Human defensiveness and powers of rationalization being as great as they are, he must be firm about his observation that circumstances cannot provide a full explanation for the behavior. People will not join the search for the more elusive, more complex, and sometimes more threatening personal "meaning" unless their rationalizations are firmly and lucidly challenged, unless the assignment of responsibility to circumstances is demonstrated to be only a partial truth.

Mrs. A could claim (see p. 68) that she was following instructions in reporting what came to her mind. But the therapist needed to insist that this was only in the letter and not in the spirit, that she was half consciously, half unconsciously inventing things to put in her mind so that she could then report them. Her reasons for discussing the place and the schedule of her appointments was ostensibly due to her conviction that they were exceptional and to a fear of being diagnosed as severely ill. This was the realistic basis of her remarks. But under the challenging questioning of the therapist, she herself acknowledged that she did not really feel the circumstances to be too exceptional and that she had no genuine apprehension of serious mental illness. The realistic basis was scant. Therefore, as the therapist intended to establish with his line of questioning, her reason for discussing the circumstances must have been something else more personal, in this case her avoidance of other material.

Perhaps the counting usher can point to objective "reasons" for his behavior: he has been assigned the task of counting the congregation, and tall people are indeed less in the way when their heads are bowed. But certain limitations perhaps also need to be pointed out to him, insofar as they are true: No one, in assigning him the task, has insisted on the supreme importance of a perfectly accurate count; the reasons for counting the congregation, whatever they are, do not require absolute accuracy. Hence, this concern for accuracy must be his own personal contribution, and as such invites inquiry.

When the rationalizations are challenged and the limitations of "realistic" meaning inisted upon, the challenge is not intended to be a scolding, or else it would be indistinguishable from challenges the person experiences "in the world." When most people challenge rationalizations, they do so as a way of criticizing the behavior which the rationalizations support. The argument is: "Your explanation is not really sufficient to account for your behavior, therefore your behavior must be wrong and must be changed." When behavior does not match circumstances, they reject the behavior. As Mrs A partially reported, her husband had already pointed out that her concern for the circumstances of her therapy appointments did not seem justified by the nature of the circumstances. We may readily suppose that he added the conclusion that therefore she should not be concerned. But the attitude of the therapist was to accept the concern because she had expressed it; if it didn't match fully with the visible circumstances, then this invited inquiry into the less visible. When the people in the back pew ask *why* the usher has to disturb the prayer, their "why" is an ejaculation of protest. Hopefully, the minister can make it clear that his "why" is quite literally and genuinely an inquiry.

It is one thing, then, to sense and mention that there seems room to find personal meaning in a resistive event. It is quite another thing to discover what that meaning may be. The former may well be the limits of a minister's responsibility and helpfulness. In any case, the former precedes the latter.

INFERRING MEANING

FROM THE SITUATIONAL CONTEXT. First establish the facts, then peruse the facts for their situational warrant for the behavior. The next step, if any, would seem to be to draw some inferences about the nature of the personal factors in the reaction. But here again, attention needs to go first to the objective situation for its clues and hints, and not to some kind of direct X-ray study of a person's psyche.

The first hunches as to what is going on in a person most plausibly come from reflecting on the situational context. "Why does he show resistance now and not at some other time?" "What are the particular characteristics of the situation to which he seems particularly responsive and resistive?" "How does this situation differ from others which are very much like it which do not seem to evoke resistance?" "How is this situation like others which may seem different in important respects, but which also evoke resistance?"

This search in the situation for clues to personal meaning needs to be distinguished from the search, discussed above, for realistic environmental meaning, though the distinction is only one of degree and hardly absolute. There we were asking what was in the situation which was "really" disturbing a person because it was actually and objectively a disturbance. Here we are asking what in the situation may be triggering motives, concerns, anxieties, desires which are already present in the person. Here we are asking not what the response of resistance says about the situation, but what the situation may say about the response. We are asking what there is in the situation which gives clues as to what is particularly disturbing for this person. The situation is "selected" for resistance by particular concerns, aspirations, apprehensions, urges and fears—motives—within the person. Which are some of the motives that might be provoked by this situation and not by others? What kinds of motives are not likely to be interacting with this situation?

To arrive at answers to such questions requires whatever intuition, empathy, and disciplined honing of insights a person can command. The insight will be greater the better known is the person or the group showing the resistance. It will be greater the more experience one has with the situation at hand, either by observation or by having been there himself. Projection of one's own likely feelings in such a situation is like any other tool a person has available to help him understand: it may guide him to sensitive insights—in which case it may be called empathy—or it may badly mislead him. The difference depends primarily on how insistently one may be compelled by his own defensive or other psychological needs to suppose that others have motives like his. Strongly motivated projection not only blinds one to contradictory clues but actually compels him to make use of these, with a twisted rationalization, to support the insistent projection. Less "needful" projection suggests insights, but doesn't insist on them.

INFERENCE FROM THE NATURE OF RESISTANCE. Beyond looking at the situational context of the resistance, one can similarly look for clues in the nature of the resistance itself. How else might a person express resistance? Instead of rambling he might be silent; instead of smiling sweet assent, he might be sullen; instead of changing the topic to one thing he might change it to another; instead of offering one set of rationalizations, he might use others. One ought to be able—again perhaps with the help of his own projection or empathy, or perhaps from past encounters with resistance—to imagine a great variety of types of behavior, all of which would be equally resistive, before he raises the question of why the resistance does take the form it does. This "why" may be another lead to clues as to the inner significance the resistance has for the resister. Such clues can be an important supplement, confirmation, or corrective to his original intuition.

Tentativeness and playfulness of inferences

Sensitization to the personal meaning, the psychological significance of behavior and events is at best a highly tentative approximation. The most that one can hope for, and be grateful for when it happens, is that he will develop several guesses, or hypotheses, about the meaning of an event, whether explicitly articulated or just intuitively felt; that these will be more or less pointing in the right direction; that they will somehow guide or enrich or sensitize one's responses so as to make them more appropriate; and that the guesses or hunches will open one to the possibility of still further interpretations. Personal events are too richly and too subtly meaningful to permit simple and single interpretation—even when one knows much more about the people and the events than most of us ever do. Differing, conflicting, even contradictory interpretations may all be equally valid since behavior itself may be inconsistent or multiply prompted, a fact recognized in Freudian terminology with the label "overdetermination." Or, multiple guesses may all be equally inaccurate and misleading. One should expect to hold multiple interpretations and to hold them extremely tentatively. There is a stereotype that the role of the psychoanalyst is to announce clearly and unmistakably the "meaning" of behavior in personal motivations and backgrounds. This stereotype must be regarded as chiefly an illusion born of our own wishes for certainty and authority in these matters. The therapist is as often adding to his range of hunches, as he is narrowing it.

Even though multiple and varied, one's inferences may still suggest some direction. They may cluster and focus. They may tend to establish a general area or range, in which one feels more justified in concentrating, without, however, excluding possibilities outside the range. One may feel that the resultant or average of his hunches is a reasonably trustworthy guide for response and further hunch.

Multiplicity and tentativeness need not inhibit action or response. A policy of action only after thorough diagnosis and planning reflects a posture which perhaps is a special malady of our prideful, scientific age. It overlooks the degree of insight and direction which comes only in the process of active response. It overlooks the ambiguities and uncertainties which remain even after the most careful analysis and planning. It overlooks the difficulties anyone has in adhering to the most carefully laid plans and programs. Especially, it overlooks those powerful resources beyond our own calculated contribution to a situation.

Probably a minister ought never to do or say anything which requires the assumption that he knows accurately what is happening within the persons involved and why. He needs to be aware constantly that there exist many sources of insight not now available to him. Some may become available to him subsequently. Some may never become available to him, but may be available to other persons involved in the event. A minister needs to act and speak so as to maximize, not foreclose, the possibility of other sources of insight. He needs to make responses which point without restricting, which direct attention but don't force it, which invite but don't insist. He can move daringly into sensitive and tentative areas, so long as he takes care not to cut off his own line of retreat, or that of others. He can find ways of speaking meaningfully, yet with a lightness and airiness and playfulness that leaves room for people to move around or move out, and not just squirm.

Examples are difficult, because the same words or actions which would follow these principles in one context would not do so in another. To mention outright one or more of one's guesses may, in the context of some personal relations and with some persons, be both restricting and threatening. For other persons, and within the context of other personal relations, it may seem a genuine and warm expression of concern and interest and a kind of playful invitation to further inquiry.

When the morning delegation from the women's altar guild threatens to delay the worship service because they are fussing so painfully in the sacristy to get each flower perfectly in place for the altarpiece, a minister may feel some confidence in understanding in a general way what meaning this way of approaching the altar has for these women, and he may feel moved to address this meaning. But how can he do it in a way that opens, not closes, inquiry and reflection? Some ministers with some women might open the way to genuinely effective pastoral and priestly functioning by blurting out, "What were you doing last night that you have to atone for with such care at the altar today?" Or, "Why do you care so much what Mrs. Phillips thinks of the altar display?" The minister chooses to suggest his "range" of hunches by focusing sharply on one hunch within that range. For women of some sophistication, and for a pastor who is able to say such things with meaning, yet lightly, comments like these might invite an exchange which comes close to confession and absolution. The women will know that he does not mean them to take literally the specific hunch he proposes. They will accept it as an invitation to reflect on the personal meaning of their behavior, and as a guidance to the general area in which the minister senses meaning. But for most pastors and most members of women's altar guilds this would not work; such a remark would hardly convey the same open and inviting mood.

Much more general and less restricting—but a response which still assumes a readiness in the women for personal inquiry—might be for a pastor to say something like, "I've noticed that when I've fussed most with something like arranging papers on my desk, I'm often troubled about something. It seems to be my version of biting fingernails or smoking." This still assumes a lightness by the pastor which lets people move around or out.

Still more generally, still playfully and invitingly, yet with some direction as to what he senses: "You can't seem to come to terms with the altar this morning." Or, "Are those flowers so stubborn, or are your hands shaking about something this morning?" Or, "You arrange those as though you think someone is going to be inspecting them a lot more closely than usual today." Or, "I'm used to your normal fussing over the flowers, but what's got into you today, I wonder." Or the minister might choose to skip any indication of his sense of personal meaning and instead make a purely situational reflection, as suggested in the preceding section: "The flowers seem to be giving you an especially bad time today."

The minister may choose to make his response at a different time, without specific link to the flowers. In preaching, discussion group, or elsewhere, with these women present, he may refer to guilt feelings, or to apprehension over others' disapproval, and to the compulsive ways we sometimes futilely try to deal with such feelings. He may choose to respond not by inviting self-inquiry, but by what will be labeled in Chapter VII as a "reply," which "speaks" to the meaning of the situation as he perceives it without explicitly identifying that meaning. He might offer some remarks about the acceptability of the flowers—and flower arrangers—regardless of their perfection. He might make this explicitly theological, again hopefully with a lightness that allows room for meaningful assimilation, and say something about God welcoming rather less than perfect flower arrangements —and people!—even though we ourselves, and perhaps others in the congregation, cannot. For example: "I wonder whether God really prefers the flowers so neat on the altar, instead of the haphazard way they naturally grow." Or, "Jesus spent so much time with the weeds of his society, I don't think you have to get those flowers so perfectly arranged in order to please Him; for that matter, we don't have to get ourselves always perfect to please Him."

GENERALITY MAY SACRIFICE PLAUSIBILITY. The risk with the more general and less personally pointed response suggested in the last two paragraphs is that it may seem to the women too general and too bland and hence "ministerial" but not personally meaningful. Even when he may be aiming his remarks or behavior fairly accurately, the women may not expect him to be understanding their situation that personally. So they may easily interpret his reassurance about the flowers simply as a kind of habitual formalized dose of clerical sweetness and optimism. Or they may interpret it as his own impatience with their delay. It is preferable not to have to resort to generality in order to demonstrate openness. The ideal is still to combine an inviting openness with personal pointedness.

PEOPLE MUST BE PREPARED TO EXPECT "HERE-AND-NOW" MINISTRY. Such ventures into on-the-spot exercise of pastoral or priestly or preaching roles, directed to specific people in specific situations, presuppose a context in which persons have come to expect such roles to be exercised. They can work only if people are already prepared to interpret the minister's remarks as expressing his intimate pastoral concerns, his sensitivity, and his "acceptance." He ought not to have to teach them what he is trying to do and persuade them of his understanding at the same time that he is trying to show them something about their behavior. This might require such specifically aimed remarks as to close off rather than to invite further reflection. The minister can hardly ask people to be simultaneously sensitive to *his* mood and to *their* feelings. If to make his posture clear the minister has to say something so specific as, "Your behavior with the flowers suggests to me some guilt feelings or anxiety toward which I feel accepting and to which I would like to direct a sense of God's forgiving grace," then he is sacrificing too much of the principle of openness and tentativeness. The training and preparation of people as to the pastor's purposes and sensibilities ought to be done in some other way and at some other time. If they understand what he is up to, he can be more general and they will still follow along.

THE AWE OF THE ORDINARY

Each of us has once been a child who has just learned to stand on his head or to recite the multiplication table, a child who has just found a bright pebble on the beach, or who has just received a new toy from a favorite uncle; and each of us has been desperately eager to demonstrate this new achievement or new treasure for whatever company of admirers he could muster. Sometimes our urge to demonstrate may have been so insistent that it intruded into adult conversation or otherwise proved "inappropriate." The possession of some understanding about the roots and the meaning of human behavior—even diffuse and general—may sometimes be like that, a new skill, or perhaps even a new toy, which one feels compelled to demonstrate, even sometimes in inappropriate situations. And perhaps books like this are an example of the expression of such an urge.

But perhaps the understanding of human behavior may more often be like another kind of childhood situation which each of us also has known. For each of us also has been in situations as a child which seemed to require particular talents which we did not have. We may have wanted to add our joke to others' or to be able to haul off with a punch. But we have not found it within us. The prospect of understanding human behavior intimately may sometimes seem an equally frustrating challenge in which we find ourselves wanting. Any insight into possible meaning of behavior—if it has any meaning at all—thoroughly eludes us; the behavior is just stubbornly there. And reading books like this, in which subtle meaning is so easily charted for every act, only enhances our irritation. If behavior is said to be like an iceberg, with nine-tenths drifting below the surface, then it sometimes seems that we are challenged to be navigators among such icebergs, required to identify every contour and crevice of these underwater masses.

But actually, close attention to human behavior ought not to imply a demand to exercise and demonstrate special talents of sleuthing and probing, or special ingenuity in devising inferences. Far more important and useful than trying to plot masses under the surface is to identify and report clearly just exactly what is on the surface. The minister's task is to reflect and respond to the obvious and visible circumstances in such a way as to testify to one's conviction that they have underlying meaning of importance, and to invite attention to or awareness of such meaning. He is to share his own awe of the ordinary.

Three levels

One might roughly distinguish three levels of obviousness or depth: the behavioral "symptom," the general disruption, the specific causes of the disruption.

In the case of the women and the altar flowers there is, first, the most visible fact that they are spending unusual time and care in the preparation.

There is, second, the inference that behind this behavior is some inner disturbance or upset or tension belonging somewhere in the very broad family of self-deprecation or guilt reactions. This may be exclusively an inference: the kind of self-restitutive behavior involved in arranging materials so carefully for the altar implies some kind of self-deprecation or anxious concern over the self. Or beyond inference, the interpretation might also be suggested or supported by more direct expressions of anxious concern or self-deprecation such as, "I can't seem to get anything right," or "Here I am, even holding up the church service."

Third, least obvious and most "deep," would be hunches as to what specially was prompting the self-concern or self-deprecation. The behavior (first level) is the reaction to an expression of some inner tension (second level); the tension in turn is the reaction to and the expression of the conflict of inner forces of some kind (third level). At this third level any hunches might be pure speculation—as well as pure projection—or might be suggested by other behavior or remarks at the time of the flower arrangements or on other occasions. For example, (1) one might suspect strong current pressures, such as concern over the opinion of the chairman of the altar guild or women in the congregation. (2) There may be actual acts of misbehavior of varying degrees of seriousness—some sense of neglect of family or housekeeping, excessive "carrying on" at the country club, lack of discipline in personal devotions. These all could generalize to the flower arranging. (3) There may be grief over a death or over another loss—a daughter getting married, a son going away to college, a sense of lost youth or beauty, the loss of husband's affection. (4) There may be a more general, diffuse, and essentially more primitive, even infantile, sense of depression and loss of personal worth. (5) There may be an inner recognition of inclination for misbehavior, even if not actually expressed in behavior—such as inclination toward sexual waywardness or inclination toward rebelliousness against housekeeping and family responsibilities.

This is the level—as the length and detail of the above paragraph suggest—which we most easily think about when we propose to be "psychologically sensitive." But it is actually the level least likely to be touched by the kind of sensitivity recommended here. The illustrations in the preceding section of how remarks directed to the altar guild might be tentative and playful ranged across all three levels. In the present context it needs to be emphasized that those with "level three" pointedness were suggested only for the situation in which they would not be taken literally but would be understood as a shorthand way of opening the range of concerns represented by level two.

SOME EXAMPLES OF RESPONSE. Remarks to the altar guild women which more clearly remain at level one might include the following: "I see that each stem, each petal has to be perfect," or "I think you are finding an excuse for bowing extra long before the altar," or "The flowers seem to be stubborn today, as though they don't want to hold their heads up in the front of the church." These are suggested as types of comments which—at least for some ministers and some women—may accomplish the tasks set here. They tend to focus on the events as being items of meaning and significance beyond the obvious and accordingly as being worth further thought and reflection. On the other hand, they are mild and light enough—a touch of humor was at least intended in the suggested remarks—that they invite rather than command inquiry; they seem to make it safe and comfortable enough to follow the general line suggested by the minister. But these general lines really have only a beginning point—in the observed event itself—with only the barest of suggestion as to the direction which reflection on that event might take.

Mrs. A's therapist said, in effect, "You seem to be hunting for topics and things to say." If he adds more, it is *"as though* you were avoiding something." With Miss N, the counselor pointed out that she was having difficulty speaking freely and asked in a general way if it meant something. In the case of the "counting usher" the minister might say something like, "You are really working harder than you need to," or "You don't have to take the prayer time for this counting; why do you insist on doing that, I wonder?" As throughout, the minister may be using words very close to those used by other people who deal with the ordinary, and who perhaps deal with it in rebuke. But the minister communicates, in his manner, his awe of the ordinary. He focuses on the ordinary, the "top level," but expresses his conviction that it is important and meaningful, important as the ordinary, and important because rooted in deeper "levels."

Why stick to the ordinary?

There are at least two good reasons for limiting one's response to the first level—or on rare occasions when it is suggested by direct observations, to the second level. Put simply, one of these reasons is that that is all you know. The other reason is that the person knows all too well, even though perhaps unconsciously, what may be going on at the lower level; events may be at "lower levels" and they may be producing the behavior seen at "top levels" just because they are too troublesome and too threatening to be acknowledged and dealt with more directly. The first reason poses the likelihood that one's reflections at the "deeper level" will be quite inaccurate. The second raises the risk that they may be accurate and thereby evoke to conscious attention matters which the person is not yet ready to handle so openly.

No matter how experienced or empathetic or skillful an observer's insights may be, he is still working on the basis of the most meager information, compared with that available to the person himself. The person can potentially recognize and "know" infinitely more of his inner feelings and corresponding outer events, present and past, of what has happened to him and how he has felt about it. As subjective and selective as his perceptions may be, compared with the relative objectivity of the observer, they are so infinitely richer as to make the observer's advantage of objectivity seem a puny gain indeed.

At the same time, the very subjective biases of the person have to be respected. If he "overlooks" concerns, it is hardly for accidental or casual reasons. Some form of repression must be operating. It must be presumed that such repression is for reasons important to the psychological well-being of the person, and these reasons must be so respected and not cavalierly disregarded. The person must be presumed to be recognizing as many of these inner urges as fully as he can and coping with them as well as he can. If he is going to do more, something will have to change; but that change will not come from the announcement of a minister's hunch as to what he is repressing. A minister's task may be to help modify conditions so that a person can more fully recognize and more completely cope with some of the inner aspects of his life. But modifying these conditions is a more subtle art than making bold announcements.

The awe one feels in the ordinary honors its positive meaningfulness

These two reasons for limiting one's response to the ordinary are related to the two elements—positive and negative—of ambivalence implied by the awe we recommend be accorded the ordinary. One holds the ordinary in awe out of respect and out of apprehension.

First, the ordinary is indeed the vehicle and expression of the depths of person and experience. The "third level" concerns do generalize and find expression in encounter with the altar flowers. The altar—with all its associations—and one's service at it provide ready occasion for the expression of such feelings of guilt and depression. The minister is provided with a special opportunity (see next chapter) just because the elements of religion and the church do evoke expressions of crucial and deep human emotions. As a general working assumption, a minister might be justified in supposing that behavior in relation to the church, perhaps more than any other institution except the family, is related to key strivings and feelings. If one could take a random sample of behavior in the church, no matter how seemingly superficial, and subject it to psychological analysis, he might well find greater richness and depth in the roots of the church behavior than in any other behavior. This enhances the confidence that one is potentially touching meaningful facets of experience when he touches even seemingly superficial behavior in the church.

But the expression of "third level" concerns in "top level" behavior is indirect and disguised, and exists at all only because it is so indirect. The generalization from a woman's "carrying on" at the country club or her dislike of home responsibilities to the altar flowers is a devious and tenuous one. When more direct confession of her feelings, at the altar or otherwise, is too anxiety-provoking, then it is only such disguised and unconscious expression which she can permit herself. This increases the caution that one must exercise in sticking close to that superficial level at which the woman is expressing her concerns. The altar and the other furniture and events of the church evoke just such fundamental concerns as a minister might most want to reach. But they are the very ones which are most troublesome to face directly so their expression in the church assumes just those garbled and tauntingly superficial forms which a minister finds most discouraging. The awe one feels in the ordinary is one of cautious respect.

LIMITS OF THE MINISTER'S RESPONSIBILITY. Both of these reasons for limiting one's response can be cast in terms of a statement about the minister's responsibility, the limits of what he is "called" to do. His responsibility is something less than delivering every soul he encounters to redemption and liberation; that responsibility, in terms of the Christian faith, lies outside any human power and authority.

In pursuing his task of bringing men and God into more intimate relationship with each other, it is often the minister's temptation, but not his legitimate task, to assume the role of one or the other of these parties. Each man is commissioned and permitted with his own resources to work out his own destiny, to make his own spiritual pilgrimage. It simply is not up to the minister, even if he could, to make that pilgrimage for a man, telling him to look here and to look there, to step here and to step there. The most that the minister can and may do is report what he sees ahead and behind, to report where he has trod and where he is bound, as best he knows. The minister is not expected to penetrate to the soul of a man with a searching, fully knowing gaze. Nor is he expected to plan each step of a man's destiny.[4] The minister speaks about the pilgrimage as best he sees it. But if, in spite of this, a person still persists in taking seemingly blind and wrong steps (or if he resists taking the next step at all) this is finally his, and not the minister's, responsibility. The minister may

[4] Such a claim and conviction is put to serious test in difficult instances where other important values are risked. These include cases of pastoral care, such as those involving potential divorce or suicide; or of community responsibility, such as those involving prospective violence; or of the role of church leader when disruption of the institution is in prospect. The prospect of the violation of important values sometimes seems to justify a radical intervention which amounts to stepping into the responsibility of other men before God, or of God Himself. But it seems perfectly clear in the case of individual men—with perhaps some qualifications in the case of corporate entities—that their responsibility and freedom must necessarily include the genuine possibility of such radical violation of important values. Furthermore, it seems clear that important as may be the preservation of the family, of life, of community, and of church, none of these may ever be regarded as an ultimate value. And the renunciation of these, as in divorce, suicide, or violence, can never remove a person beyond the pale of God's redemptive grace. By the same token, it of course must be acknowledged that neither can the assault on a man's integrity and responsibility—as by insistent probing into his soul, or physical restraint (as from suicide) or the equivalent in forceful arbitrary commands and prohibitions—necessarily remove a person from the possibility of divine healing and redemption. But it is believed that such an assault can seriously injure and cripple him for his pilgrimage.

sorrow, he may endeavor to walk alongside as best and as companionably as he can. But it is not finally his responsibility either to provide the healing or to accept it on behalf of another.

Such a contention would seem to be nonetheless true even though it were supposed that a person's decisions in these matters are largely determined unconsciously. In the final analysis, unconscious processes and directions are as much a part of a person, and part of his freedom and responsibility, as conscious processes. And they must be accepted and respected as such. Like the preservation of the family and of life, heightened conscious surveillance and control by a person over his affairs may be regarded as an important value. But it is hardly ultimate, or critically decisive of a person's redemption or damnation. So probing level three—making the unconscious conscious—is far from a minister's religious calling.

It is the minister's task and faith to look on each ordinary event with eyes ready to see significance in it; to invite another to share such a readiness with him; to provide those conditions of support and security which may encourage a person to pursue prospective meaning; and to accompany the person in such a search. But the person himself must be relied upon to provide the important clues as to the meaning and significance, and to pace himself or to dose himself with insight into the deeper and probably more troublesome levels, according to his own inner wisdom as to how much he can safely and profitably consider. The minister may never come to understand the significance of events at the deeper levels and still have been instrumental in promoting their discovery and more satisfactory coping with them. In the marvelous workings of a person's own inner perceptions and reactions, he may well discover and "solve" a problem long before it ever becomes explicitly articulated, and so it never does. This will be illustrated shortly.

This must be one point at which a difference between a minister and a psychotherapist clearly emerges. It may be the task of a psychotherapist on occasion—though less universally than may be popularly supposed—to achieve and to promote accurate insights into the deeper layers. It is the task of the minister to deal with events as ordinary events as they occur and as they are experienced, but he deals with them with the awe based on his recognition (1) that any event is more than it seems on the surface and is the carrier of significant meaning, and (2) that such ordinary events are the means by which people actually are working out their destinies on the deeper levels. This awe of the ordinary, the recognition and the acceptance of it, is perhaps what ought to distinguish the minister and the church community from other confrontations with the ordinary which persons have in everyday experience.

SURFACE CLUES FOR SELECTIVE AWE

One's response to the obvious is, of course, selective and focused. Some events of the ordinary inspire more awe than others. To attend to and to respond to the visible does not imply a passive mechanical rendering of every detail of every event. It is hardly recommended that a minister become a kind of unobtrusive Polaroid sound-movie camera—any more than a portrait painter strives for snapshot fidelity, or any more than a "nondirective, client-centered" counselor parrots like a faithful echo everything his client says. That exists only in caricature. A minister communicating his awe of the obvious to his people and inviting their awe selects, focuses, and highlights some events rather than others. His task must be like that of a portrait painter who highlights aspects of the obvious (where he is convinced the significance lies) in a way that lets inner "significance" show forth.

The third ear must be tuned. The inner eye must be focused. Intuition must be practiced. But how? Partly, "selective awe" of surface events is inevitably based on intuitive hunches as to what is going on at the "deeper" levels. Some behavior just seems a revealing expression of important psychic patterns.[5] But one can get along

---

[5] Among these may especially be encounters with the symbols and purposes and programs of the church. This is why a minister may look to reactions—even resistive reactions—to the programs of the church as a basis for advancing these programs. This is why the recommendation of the next chapter to "stick to religion" is more likely to steer one toward rather than away from significant psychological events at deeper levels. Extra attention to or avoidance of the altar or prayer raises too strong a possibility to overlook some dis-ease in a person's attitude

without being tuned to the depths. One might effectively highlight important events so as to help people deal more effectively with their underlying meanings without ever having hunches as to what the meaning is.

The surface levels of the events themselves have characteristics which betray, if one becomes sensitive to them, the existence of some significant inner thrust. One can navigate along the river by attending carefully to the ripples and currents on the surface without ever knowing or needing to know what types of sandbars or debris or channels have produced them. It may be more important for the navigator to learn to attend carefully to the slightest ripples which show that "something is up," rather than to become an expert at knowing what under the surface produces particular kinds of ripples. There are clues on the surface of events which can reliably be trusted as crying out for attention. They seem to be saying, "Something important is going on here." The rest of this chapter will consider several such clues among the ripples.

Inappropriateness

The most important of these surface clues is the simple fact of inappropriateness. The behavior doesn't seem to fit what might ordinarily be expected under the circumstances. This misfit is, from the minister's point of view, frustration and obstacle. But it is also the clue that something within the person is important enough and compelling enough to deflect his behavior from what it might otherwise be. His behavior is a discrepancy from a "baseline" or "norm," based on general cultural and subcultural expectations, and on personal habits and customs, which suggests, for example, just how perfect a flower arrangement has to be. Normally it can be supposed that the desire for a good arrangement of flowers is subordinated to the larger purposes of the worship service and is not so

toward himself, his posture before others and before God. Resistance to the more intimate confrontation with persons of different social groups, as in the inner city, or with persons of one's own social group, such as in Bible discussion groups, too naturally suggests a fearfully and precariously defended sense of well-being.

strong a value that it would interfere with the worship service. When women who have been arranging flowers at a certain pace and with certain criteria on one Sunday change and seem to show an excessive concern for perfection, as measured by these criteria, one can reasonably suppose that something within them is deflecting and modifying their behavior, and that this something may be personally meaningful and significant. To the discrepancy between what happens and what one might "naturally" or "normally" expect to happen, whether with an individual or with groups, whether it is devastatingly frustrating or just curiously surprising, an appropriate response would seem to be an earnest, "Why?" Not the "why" of irritation and protest with which our despair so commonly mocks the prospect of an answer, but rather the "why" of genuine inquiry.

This discrepancy may be detected in several ways. The remaining sections of this chapter all illustrate, in a sense, different forms of inappropriateness. But it can seriously be recommended that one principally pay attention to his own inner experience of *frustration*. One's inner emotional reactions *may* be sensitive, reliable clues that expectations have not been matched by outcome and that this deflecting *may* be attributable to important characteristics worth knowing more about. But the "may" needs to be underlined. For, though this recommendation is made seriously, it is also made in the face of risk. Feelings of frustration may so easily arise from circumstances other than important and meaningful characteristics within other people; the imputation of such characteristics can so easily become one more blinding and hostile reaction to the frustration. If inner frustration is to be used as a reliable index of the presence of important self-deflected characteristics in other people, at least two assumptions must be met. One is that one's own expectations have been realistic and so in fact do provide a reliable "baseline" of what one might naturally and normally expect. The other assumption is that the discrepancy between expectation and outcome is not attributable to something more external and circumstantial. It might be recommended then that one develop the habit of responding to (professional) frustrations with the question, "Why?" and then carefully checking two possible answers to this question: (1) in the unrealisticness of his own expectations, and (2) in the external circumstances, perhaps of his own making. These having been honestly considered and rejected as adequate explanations, there remains the real likelihood of significant deflecting characteristics within the other persons, and the situation may be worth directing attention to with this in mind.

Undue repetition

Another possible clue in surface behavior and an avenue toward "deeper levels" is insistent repetition—or the repeated association between some event and a reaction. Here the baseline of expectation against which the reaction is being measured is one that might be called "chance" or "randomness." Tardiness at a board meeting once is hardly worth noticing. Repeated tardiness may make one begin to wonder if this is a kind of clue behavior. Tardiness only at board meetings and not other activities, or tardiness only at board meetings with an agenda planned to include discussion of work in the inner city begins to suggest that the tardiness is a meaningful response.

When a minister hears a speech once on the history of the parish under past ministers, he overlooks it—or may even benefit from it. When he repeatedly hears the same speech, in the same words and from the same person, he may reasonably expect that the repetition means something. He may expect so even more when the speech seems to be evoked consistently by his discussion of foreign policy, national economic issues, and community politics. He may reasonably suppose that lodging his views on these issues will be enhanced by working through whatever meaning may lie behind this repeated reaction, not in irritatedly trying to get around it.

A minister noticed that in a Bible discussion group one man's comments were invariably followed by those of his wife, sometimes supplementing his remarks, sometimes contradicting them, and sometimes simply not relevant to what he had said. In itself, this was hardly anything exceptional for a Bible study group—except in the startling repetition of the husband-then-wife sequence. (Further conviction as to the likely meaningfulness would have come if the

minister had established that this happened only in the Bible
discussion group, or only when particular biblical themes were under
discussion.) Repetition is a "safe" external characteristic that a
minister can easily and guilelessly call attention to without making
threatening implications that he sees some deeper meaning. In this
case, the minister made a light but pointed remark at the end of the
evening to the couple about "getting two for the price of one." The
wife ignored the remark, but the man made a confirming but
similarly light remark about getting a stiff neck from turning to look
at his wife every time he finished talking. When the woman missed
the next several meetings of the group, the minister recognized,
guiltily at the time, that this absence was her meaningful response to
his intervention. When she later resigned as assistant superintendent
of the Sunday school, he feared he had blundered onto very sensitive
matters. However, about three months after the episode, she sought
the minister and asked for help in finding some point of useful service with deprived groups in the city, which she then pursued
faithfully and without fanfare. She told the minister something
casually about not needing to "prove" herself by running things any
more. He suspected this had something to do with his earlier remarks, but he never knew. He never knew what went on within the
woman, between the woman and her husband, or between the
woman and any counselor she may have sought (in this case not
himself). Apparently his remark had precipitated something of a
stark reorientation. He did feel confident afterward that her work in
church activities was a much more spontaneous, well-directed, genuine service, much less compulsively busy and organization-oriented.

Relentless persistence

A form of repetition which may be especially useful "clue behavior" is a persistence in spite of changing circumstances. On some
occasions one might call it rigidity, except that rigidity implies a
passive, unbending stubbornness, and what is being remarked on here
is more of an active insistence. What may not seem inappropriate or
otherwise significant on one occasion may begin to arouse more inter-

est when it becomes repeated, and especially when under highly diverse circumstances. A woman captures a minister after an evening meeting to voice a long and detailed complaint that the church school and the Sunday evening youth program are not providing her teen-age daughter with enough "solid religious content." The first time that this happens, it might mean almost anything, including the possibility that her analysis is absolutely correct and should be heeded in its own terms! When it happens a second time and even a third, in almost the same language and even after the youth program has, in fact, begun to include precisely the kind of material she requested, then one begins to suspect that something within the woman is driving these complaints, rather than that they are simply a response to the situation.

The response to such a woman is to focus on this persistence in a way that turns her attention toward its possible inner sources. As always, the crucial factor is that this is done as an expression of genuine concern for her, not criticism of her behavior: it must be as though one says, "This persistence raises a mystery; there is something related to it within you which is worth knowing," not "This persistence is not objectively justified; it shows there is something wrong with you." Assuming a prior relationship in which the minister's acceptance and concern has been established, he may well try to focus precisely on her persistence: "I begin to think you're never going to get off my back about the way we are treating Marilyn." Or, "Nothing we do is right; I just don't think you trust us with Marilyn."

The same kind of interpretation and response can be made when the persistence is not in the face of change of circumstances so much as in the face of changed "interpretation of the circumstances," although this type of encounter obviously runs great risk of degenerating into rebuke, battle, and argument in the fashion of the world. It might be that the minister is able to answer the woman's objections, not by changing the program in the coming weeks, but by pointing out to her that the program already includes what she is asking for. To the degree that her complaints continue, and assuming that, taken at face value, they have been sufficiently countered by the new interpretation, then one may be justified in looking at them as clue behavior. This strategy is one of measuring the degree of personal push behind her behavior by testing it against changed perspectives of the external circumstances and finding it essentially unresponsive to these.

This persistence can be responded to without any clear hunches—either beforehand or perhaps even afterward—as to what it is within the woman which might be generating this persistence. But for the sake of plausibility in this presentation, it may be reported that later conversations with the woman who provided the basis for the above example suggested that her concern for her daughter's welfare in religious and moral matters had much to do with her own intense apprehensions about the example and training she herself had provided for her daughter. This happened to surprise the minister involved, since his first hunches about the "meaning" of her behavior were more along the lines of suspecting a rebellious resentment against men, ministers, and other seemingly incompetent and arbitrary authorities in her life. But since his hunches made no difference in the way he highlighted the persistence itself—except to bolster his own feeling that there must be some meaning in the persistence—she was left free to discover what meaning there was in this clue behavior, once she recognized it as a clue to meaning.

Talking past each other

Every minister knows the agonizing frustration of trying desperately hard to follow and respond to someone's earnest expressions but always seeming to miss the mark. He tries to reflect on what is being said, but the response is never acknowledged as correct. The person always seems to mean something slightly different.

This type of frustration may be another important clue to strong pushes within the person. Perhaps he is trying to express something for which he just can't find any adequate words. Perhaps the experience is one of alienation from or resentment toward the minister, or perhaps toward people more generally, which expresses itself by never consenting to communication. Perhaps he is so habitually used to being misunderstood that he doesn't really stop to listen to the understanding now offered to him. The frustrating and meaningful fact of the talking past is what the minister needs to be attentive to, more than the elusive content of the words themselves.

In the nature of the case, since verbal communication and rapport is not good in such circumstances, it is difficult to respond to this obstacle by directly focusing on it in so many words. The more subtle and less serious the "talking past," probably the more easily it can be verbalized and talked about. "Sometimes I get the feeling that one of us is determined to misunderstand the other." In a proper context where one is prepared for it, such a remark can shift attention to the interpersonal relationship, which may turn out to represent an important problem that *can* be discussed coherently. It may spare both parties the frustration of the continued sparring.

But most often such "talking past" should probably be left as a clue behavior which a minister makes note of and to which he may eventually respond in some way, but not immediately and not verbally.

Intensity

The intensity of a person's behavior may also be a clue to the particular personal pushes which are driving him. This may refer simply to the physical energy involved. A louder than necessary voice, a firmer than ordinary handshake, for the counting usher a determined nod of the head at each count—these may be clues to extra horse-power within the person, to extra meaning which the behavior has for him internally, beyond the apparent and obvious. Such physical vigor and intensity is not too promising a topic on which to focus verbal reflection. The person's translation of his inner concerns into the physical intensity is likely to be a highly unconscious one, and the path backward—from physical intensity to inner concerns—is not an easy one to trace. It is harder for him to accept the physical intensity as potentially meaningful, and it is harder for him to recognize in himself any potential meaning which the intensity may have. It is therefore easier for him to regard mention of it as rebuke or affront rather than sympathetic curiosity. The translation of emotions into physical expressions is a way of bypassing acknowledgment of the emotional. So there is less profit in reflecting simply on the physical intensity, as though such reflection in itself will invite self-inquiry. The exception may be those signs of intense physical expressions which a culture, or moderately sophisticated persons within it, comes to regard just in the sense we are here discussing. The comment, "You are shouting," or the quotation from Shakespeare, "Methinks the lady doth protest too much," may become a comment which means clearly and intelligibly in certain circles something like, "You must mean something other than what you're saying," or "You must not believe what you're saying or you wouldn't have to shout."

But intensity which is not purely physical vigor may be more open to verbal reflection. There may be a kind of excessive earnestness. The counting usher may not only doggedly confirm each counted person with a determined physical gesture, he may also fuss about getting into just the proper position ahead of time for making his count. There may be a kind of exaggeration. The arguments against inner-city involvement by the church, or for more Bible study in teenage classes, may invoke extreme, unfactual, contradictory claims and argument. There may be an enthusiasm, for or against. The plans for a women's fair or a men's breakfast, the minister's remarks in his sermons on family life or on racial questions, may arouse feverish loyalty or equally fervent opposition, to a degree which no fair or breakfast or sermon actually warrants. If this happens, it suggests some important (symbolic) meaning and function which these things have for the individual. Such reactions as these, which ministers so often inveigh against as misplaced loyalties or stubborn opposition, may be worth further inquiry and reflection. They are more accessibly related than physical vigor to the concerns which are prompting them. One can hardly imagine any fruitfulness in pointing out to a congregant after church that he is shaking your hand hard. But if he is proclaiming fervently his approval of your remarks on the sanctity of family life, one might consider pointing out that he has latched more vigorously onto one small section of the sermon, which didn't after all say anything particularly unique or remarkable: "I should have let you preach the sermon; you seem to see more in that than I did."

Inappropriate emotion

Although patterns of how one expresses emotions, and toward what, vary widely in man's experience by place and time, every group has worked out fairly clearcut codes and patterns of emotional expressions—just as of language—by which they communicate with each other. And most persons in a group confirm their acceptance of these codes by their usual patterns of behavior. People in any one group agree pretty well on what is outrageous, humorous, sorrowful, fearful. And they agree pretty well on the patterns of gesture and language by which one expresses outrage, humor, sorrow, or fear. When someone who otherwise appears to accept his group's conventions of emotional expression shows unusual affect, we may suspect this also to be a sign of inner promptings. Being amused or fearful at something which is not, by apparent objective or social standards, amusing or fearful; failing to be amused or frightened at what is, by these same standards, actually amusing or fearful; showing emotions appropriate to the circumstances but to an exaggerated degree and intensity— these represent another clue that something within the person is affecting and deflecting his behavior beyond what is attributable to obvious and apparent causes. That something—as in all these other cases—is probably pertinent to attend to. It may be discerned by following the leads back from the clues of the surprising emotional reaction.

For several reasons this is perhaps the most difficult sign to respond to. Judgment is necessarily very shaky as to what is surprising or unsurprising, appropriate or inappropriate emotional response. Persons are especially sensitive to observations of their emotional life and may regard comments as unwarranted intrusion on their privacy, even from a minister from whom they would not resent many of the comments suggested in the preceding paragraphs. Or else they may regard the observation, especially from a professional person, as equivalent to something like a diagnosis of abnormality. Finally, emotional disturbances, especially if they are general over many situations or extremely intense, may indeed betray personal struggles and difficulties, but to a degree beyond what may be pertinent to the minister's concerns or competence.

In summary: Many ripples make a big wave

These types of clue behavior may occur independently and separately, but it is perhaps more likely that one person or one incident will betray several of them at once. This multiplication of the intrusion and deflection of inner promptings is what makes some persons escalate, in the eyes of their ministers, from showing resistance to being a nuisance. The "difficult people" of the church are difficult because they are repetitious, persistent, and intense in their resistance, and because they are difficult to "relate to" in ways that are described above as "talking past" and showing surprising emotion. This simply means that the same factors that are producing one ripple are producing others. If it is desirable that the minister respond to one of these signs with the prospect of understanding it as meaningfully caused, it is all the more desirable—but also all the more personally difficult—to regard a confluence of these signs as representing even greater likelihood of meaningful cause.

Psychologists are sometimes accused of being overly preoccupied with the abnormal and with basing comprehensive psychological theories too exclusively on abnormal cases. Most notably, Freud's still dominant framework of theories was developed out of his observation of neurotic patients. Although it is only *partly* true that contemporary psychological theories are based on abnormal phenomena, it *is* partly true. Psychologists are especially interested in the unusual. It is precisely at the point of the unexpected, of the novel, of individual difference that curiosity is aroused. The surprising and the extraordinary begs for explanation as the routine and the expected does not. When a person's behavior is inconsistent with what a situation most obviously demands, this is the clue of the intrusion of individual psychological variables, and the attention of a psychologist is aroused, whether or not he stops to call it abnormal. Indeed, many of the clues discussed above bear some resemblance to what might sometimes be regarded as indicators of mental abnormality. This coincidence, though inevitable and intended, is more apparent than important. If behavior is unusual or odd or disrupting or frustrating or "abnormal," that is a judgment which is far less important—and perhaps not even worth making—than the recognition that this behavior is thereby particularly meaningful and potentially revealing of pertinent central reactions of the individual (or the group) to the situation set before him.

VI

Religiosity: Impotent Residue or Remnant of Power?

Almost within living memory, the minister was still *the* person —the Parson—the church was still the dominant social institution, Sunday gathering for worship was still the highpoint of the week for family and community, the minister's sermon was still the most decisive word heard in the community, and theological debate could still make big news. With rare exceptions, these things are no longer true. The most loudly heard explanation, offered in mounting crescendos since World War II, is that Christianity is finished (the "post-Christian era"), all religion is finished (the "secular age"), and finally, that God is finished. These claims, to say the least, seem rather broad generalizations from the data.

The minister, viewing from within the church, has all the more reason than the critics viewing from outside to be concerned about the impotence of religious forms, religious language, and the religious institution. He can see not only how these are steadfastly ignored by those who stay away, but also how they are trivialized by those who come. He can see how God's holy demands and His assurances are emasculated by the language of piety, the jargon of theology, cultish rituals, whether in sanctuary or in church kitchen, literalism of Scriptures, priestly expectations of a minister's office, and the intense narrowness of institutional loyalties. God's word is attenuated and

226

Christ's body is atrophied fully as much by those who are half informed, half committed, half participating, as by those who stay away
altogether.

The resistive use of religious forms may distress a minister because
he is convinced of the potential power of these forms. He is disturbed by the disparity between the potential constructive power of
the forms and their use for mere resistive purposes. This was discussed in Chapter IV. Here we pose a far more threatening form of
distress. The minister may be disturbed even more over the resistive
use of religious forms when this use echoes his own otherwise un-
expressed sense of the impotence and futility of the forms: "Maybe
resistance is all that they are good for." There may indeed be, as
argued in Chapter IV, power and vitality in the resisters, but none
left in the forms. Maybe the strategy is to unleash the vitality from
the religiosity which imprisons it and turn it loose into more vital
channels. In an electrical circuit, resistors are necessary to produce
light, heat, and motion, but only if in suitable apparatus and
connected to a source of power. If the resistance is part of a small
isolated electrical circuit which is linked neither to major power
sources nor to any apparatus capable of performing useful work, then
it should be removed into a more productive circuit.

When a minister, who is bound by his role, training, and even
commitment to the forms of religiosity, hears voices, both within and
without, telling him of the futility and impotence of this religiosity,
he commonly follows one of four courses. First, he can ignore the
voices, pretend that the facts and the times have not changed, and
persist in the forms of religiosity as though they carry all the power
they are supposed to and once apparently did. To the difficulties in
this option, this book is not addressed, because enough other books
are.

Second, he can echo these voices as though the facts they describe
are so, but denounce the decline of religion which they announce.
Neither is this book addressed to those who denounce the loss, any
more than it is to those who deny it.

Third, a minister can amplify the voices and celebrate the demise
of religiosity. Those who celebrate the demise usually go searching for

new sensations of relevance and potency beyond the confines of religiosity. They are likely to develop elaborate rationale as to how God has accompanied them—or preceded them—into the secular realm. The entire secular becomes so blessed, without criteria or norms or discrimination, that whatever such a liberated minister touches becomes thereby divine. In this mood of normless secularism, God can be found at work in whatever gives a man a sensation of relevance and power—just as in the parallel mood of normless, existential situational ethics, God can be found willing whatever gives a man a sense of reasonable satisfaction.

Since World War II the two most appealing lures have been the Couch and the City—the power in reshaping individual lives represented by psychiatric techniques, and the power over social forces represented by political, economic, and direct action. The couch was perhaps more popular in the fifties, the city in the sixties. (However, the flourishing of such essentially secularized forces as the American Association of Pastoral Counselors and the American Foundation of Religion and Psychiatry is testimony that the lure of the couch is far from dead.) [1]

Fourth—and perhaps the most common response—a minister continues through the motions of religiosity but with strong longing and envy for the arenas in which he thinks the action has moved. This, again, usually means the couch or the city. Sometimes more consciously than at other times, he is dogged by what he feels as a stinging contrast between the seemingly puny hold the church and its forms have on people, its meager appeal, its clumsy ability to affect them, as compared with the throbbing power revealed on the couch and in the city.

[1] Since this book is written from a psychological point of view, there is the risk that it may be misperceived as simply a plea for the psychologically discernible secular over the sociologically discernible secular, for the couch vs. the city. This is not true. We are not asking minister-politicians and minister-social workers to become minister-therapists. Instead we ask them to consider carefully whether they can't just be ministers—ministers of that institution which still claims a peculiar and uniquely potent role as called by God to be the body of Christ. To make clear that we are not pleading just for the psychologically tuned secular, this chapter will tend to emphasize the difference between ministry as conceived here and that particular lure, rather than the difference between ministry and a sociologically tuned secularism.

This book proposes, however, what amounts to a fifth choice. The power which the religious holds may be evident now in newer and starker fashion, for example, in what this book calls "resistance," rather than in more conventional reactions. But it is still there. The relevance and the meaning of the religious forms and symbols and language and atmosphere may have shifted expression, but it is nonetheless real. This book urges ministers to look for it and respond to it in these new modes. This chapter in particular attempts to argue for and to demonstrate that responses to religiosity, despite their unexpected or vexingly resistive form, still betray the awesome and gripping power which religious symbols hold.

Religious forms, patterns, and concepts are hardly superficial or casual accretions of human culture. They are what they are, and they have persisted through the centuries precisely because they touch, evoke, and focus intense and intimate human concerns. When a minister feels some sense of inferiority or irrelevance beside the psychotherapist or the city planner because the latter seem to be dealing so competently with basic and critical dimensions of human experience, this itself may arouse our curiosity, but the attitude is hardly justified by the reality of the situation. The minister doesn't have to abandon religious material in order to touch the throbbing and dynamic centers of human life.

In a sense, the present chapter is only a specific continuation of the last, which contended that the ordinary and obvious surfaces of life are intimately enough related with its depths to convey the important meaning of these depths and to deserve the awe sometimes reserved for the depths. Perhaps religiosity is best seen as a special instance of the ordinary. From one point of view, nothing could be more ordinary and superficial than most of the common religiosity to be observed in our churches. At the same time, this religiosity is using forms and symbols and behaviors which are uniquely well tried and suited to capture, at the surface manifestation, some of the deepest throbbings of human life. This is as true in the resistive responses to religious forms as in the more conventionally religious responses.

This chapter has two portions. The first is a brief general discussion of the significance of religious forms and language, developed strictly from a naturalistic psychological and anthropological point of view. It says in effect to the minister: "Okay, if the secular, in this case particularly the psychological secular, seems to you to be in intimate touch with meaningful realities, let us accept its approach provisionally. Let's see what can be said, even from this point of view, about religiosity. Let's see whether a naturalistic point of view can so easily agree with those of your own subjective feelings which would contend for the impotence of religiosity." The larger second portion consists of an analysis of three specific instances of religiosity, seen at first as trivial and resistive, and on second look as suggesting the power of the religious even within the trivial and resistant.

WHAT IS RELIGION?

One's self, and the surging and seething forces within and without with which he must contend—these provide the persistent focus of the central, even ultimate, concerns of the human predicament. They may be cast in the language of psychology or of religion, or in the unrefined, crude language of raw experience: What am I? What am I supposed to be? How do I fit into the scheme of things? This stubborn and decisive Otherness in which I find myself—what is its character, its attitude toward me, its requirements of me? Is it benign or indifferent or malevolent? Is it one or many, intelligent or purposeless? These are the typical primordial questions which persist through the generations, sometimes stated with more sophistication, sometimes less, sometimes posed calmly, sometimes fervently, sometimes buried for half a lifetime under answers too pat or too frivolous to last longer than that, but, whether acknowledged or not, always giving energy and urgency to the human pilgrimage.

Primitively, these questions are asked about the *natural* forces which surround one and seem to control his fate: the destructive forces—earthquake, lightning, disease, airplane crashes, enemy's bullets; the precarious life-giving forces—sun, rain, fire, good crops, stars to steer by. Beyond this, the questions are asked of the more subtle, still decisive, forces of the *social* Other: those with near impact—family, tribe, neighborhood, work group—and the enigmatic worldwide forces of social, economic, and political events. How do I stand with them? How do I treat them? Parents first, then peers, and maybe finally the world beyond. The questions are also asked of those internal *personal* forces which, while one's own, also seem alien and mysterious, often threatening, and have been labeled in various times (unclean) spirits, demons, unconscious. How will they treat me, and I them? And, whatever the natural, social, or personal particulars which provoke the questions, they are simultaneously being asked about the *supra*natural, *supra*social, *supra*personal core, or essence, or ground, or principle, which is seen to be underlying, running through or behind, transcending the particular phenomena.

But really these questions are not so much asked about the Other as they are about one's relation with it. It is the urgency of this personal question which distinguishes religion from the philosophical enterprise and its offshoot, science, including psychological science. What must I do to cope with these forces, to align myself with them, or them with me? Are there clear rules I can follow to accomplish this alignment (perhaps to be called rituals or morals or magic)? Are there more subtle, more tentative guidelines in situations to which I can respond and from which I can find direction and aim? Are the forces arbitrary or whimsical so that I must plead, cajole, bribe? Must I struggle harder than that against odds and rebel? Must I be more patient, perhaps resigning myself to the inevitability? May I trust that despite the vicissitudes of occasional apparent hostility and indifference, in the long run and ultimately the Other is benign and supportive, and one can feel worthy, regarded, and at home? Must one be still more patient and wait for eventual affirmation, alignment, and at-homeness in a moment which is somehow radically beyond or outside these forces and which compensates for them?

Religious formulations

These yearnings and apprehensions of the human spirit are stated above in a general and phenomenological way. They are processes which contemporary psychology, in certain limited ways, has been able to detect and describe with such terms as acceptance, actualization, adjustment, anxiety, and so on through the glossary.

They are processes sociology describes with its own words: accommodation, adaptation, etc. They are also processes long since captured and addressed by religious symbols, postures, concepts, and activities, ranging from the most primitive in field, forest, or campfire, to the most sophisticated formalities of liturgy, legalism, and theology. Even in the homely and humdrum forms, lukewarm and warmed over, in which most suburban Americans know their religion, there is still a vital remnant of relevance.

If anything, religious language provides a greater immediacy and vitality than psychological language, which is more remote and abstract. Psychological language in psychotherapy, for example, talks *about* relations with parents. Religious language in the church *expresses* such relations. Psychology offers conceptualizations about the human predicament as an objective scientific discipline. Religion also offers conceptualizations, but as these have emerged directly out of men's experience. Religious and even theological concepts tend to be derived from existential searchings and encounters; the psychological concepts are in answer to more abstract analytic questions. And beyond conceptualizations, religion provides the symbols and forms for a continually living encounter. When a minister finds the psychological language—or more technical theological jargon—particularly congenial, one reason may be that he finds the role of objective analyst more congenial than that of fellow pilgrim.[2]

LANGUAGE OF THE FAMILY. Religious vocabulary, for example, like that of psychology, uses much of the language of the family, since for each person the first searching questions and perhaps even the decisive answers about his relations with controlling forces are worked out in relation to the immensely concentrated power and otherness which each infant finds in his own parents. Styles, moods, and language adopted with respect to parents and family persist even as the parents are gradually supplanted or supplemented by an

[2] The argument deliberately proceeds from the minimum of psychological considerations. Assumptions about the revealed character of religious forms and concepts would not be inconsistent with this psychological argument and would, to say the least, considerably enhance the argument for relevance—either the relevance of the forms as ideally used or the residual relevance and power of the forms even in their attenuation and distortion.

expanding universe of otherness. It should occasion neither surprise nor apology that the most comprehensive and ultimate references to the Otherness in which one feels his life rooted still retain references to the family. Some of it is in explicit language, as of "father God" and "mother church." Some of it is in more implicit evocations of family relations, as in the blended perceptions of God (e.g., as both nurturant and demanding) or the blending of obedient and rebellious responses to God, or the attitudes toward social responsibilities which partake of ambivalent feelings toward brothers. The residue of relations with parents and siblings is evidence of the vitality and essential relevance of the religious symbols, not of their triviality. A religious system that tried to move away from such family symbols would be abandoning not an arbitrary symbol, not an infantile, regressive crutch, not an illusory projection reducible to psychological analysis, but the vehicle by which most persons in our culture are able to express and develop their root orientation toward the fundamental forces of reality among which they live their lives. Whether and how a person ever moves out into productive relations with particular realities in his adult world still reflects the root relationship he first forged with what once comprised his entire world, namely his parents; and it is with this language that he may still express the basic orientation from which he moves.

Even as resistance

But what of the religious forms in their attenuation and distortion, as they become resistive blocks to just such productive expression as has been claimed for them? Even in distortion and misuse, we suggest here, there may well be an attraction and power in the elements of religion which need to be taken seriously and taken as a starting point, not discounted and neglected. This resistive use of the forms may still represent an encounter with their meaning and may disclose just how a person stands in his evolving relation to that meaning.

Even in the woman ostentatiously sporting her new hat on Sunday morning, even in the man stubbornly fighting for his familiar pew, even in the child eagerly flipping hymnbook pages during the invocation in order to find the first hymn—even in such trivial distortions of elements of worship, people may be heeding, *in their own way of the moment,* the meaning which is in those elements and their context. This may be, as it were, their personal religious ritual, unconsciously expressing something of how they perceive themselves standing before God at this moment in their lives. The forms of worship in the context of the church may evoke just these particular reactions. True, people show off hats, fight for seats, and find pages in many other contexts than that of worship. But it is just possible that such behavior may happen more often in church. This is the ironic possibility that most vexes the minister struggling for the ideal use of the forms and almost pleases the critics of the church because it seems to confirm their accusations of the church's corruptibility. But if such behavior is more frequent in the church it may be because the power of the church forms elicits starker responses. When such behavior happens in church, it may have a special or surplus meaning it doesn't have elsewhere. Elicited in the context of these religious symbols, the same behavior may express something that it would not in another context.

This is not always true of course. The behavior may be just what it seems to be, so much feminine display, male pride, or childish immaturity. The purpose here is only to argue enough for the *possibility* of such essentially religious meaning in the resistive use of religious forms as to make a minister look more carefully before he discounts it as mere resistance. If we here seem optimistically prejudiced in favor of the possibility of finding meaning, it is to counteract the more prevailing pessimistic prejudice.

What might our hypothetical examples of hat, pew, and hymnbook mean? Of course, they can be analyzed in psychological terms such as "need for social recognition" (in the case of the hat and pew) or "compulsiveness" (in the case of pew and hymnbook). They can evoke sociological terms such as "status symbols" and "middle-class values." These may well be accurate for any particular case. This represents the *personal* factor of the scheme introduced in Chapter I. We would expect such compulsiveness or such needs to be promi-

nent in nonchurch situations as well. But what of the personal
reaction to the situation, which the behavior represents? Here is
where we may look for special meaning unique to the worship
context.

HOW CAN A SUNDAY HAT BE RELIGIOUS? If we were somehow to
tap the unconscious associations of the woman with the hat, we
might well discover such thoughts as these: "Sunday . . . everyone
there . . . can rest a while this morning . . . a day off for the
Lord . . . everyone but me . . . I still have to bustle to get them all
dressed and fed . . . if it wasn't for me, they wouldn't all shine that
much . . . but nobody mentions that . . . I'll make them mention
this hat . . . how far forward dare I walk. . . ." If these are
plausible associations by the hat wearer, we can notice a degree of
comprehensiveness and depth which is not so likely to be evoked in
any context but church. Partly this is personal response to the intrinsic character of the worship; mostly it is built in by social custom:
"everyone" there, reflective pause from routine, cravings for "notice,"
reservations about approaching the "front" of the church (one of the
most respected taboos in Protestant churches). It's hard to imagine
just such associations any place but church. The woman and her
family report for their weekly "inspection," if not before God, before
"everyone" (and in this case one may wonder how important is the
distinction). Her family passes, on her merits; but she has to
demonstrate extra merits, good works, to pass. "Notice" doesn't seem
freely offered; it can't even be earned, but has to be struggled for. But
this effort at self-justification has its taint, too, and with it she can't
quite dare approach the altar or front pew in freedom, just because
there's too much noticeable pride in it (if noticeable to her unconsciously, then probably to others too; therefore it is to be covered up
by staying part way back).

"Need for social recognition" and "status symbol" seem a bit pale
as explanations here. The particular context—the weekly inspection,
as the church service seems to be to such a woman—gives this "need"
a special quality and texture. Such feelings are inseparable from the
particular kind of "religious" stimulus she finds the worship service to
be, and they lend themselves easily to understanding in theological

categories. If one were to discuss the episode with her—let us for the
moment ignore the practical question of how to arrange such a
conversation—in such terms as self-justification by God, grace, and
freedom, these terms might come much closer to being recognizable
in her experience than would, say, corresponding psychological terms.

CAN A HYMN NUMBER BE RELIGIOUS? What might a child be feeling as he sits in the pew, sees the posted numbers, and starts flipping
through the hymnbook? Maybe this: "This must be important and
impressive; everyone's quiet and looking up or bowing their heads
. . . dressed up, music, lights, decorations up front . . . God made
me . . . God can hear everyone at the same time, all over the city,
all over the world . . . I don't get it . . . I can't understand what
the minister's saying either." Impressed, baffled, wanting to participate—is it any more complicated than that? Is it any more—or
less—a worshipful response of the child to the worship symbols when
he reaches for the hymnbook to find the next hymn? He simply
wants some concrete evidence that he belongs in this, that he too *can*
be part of this important proceeding. Who's to say that the satisfaction of finding the right number is, for this child at this time, different from an experience of grace?

THE ALTAR GUILD AGAIN. An altar still carries associations of
purity, dedication, sacrifice by or on behalf of one's self, associations
imbedded in it centuries before Christians began imbedding martyrs'
relics in altars. Though not sanctioned by stanch Protestant ideology,
such associations are still encouraged by most Protestant practice:
elevated position; fresh, virgin flowers; clean linen or polished wood;
burning candles; cross; offering plates; the white pages of the Holy
Word. Even Protestant churches lacking an altar still have the
psychological equivalent of the "holy place" in window, pulpit,
chancel, communion rail; the need for the sense of order and power
and goodness, concretized and localized, to which one can relate (as
in purity and humility and sacrifice) is too great to be silenced by
"reformed" institutional scruples. So, an altar will evoke feelings and
occasion events which may have their "religious" elements subdued
or disguised but which are still not nearly so likely to happen in any
other place than at the altar. Women indeed may, and do, fuss un-

duly with flower arrangements in other places, and for similar reasons, but there is likely to be a special urgency and prominence to this fussing when it is, as they say, "for the church." The altar is insistently evocative of questions of one's own worth and goodness. We may also suggest here that it is up to the Christian minister to let the altar also speak, in its own terms, its affirmative answer to these questions it evokes.

To be simultaneously tentative, inviting, accepting, obvious—and now perhaps more "religious" than in our earlier suggestions—a minister might find his reactions following some such line as this, adapted of course for particular persons and situations: "You remind me of the way I usually fuss with my sermon before going into the pulpit, working with the notes to see if I can't get it a little more perfect. It's no strain at all to speak to the largest groups about any subject without getting so fussy, but there is something special about standing there in the chancel beside the cross and the altar and dealing with the holy word. I guess flowers have to be just so when they're going to be on the altar. . . ." (So far he reflects the question the altar seems to be raising for the women. Now he goes on to point to its "answer.") "But I have noticed that at times when I am most conscious or even fearful of the altar and the holy word, and most uncertain about the adequacy of what I have to say—those are the times when the sermon seems to jump off from the notes and take care of itself. I suspect that the altar does something like that for the flowers, not to mention each of us personally. It makes us especially humble, even fearful, to have to prepare something for the altar; but the altar may also complete and improve what we put on it. I suspect the flowers look better there on the altar than they do here while you're arranging them."

THREE EXTENDED EXAMPLES

A religiously tainted debate

An official board of the church is debating how to spend some unexpected income. About two-thirds of the board want to redecorate and refurnish the church office and minister's study, which have been left untouched in recent redecoration of other rooms. The others want to support a new project in the nearby city, where many of them work, by contributing to the salary of a minister to work in a large low-rent housing project. Regardless of the minister's own preference—and given such a choice, his feelings may be mixed, or perhaps quite decided!—it is the contention of this book that he is not primarily called to use the occasion to press for a decision one way or another. Rather, his task is to permit the board members to learn about themselves, individually and as a group, what their loyalties are, and how they can discover loyalties and pursue commitments. He is less concerned to have this decision come out "right" or "Christian" than he is to have these men, either as a board or in some other role, better prepared at another time to make a "right" or "Christian" decision. It is the contention of this chapter that the minister can do this without abandoning the jargon, symbols, and forms of religiosity. The long-range objective—advancing men's knowledge of and responsibility to God—might in the long run be served by either improved working space in the church office or a new minister in the housing project. It can also be served, perhaps even more effectively, right here in this meeting, using the very materials of the debate. In so doing, the minister might respond to any one of several characteristics of the situation. Here we emphasize one in particular.

The minister might be disturbed by the fact that the debate derives an urgency and a kind of holy hue from the religious argumentation, or rationalization, which crops up. On one side: The church of all places deserves to have an attractive and efficient nerve center. We shouldn't ask the minister to search out God's word in that storeroom he has now. How can people respect the church the way they ought when this is the kind of office they walk into? The church is God's house and this is where we should spend His money, not on somebody wandering around other people's houses. On the other side: Christians are supposed to be helping other people, not themselves; we ought to get a church started among the people in that housing project; they need it, just as the people in Africa and Asia have needed the civilizing influence of missionaries.

A minister might be irritated at the degree to which the board members use such religious argumentation as a patent rationalization to cover already well-entrenched positions. The use as rationalization trivializes and prostitutes the very arguments they invoke. He might desperately want to slash away this covering rationalization with which the men fill the meeting and look at the more fundamental bases of their positions, such as the unwarranted personal pride they feel in their institution, or the fearful distance they feel from the low-income inner-city residents, a distance measured equally by their shunning or by their patronizing. He might like to expose this process of rationalization, to help the men see how they, like everyone, tend to invoke the name of God and other high-sounding principles to bolster their own positions. Or he may feel like exposing it less calmly, and angrily invoking the wrath of God upon such hypocrites.

ELEVATE THE RELIGIOUS IN THE RELIGIOSITY. Without arguing that any one of these reactions would not be appropriate on occasion, it is still possible to consider an alternative point of view.[3] Assuming that the religious references are indeed rationalizations, like all rationalizations they must have some truth in them. A rationalization always says something, as well as covers up something. It may serve the function of obscuring other facts, but it still is based on something genuine, not pulled out of the air. Pure inventions could hardly serve the purpose of a rationalization; it must appear plausible enough to stand, and in our sophisticated times, even the rationalizer subjects his own rationalizations to the screening of a certain logical scrutiny. The truth here must be in the degree to which such men do feel an importance about their relation with God, however attenuated may be their feeling and statement of it, and however subdued it may be by loyalties to church, or to minister, or to doing good. There is indeed an urgency and an intensity to their participa-

[3] As suggested in Chapters IV and VII, the decision on strategy may depend, among other things, on the minister's intuitive assessment as to how much reality versus how much defensiveness is represented by the rationalization. The reaction proposed here assumes a fair proportion of "truth." If the fact of cover-up and denial and defensiveness seems overwhelmingly predominant and the "reality" in the rationalization only incidental, then the appropriate reaction may be to focus on the defensiveness.

tion in such meetings and to their battle for particular positions—an intensity which is true and is truly a religious one, however disguised and obscured it may be.

Why do already busy men get "involved," as they say, giving time and energy to meetings and to issues? (If their participation is reluctant, as it often is, this is only further evidence that some substantial motivation is prompting their participation, enough motivation to compete with the reluctance, or else they would not be there at all.) Diverse and multiple as these motives are, for most men there must be a substantial component of something recognizable as religious motivation, as discussed earlier in this chapter. All men, in one way or another, want to get their lives more clearly in touch with and aligned with the fundamental, creative, meaning-giving, controlling Otherness in which they live their lives. The church by its own claim and by public acknowledgment—though these two may differ in terms of the statement—appears as a representative of this Otherness and provides a natural means of achieving this relation with it.

To be sure, this motivation and this relationship may have a form which in its partialness makes it less than ideally or wholly religious. It may well seem more magical or superstitious than religious. It may well seem more like a desperate self-justification than an acquiescence to God's sovereign grace. For one man, it may be an alignment with a "good" institution, in order to quell guilt feelings for practices in other institutions during the week. For another, it may be a kind of prideful glorying in the exercise of authority, to compensate for the frustrations of inferior status at home or at work. And so on. But even as the specifics can be analyzed and judged for their desperation and partialness, one ought not to overlook the general element which they have in common: this is where each man is on his own stumbling pilgrimage. Each man is relating, in the style and mode which is his, to the institution and forms and language which he recognizes, however uncertainly, as representing something he needs and wants, however confusedly. Even though his particular floundering steps may not seem to have the pace and direction of a pilgrim's, or even though he seems to be standing firmly still, as though his present stepping-stone were truly the end of all pilgrimage and searching, he is still on pilgrimage. Floundering or stubborn clinging are simply the nature of some stages of pilgrimage.

When these religious arguments are made, perhaps half in stereotyped, formalized cover-up, but also half in indication that fundamental religious searching is somewhere involved in the enterprise, a minister may, quite understandably, be peevishly annoyed at the cover-up. But why should he not take the second half seriously, and unashamedly elevate these religious references to a topic of more clear and more central focus? "So you allude to what you owe God and His church. Okay, let's talk about that," he may retort in one way or another. He is not calling a bluff, or laying down a challenge, or wearing a chip on his shoulder, or finding a pretext to deliver a sermon or to sink psychological probes. He is acknowledging, or assuming, that there is something personally important represented by these references, even though neither he nor the man who made them may know exactly what that importance is. But the meaning and importance is still a personal one, not abstract and systematic. To elevate to attention references to God and to church and to obligations does not necessarily mean to launch a systematic discussion in theology, ecclesiology, or ethics. What is of primary and initial significance is whatever meanings and implications and associations these references have for the men who make them.

HOW THE MINISTER MINISTERS. A simple highlighting and reflection may do much. "I'm interested in the way you put that," the minister says to one of the men arguing for decorating the office, "that we owe this much to God and His church." (He might say the same thing to one of the men arguing for the inner-city minister.) This may be emphasizing the point more than the man consciously intended when he made the remark, but it is hardly exaggerating the gist of the remark beyond attitudes and feelings the man has and is ready to talk about. Nor is it exaggerating beyond what is appropriate for this time and place; after all, such religious language reflects what they are gathered for, both consciously, and also, as just suggested, more fundamentally and unconsciously.

Such an intervention by the minister elicits ready reply and discussion. "Sure, compare what our church rooms look like with the lobby of any movie theater or hotel, or even most bars." "Or with the carpets you just put in your own office," another trustee retorts to the first.

To provoke them into making more explicit what they have in mind, the minister rejoins, "Well, so what? Is God in a beauty contest or something?"

His provocation is successful. "Well, no, but it just doesn't feel right. It's like I wore my oldest clothes to church, or gave less money to the church than I spend on liquor." Already, half as analogy, half as a personal deepening of the discussion, the trustee has acknowledged that the urge to decorate is less an objective requirement by God than it is an internal motivation to "feel right."

The minister, still being personal and not dogmatic, but religious and not psychological, accepts this and pushes the inquiry. "I suppose most of us feel that way, but I sometimes wonder why."

The question is avoided, and instead, other trustees pursue tangents or rehearse points already made. "I think a lot of us do spend more on liquor than we give to the church." "Not me, that's the one thing you can't accuse me of," the board's teetotaler adds, only to be challenged, "But I'll bet you spend more on golf than on the church." "But never on Sundays!"

"I know I spent more decorating this church for my daughter's wedding than I intended to," another trustee nurses an old but unhealed wound. "Jane is your only daughter; I have three," another chimes in, "but for each of them it's only once in a lifetime, so I suppose it's worth it." "It's the only one for Jane I'm going to pay for," the former grumbles.

This makes one trustee want to raise the question of the church's attitudes toward remarriage, whether it permits a full ceremony, etc. The discussion of a wedding leads another one to say, "I think couples should have a nice wedding to look back to, not just if, but especially if they are going to move back into a drab apartment. I think that way about the church, too. I think it ought to look good in here, not to *keep up* with the bars and the movies but because so much around it is so shabby."

"Sure, when I greet visitors Sunday morning and hand them a

program," one of the earlier speakers adds, "I want the place and the program to look nice enough so they know that I know God's business is important business. Why don't we ever have printed programs?"

"I wasn't thinking so much of how you feel," is the mildly sarcastic reply, "but of how people themselves might feel when they walk off the street into our building."

By now the minister is faced with reactions at several levels and cannot pursue them all simultaneously. There is, first of all, the apparent resistance to his direct question of why it "feels right" to support and decorate the church and to be well-dressed in it. But since this question was addressed to one man before the others in the group were really ready for it, their reactions can perhaps be regarded not so much as resistance to the question as catching up with the first speaker. If the minister now repeats such a question, only to have it evaded by a continuation of the same conversation, then he will be in a position to demonstrate this as resistance and to discuss it directly as such.

Second, he thinks it curious that in none of the comparison between the church and other buildings has there been any mention of the men's homes. He speculates to himself that this may be because they identify the church and their homes too closely with each other to warrant a comparison. The arguments they use for decorating the church may be very similar to the arguments they use to justify their elegant homes. In some ways, the church may seem to them an extension of their homes. Or more importantly it may be that their homes are extensions of the church, in the sense that they may also be seeking in their homes and family life the kind of saving reassurance or purpose which is essentially a religious quest. Whether the minister is right about this speculation or not, this omission of the home from comparison may be worth mentioning in later discussion. The discussion, however, is not yet well enough defined or established to be able to identify convincingly and to develop productively the omissions and resistances.

Instead, the minister chooses to focus on the most obvious level of this discussion. Provoked by this mild pushing of a "religious" question, the men have, in fact, given many hints of the several different ways in which they feel related to God and of where they feel they are in their religious pilgrimage. There are, for example, hints of legalism and obedience to expectations from "on high" in some of the ways they talk about the decoration, and also about Sunday golf and second marriages. There is also a certain degree of ecclesiolatry involved in the way that some have gained satisfaction and assurance from identifying closely with a church they "can be proud of." There is some suggestion that religion and the visible church provide compensations for the otherwise shabbiness of one's life.

The minister chooses to reflect these overtones he has detected in the discussion. Because it is still a young discussion and because there is a group involved, he chooses not to reflect directly or exactly what has been said, or to identify remarks with speakers. He speaks more indirectly: "I can think of several reasons for wanting to have the church rooms attractive . . ." and he then summarizes those he has heard in the discussion above. Since it is truly a reflection, even though phrased indirectly, of the discussion, he has reason to think it will register and evoke responses in a way which might not be true if he simply offered speculation pulled out of more remote experiences. He may be emphasizing these religious meanings more than the men intended, but not more than is really there.

Such reflection to a group, rather than to an individual, despite the loss of immediacy and intimacy, does have some advantages. For one, it permits any who want to be silent and to reflect an opportunity to do so while others speak. By casting a wide net in his reflections, responding to themes expressed by several persons, the minister provokes some to verbal reply and perhaps others to silent, parallel reflection. Themes not responded to aloud are not necessarily fruitless. (On the other hand, by the same token the group situation does permit defensively inclined persons a chance to ignore without challenge reflections relevant to them, and to escape into the discussion of somebody else's theme. But this also may, in time, be reflected.) Another advantage of the group is that the reflections are able to evoke the multiplied, collective resources of the group, combined and mutually facilitative abilities for insight, analysis, and judgment. Judgments that they are too narrow in their loyalties and in their interpretation of God's demands, for example, are already available within the resources of some if not all members of the group. With a group, there is even less need or excuse than with an individual for a minister to turn preacher and to insist on the lessons to be learned and the judgments to be pronounced.

In this case, one of the minister's reflections is picked up immediately and the others are perhaps left to simmer. "Sure, don't we do things for God and the church because we're supposed to, because He expects us to come to church, give money to the church, even give time for meetings like this?" Another supplies a corrective: "I don't think these things are any good if you do them because you think you have to. You're just trying to buy off your conscience. I think you have to want to do them."

So the discussion goes, the men discovering, or rediscovering, gradually, some more than others, that both God's demands and His assurances are greater than their narrow focus would make them. The decoration of the church office (or the remote and uninvolving act of hiring a minister as one's representative in the inner city) hardly exhausts, maybe hardly touches, the richness and fullness of one's relations with God and one's responsibilities to Him, comfortable and convenient as it is to try to contract one's religious quest to such easy and narrow scope. The direction of the discussion is toward this realization.

Such religious, indeed theological, discussion could be translated into more or less equivalent psychological terms: motives for identity, esteem, acceptance, self-actualization, security, guilt-reduction; constricted compulsiveness, defensiveness, anxiety, etc. So could the outcome of the discussion be analyzed in psychological terms. Discussion of God, making Him seem more real—real enough to talk about seriously "even in a trustee's meeting"; shared discussion of misgivings; shared confession of anxiety-narrowed or anxiety-intensified loyalties; testimonials, of a sort, of different ways in which men have found "God"—this could all be analyzed as providing greater assurance and security, release from some anxiety, increased willingness to break loose from clung-to postures and to venture more freely. But why bother with such psychological translation or psychological analysis, except as psychological language itself may, for example, provide a kind of idolatrous commitment and assurance for a minister not too unlike office-decorating for his trustees? Psychological language provides only one kind of derived abstraction. The language of religion may be at least as primary and immediate. "Anxiety" and "compulsiveness" may be inferior substitutes for "estrangement" and "idolatry," rather than, as some defensively suppose these days, vice versa.

Too holy a ministry

There is another common instance in which a minister may feel impeded or annoyed by what he considers an excessive or inappropriate religiosity. This has to do with his parishioners' attitude toward his own role, and the ways in which they set him apart as a holy man, ways which he neither personally welcomes nor regards as doctrinally justifiable. In a wide range of situations, parishioners show that they regard the minister as having special access to and possession of moral and religious qualities which the laymen themselves lack.

The minister is still, though decreasingly these days, set outside or above the vicissitudes and routines of normal, everyday life. Money is considered too tainted and below his proper concerns, so that the trustees may feel more comfortable dismissing him from budget-making or money-raising activities; he is to take care of the higher things less accessible to them. Merchants may offer him discounts, perhaps because earning a good salary is thought to be beneath him or perhaps as a reward for keeping himself a holy man. Priests and priestesses at least since the Vestal Virgins and the kings-for-a-year of early cultures have been rewarded handsomely with goods and prerogatives by a society which expects them to deny some of their normal humanity, typically sex or even life itself, on behalf of them. The minister is expected to be a moral and religious model; he must practice a personal piety abandoned by others and must refrain from loss of temper, family conflicts, mental illness, and other lapses from perfection which are permitted other men. He is sometimes thought too tender or too ignorant to be exposed to locker-room stories, profanity, or shop talk from the business world. Counselees sometimes seem to feel an obligation to spare their minister an account of their more sordid doings. Whatever men may feel most (or even a little) guilty or apologetic or tainted about, they would keep separate from their contact with the holy man.

In Sunday morning worship, laymen are ready to ascribe to the minister more of a priestly role than is comfortable for any man to accept, unless he is bolstered by a Roman Catholic conception of ordination and sacramental worship. Regardless of Protestant doctrines and regardless of the minister's own expressed views, the laymen still seem to want to regard him as one with an especially direct access to God on behalf of all of them. He is not only to be an expert about the faith, but a model of faith. He knows God, His word and His will, in an intimate and authoritative way. He can communicate with God in prayer in a way in which laymen feel they cannot. Although he is without the Catholic priest's sacramental powers to make God present, the Protestant minister is often expected to do the same thing with his personal charisma and homiletical prowess. By his mighty and unique force of word and personal power, he is expected to make God living and real for people who cannot otherwise know Him and whose only contribution to this encounter is the passive reception of what the minister alone is able to deliver. At the same time, the minister's sermons and public statements, like his private ones, are sometimes supposed to be pure and untainted by worldly affairs, such as the church budget, politics, or sex.

CORRECT THE "ERROR"? When a minister is inappropriately endowed with being holy or religious, he may be especially aware that this is an impediment, that such a role-attribution interferes with developing the kind of relationship with his people which he feels is appropriate and with doing the kind of work which he feels called to do. He then may feel called to undertake corrective measures. He may decide to lecture to them, from the pulpit or privately, to instruct them on the proper attitude to take toward a Protestant clergyman. He may plead with them to let him "live a normal life." He

may decide boldly to act out a denial of this holy role and to prove
publicly that his life is no more sheltered or pious or pure than anyone else's.

Unfortunately, this posture of lecturing or pleading or defiant
worldliness does not represent any more than does the holiness the
relationship he wants with parishioners. It does not comprise the
work with them which he feels called to do any more than does being
a "holy man."

Such a reaction might be appropriate for those in other professions
who found themselves victims of unwanted role-attributions, but it is
not appropriate for the minister. A schoolteacher, for example, might
find that his teaching of mathematics is handicapped by discipline
problems in the classroom occasioned by the students' lack of respect
for the kind of car he drives and the clothes he wears, or by their
parents' mistrust of his political views, or by the infatuation a girl in
the class has for him. Such problems are clearly irrelevant to his
objectives in teaching mathematics, strictly conceived, and the solutions to these problems are hardly likely to take the form of mathematical formulae or to enhance the students' understanding of
mathematical principles. The solutions will go on independently of
the process of teaching and will be purely instrumental to it, not
partaking of it.

The minister's calling and purposes, however, are such that no
misperception of his ministerial role, or the correction of that
misperception, can be irrelevant to them. This misperception cannot
be thought of as being accidental or incidental but rather as being a
meaningful and important statement of something about the religious state of the persons who make it. And his response to this
perception, whether he likes it or not, is inevitably a ministry to this
religious state, whether a sensitive and helpful ministry or a deficient
one. Their religious state, their relation with God and their understanding of this relation, is going to be affected by what the minister
does in this situation, whether he wants to regard his response as
relevant to his ministry or not.

MINISTERING TO THE MEANING IN THE "ERROR." Just what kind
of relevance or significance may a minister see in the misperception of

his role? Some ministers in these days may be quick to infer meaning in psychological terms: feelings of guilt or inferiority being compensated for by identification with a good man; ambivalence toward fatherlike authorities expressed in the estrangement from God implied by the need for a priestly intruder-mediator and in loyalty to the priest; "capturing" of an otherwise remote and threatening God by having His emissary in one's own employ. Such psychological inferences may or may not be accurate for any particular individual. They may or may not be very close to the "religious" meaning, which will be suggested below.

Why not understand these persons' reaction more directly, just as it presents itself in their tendency to make their minister a holy man. Perhaps such attitudes toward the minister as we have described can be appropriately and helpfully understood as representing persons' yearning to know holiness, to elevate life out of the cloying feelings of taintedness and partialness into touch with divinity, to purify life, to belong to goodness. Such language, and its more technical theological counterpart, is sufficiently rich, familiar, and valid. Maybe a minister and his people can take seriously enough, without apology, as suitable and useful for everyday discussion, the kind of language the minister often reserves for the pulpit.

Consider the example of a group of lay leaders who are planning a dinner meeting to celebrate and encourage the "laymen's role in the church," as "ministers of the church in their everyday life." Several of the men are to give small testimonials as to how they "practice Christianity" in their business, and there are to be small discussion groups on this theme. In planning the order of events, the chairman proposes routinely that the minister's grace come before the men sit down, and he is about to pass on to the rest of the program when the minister interrupts him. "Why am I giving the grace? I thought this was a program for lay Christians." This is at first taken as a harmless joke—at least as good a joke as a minister can muster—and quickly passed over. But the minister is determined that this is an occasion for ministering to this "holy man" imputation and whatever lies behind it, and he persists. "I'm serious. Why shouldn't one of you say grace at this dinner?" The replies include the following:

"Everyone expects you to. You always do. Isn't that what a minister is for? . . . We need to make a good impression at this thing. What are we paying you for? . . . Walter can do it, but count me out. I feel awkward enough at home when my wife gets me to ask a blessing. . . . If you leave it to me, I'll take the way out I do at home and have a silent Quaker grace."

In the course of the discussion, the minister offers a series of comments and interpretations along the following lines:

"When the chips are down, this talk about lay Christianity seems to be just so much talk. I think you still have some kind of feeling that there's something about me or my title or my job that gives me a direct pipeline to God which you can't have but which you'd like to hook up with. I think you really feel that there is something about you which is bogged down so that your word can't soar up to heaven the way you think mine can. Maybe you think I have a halo around my head and you have a kind of veil around yours that keeps you from seeing God and talking with him. You feel so far away from the throne you need someone else to carry the message."

In such general terms as these, the men do acknowledge the minister's reflections of the ways in which they feel uncertain and unworthy to pray in public, and the ease and satisfaction they feel about having the pro do it. With their own feelings and attitudes held up to scrutiny in this way, the men themselves also suggest some defects in this self-perception: official doctrine which they also accept, and which they are in fact celebrating with this dinner, proposes an alternative view. When they look at themselves more objectively, they don't, some of them anyhow, feel quite as unworthy or feel God quite as inaccessible as they instinctively thought they did. There is, in short, a small skirmish in which some of the men reappraise—or perhaps simply appraise—how they feel about themselves and their relation with God.

Beyond this, there is some further discussion of what amounts to a doctrine of ministry. One of the men asks, "Suppose I do say grace at this dinner, where do we stop?" On another occasion the deacons continue this discussion, virtually in these terms, and do agree to leave the sermon and communion to the minister, but suggest that it would be more appropriate for the ushers to take the offering to the altar and offer prayer there themselves. When this plan is actually introduced, there is enough startled reaction to provide many other occasions for the minister to discuss with his people his role, and beyond this, what his role means to them and why. Some of these turn into frank psychological or "personal" counseling situations where the discussion of the altar, prayer, and the holy man evoke specific reports of guilt feelings and intense unworthiness approaching depression. Most discussions remain at the level of meaningful religious encounter.

Parents Anonymous—a case of evangelism

Others who express resistance in religious language that may be particularly annoying and particularly difficult for a minister is that group of parents whose only relation with the church is to send, sometimes bring, their children to church school, and maybe occasionally to send a small check as token payment for these services. They will say, if approached, that they think their children "need religious training." A minister can be understandably annoyed at the apparent hypocrisy, when such parents show no other sign of respect for religion, the church, or the minister. He may suspect in his annoyance, with perhaps a touch of unconscious envy, that the sending and the explanation are only a pretext and a rationalization for the parents to enjoy a more leisurely and private Sunday morning at home.

The minister may go beyond such annoyance to raise the question, at least with himself, as to what could propel parents into action which is so obviously inconsistent and so obviously vulnerable to unflattering interpretation. The minister's tempted rejoinders of "hypocrisy" and "self-indulgence" must be at least equally apparent to the parents themselves. Their behavior must be in spite of and in the face of the risk of such judgment, by themselves if by no one else. So these snap judgments to which the minister is tempted are perhaps best seen as a measure of the degree to which something else is pushing this behavior. It is these "weights" on one side of the scale which must be borne up by whatever force is producing the behavior.

If he asks questions of this kind to get behind his immediate judgments, then the minister may develop psychological hypotheses. He may, especially if there is other supporting evidence, speculate that this behavior represents some kind of misgivings the parents may have about their own role as parents. Perhaps the statement, "The children need religious training," should be translated to mean, "I recognize that the children need something fundamental—love and support, direction and guidance—which I don't feel adequate to supply." Perhaps it should be translated, "My children should be exposed to better models than I feel my life provides, especially with a Sunday morning hangover." It may mean, "Maybe my parents were right after all about church and about a lot of other things against which I rebelled, and I want to try to recover some of the values and perspectives they stood for." Such a psychological interpretation of sense of duty or sense of inadequacy is not alien to a religious perspective, but it is likely to be alien to the way the parent thinks about himself—at least in initial encounters with the minister.

Why should a minister not pursue his contacts with such parents in terms which they choose? Why not develop the topic and the relationship directly from the starting point that "children need religious training"? He does this, not ignorant of such psychological musings as have been proposed above, but sensitized in a general way by them as to what these people may be like. Neither does he abandon whatever convictions he may have acquired in his brushes with the principles of psychological counseling about respecting the position of another person and about the futility and irresponsibility of trying to impose one's own viewpoints on him. But the statement and the terms for discussion remain, until changed by the parents themselves: "Children need religious training." "Religion," whatever it means to the parents, is likely to be fruitful and vital enough an area of encounter.

HOW MINISTER WITHOUT A CONTEXT OF RELATIONSHIP? This particular example raises a keen difficulty, more relevant to Chapter III: how to develop any convincing context of acceptance with persons so tenuously related to the church and the minister, and about a topic on which they are so readily vulnerable to feelings of judgment. Even assuming that the minister is genuinely more concerned with the spiritual welfare of such persons—what their response to the church means to them—than with strengthening the institution of the church—what their response to the church means to *him*—and assuming that he can fully accept them personally in their present status and not be personally upset if they stay outside his formal church programs—even assuming that the minister feels such acceptance, how can he communicate it? How can he ask them why they want their children to have religious training, and have this "Why?" understood as genuine curiosity and not immediately interpreted as an attack, or as the entering wedge of an argument, inevitably leading to the conclusion, "You should come to church." Even more difficult—if the parents do become defensive, how can he presuppose enough perceived acceptance to deal with this very defensiveness as a starting point for fruitful discussion, as he might do with someone with whom he had firmer relations?

Perhaps approaching a group of such parents would be less threatening than approaching individuals. This provides them with the security of outnumbering the minister and with the opportunity of retreating into a kind of anonymity within the group. A group more or less identified as non-church-attending parents of Sunday school children also provides the added potential advantage of forthrightly accepting this status as one to be legitimatized and celebrated, in the American fashion, by having a group meeting and perhaps even an organization. Perhaps the minister invites a group of such parents to meet with him. He does not disguise but, rather, openly acknowledges and presumably accepts, the nature of this group. Perhaps he lightly labels the meeting as one for "parents who like peaceful Sunday mornings" or a "church meeting for parents who don't like church meetings" or perhaps most simply "Parents Anonymous." However, a minister may not feel that he can call such a group to meet without seeming to identify them as a band of culprits more than to celebrate their peculiar status. He may prefer to deal with individual parents but still acknowledge and accept their status by making clear to them that they are not singled out. He may refer, lightly, to his hypothetical "club of Parents Anonymous."

The relationship and mutual regard between parents and minister may be greater if a minister honestly accepts the role which he has for such persons as a representative of the church from which they feel some estrangement, and if the minister can acknowledge the fact that their relationship starts—even if it doesn't end—with the fact that they are sending their children to "his" church for "religious training," but not attending themselves. If they have despaired of finding in church participation serious help in their own religious quest, they may find new respect and new hope within the very candor and integrity with which the minister approaches them. They are encouraged to attack their problem—their ambivalent estrangement from the church, represented by sending the children but staying away themselves—if he can face *his* problem (namely, them) with a straightforward assurance, and if he can approach them with an unembarrassed discussion of religious questions in terms relevant and recognizable to them. He sticks to his business, as they see it, religion, and to his real basis for approaching them at all. He does not insinuate himself in the guise of a witty and sociable fellow, or as a psychological expert in raising children, or as a community leader marshaling support for a new town project, roles which he might think more acceptable and ingratiating to the parents than that of a minister-discussing-religion-and-the-church. To adopt one of these roles may be a successful foot-in-the-door tactic. It may make the minister feel more comfortable, bypassing the subject of religion and the church, over which he may anticipate tension. But such a tactic also evidences—for all to see—a temporizing and timidity which cuts the ground from under further real encounter. Under such circumstances the parents can hardly conclude anything except, "If this minister can't face questions of religion and the church directly, how can I be expected to?" Or at least, "How can he help me?"

Ministry is not like television advertising. In a task as peripheral from central human concerns as selling a brand of cigarettes, it may be possible to plan two different tactics, one for getting attention, and the other for selling the product, without having these interact.

Whatever devices one uses to get the attention of an audience will not necessarily affect the impact of the devices one uses to sell the product. But we can note, too, even in the case of this example, as cigarettes have become more closely associated in recent years with questions about a more basic human value, that of health, the "approach" which an advertiser uses is more carefully scrutinized and is regarded as relevant to the confidence one puts in his message. Similarly, advertisers whose goal is more the "public relations" task of affecting personal attitudes toward an institution or a policy, not just affecting relatively superficial buying choice, must pay much more careful attention to the means they employ to gain access to persons' attention. They consider carefully, for example, the types of television programs which are "vehicles" for their messages. If approach and substance interact in the relatively superficial process of building an institutional image or winning support for policies, how much less can they be separated when dealing with the most fundamental questions of life about which persons are particularly vigilant and sensitive.

The problem with the parents on the fringe poses an extreme instance of the minister's common feeling of not enough rapport with persons to support ministry as he wants to exercise it. The example poses the common temptation of the minister to adopt a preliminary strategy to win rapport before he can exercise ministry. The example also points out that even in such an extreme case, there is in fact a relationship, which, when directly acknowledged, provides sufficient basis for ministry.

HOW MINISTER WITHOUT A CONTEXT OF RELIGIOSITY? How can one respond to and exploit the ostensible religiousness of such a case, when there is so little of it? How does one discuss religion with persons who neither have a religious vocabulary nor are particularly inclined to acknowledge its relevance or importance? The "Parents Anonymous" again highlights the temptation to suppose that preliminary remedial work is necessary to bring persons to the point where ministry can be exercised—not to develop relationship this time, but to develop religious sophistication. People on or beyond the fringe of the church present an extreme case of the lack a minister may feel all his people have; he may feel that they need to be trained to recognize and discuss religious problems in appropriate terms before a real discussion can take place or before he can offer real help. This feeling can be interpreted in some cases as representing the timidity of the minister in venturing beyond the narrow confines of the perspective and terminology with which he has learned to feel comfortable in seminary classroom and bull session. Or it can be interpreted as a regretful recognition by the minister of the relative poverty and crudeness of understanding and faith available to such a person compared with the richness of understanding that a more refined language permits.

It may be hard for a person accustomed to so much more refined and precise language to understand that important questions of personal orientation and fundamental attitudes—in short, of religious pilgrimage—can be expressed in such seemingly superficial and unreflective language as, "I always think it's good for children to have a chance to have some religious training." To stick to religion with such people may mean, for some time, to talk about the church as an institution, their experiences in it and attitudes toward it; for the vast majority of the population, the church building, its program, and its professional ministry represent the major defining characteristics of religion. Or it may mean a long period of talking *about* religion as a general objective phenomenon, rather than developing or using the language which religion provides to talk about oneself and the relations and responsibilities one has toward what he finds around him. But such language cannot be denied the possibility of expressing, even so imperfectly and inelegantly, central strivings, yearnings, apprehensions, and convictions of a fundamentally religious nature. Attitudes toward the church and the objective, though remote, phenomena of religion, may provide a concretization and a focus for otherwise vaguely felt attitudes of confidence or mistrust, responsibility or rebellion, toward God. We recognize this for people within the church; why not all the more so for those on the edge of it? The church, after all, is supposed to be the continuing body of the Christ by which men know God, however remotely.

MINISTERING TO THE MEANING IN THE ESTRANGEMENT. A minister

might decide to reflect the parents' statement of their children's need for religious training, to probe their own understanding of this statement, and at the same time to try to indicate that his own attitude was one of open inquiry and not condemnation, by some approach such as this: "You say that your children need religious training, but I'm really not sure that they do—at least not the kind that we are able to give, with limited time, space, staff, and so forth. It's a pretty patched up affair. I really wonder sometimes what the kids get out of it." Taking their statement at face value, he gives his own honest response to it.

What kind of responses might this kind of probing, reflection, and confession elicit? How might each be interpreted and pursued? Here are some responses, which may come singly or in combination.

"It's more than they get at home." The minister's confession evokes a counterconfession and an apparent readiness to discuss a sense of religious deficiency in the family and something about the expectations and norms by which these deficiencies are measured.

"Well, they learn something about the Bible and Golden Rule." Or, "They learn to say the Lord's Prayer; they can't do that in school any more." Perhaps these elements are what the parents think the essence of religion is. It is more likely in this context that these are the elements which the parents believe the minister may regard as basic; their reply is perhaps to be interpreted as a bid to identify themselves with the minister and with the religion he represents. Like the first reply, it might be an effort to reassure the minister about his own misgivings, a positive, personal gesture, if not too condescending. More likely, rather than showing themselves on the minister's side, the parents are making an effort to get the minister on their side. Their reply may be something of a bid for the minister's approval or an escape from his condemnation, a demonstration that they too are "religious." Maybe it is purely a defensive I'll-beat-off-your-criticism-by-doing-it-myself-first (a version of, "You can't fire me, I quit"), i.e., "identification with the aggressor." ("We know what religion is and, like you, are in favor of it, against the secular schools.") The appropriate response here might be to acknowledge just this characteristic of what the parents seem to be saying.

"Well, at least they get a Sunday school paper which they leave lying around, or sometimes a picture of some flowers they make me tape up on my refrigerator." This is a kind of defiance which outwardly might seem to cut off discussion and send the minister packing in a hurry. But the minister actually, if he can withstand the first blast, should regard this as a most promising rejoinder. The woman has taken him on his own terms of candor and integrity and has told him, in so many words, just what she thinks of religion and his church. The minister's reply should recognize her attitude. Presumably it will be somewhere between a too narrow reflection, "Do you find this Sunday school debris a nuisance?" and an overadventurous interpretation, "And you'd probably just as soon not have me hanging around here any more than the so-called flowers." Toward the narrower side he might reflect, "That's pretty meager reward for having to get them all dressed up with faces washed and money in their pockets." To make it more general he might say, "It all seems such a bother, and for what!" To this, the minister may hear more discussion about the Sunday school, to which he will make similar reply. Or he may already have earned something like, "I feel that way about the church service, too. It's a nuisance to have to look bright on Sunday morning and to get there and try to figure out what's going on. And for what? Or those insipid women's fairs that they got me to help on one year!" If the minister has withstood these assaults, he has been offered a chance to explore some fundamental attitudes. Something has tripped up this woman on her religious pilgrimage, and he may not be too far from finding out with her what it is and what is to be done about it.

Perhaps the defiance is less direct, but also less accessible. A man may slough off the minister's remarks with something like, "Oh, I think the Sunday school is doing okay." He just doesn't want to get involved in a discussion with the minister. If this seems to be an accurate interpretation, the minister might as well say so, "There doesn't seem to be much to talk about." To this he may get a noncommital, maybe gruntlike response, confirming that discussion is at a close, or one may just as likely find the invitation accepted to talk about not talking about religion, "Yeah, I never have understood this

religion business and I seem to be getting along okay without it."
Past experience is now open for exploration and ministry.

Defiance in another form may be, "I think the church is okay at
teaching kids and helping them get started." If the minister acknowledges the implied corollary that the church seems irrelevant beyond
childhood, this may be the first experience that the father has had for
a long time that the church and the minister don't "miss the
point."

Or there may be more straightforward replies, easier and more
rewarding for the minister because they more overtly seem to accept,
even invite, further discussion of religious attitudes. "My parents
always took me to Sunday school and I want to do at least as much
for my own children." "Well, I've decided that there isn't much to
this religion business—God is dead, and all that. But, you know, I
could be wrong. And I think everybody ought to have a right to
decide for himself. I talk to my kids about their Sunday school lessons when they come home to try to help them decide."

These parents may be able to accept the implied invitation to
specify some of the "religious needs" which they want the Sunday
school to provide for their children and, hence, to indicate indirectly
something about their own religious aspirations. "To know the Bible
better, to know how to pray, to get them started straight and to help
them over rough times, to help them learn to choose between good
and bad, to give them the courage to do the good"—all these may be
regarded as kinds of projections of their own religious pilgrimage.

Whatever it specifically turns out to mean for any particular
parents, the act of sending but not following their children to church
does mean something. However much that act at first seems to
contradict the possibility of ministry ideally conceived, the minister
who is open to whatever relationship is actually in the act may discover that its meaning is not so remote after all from the parents'
religious quest or his own purposes of ministry.

VII

Responses to Resistance

The psychotherapist and the minister are both men of words. This is one reason that it is appropriate to look, as this book has, to the experience of the former for hints the other can use. The major activity of each is in listening to and speaking words, and sometimes reading and writing them. Their main relationship with people lies in what they say to each other.

To rely on words is appropriate. The psychotherapist may understand this largely on the basis that words represent the most highly developed tool of the ego, whose resources (both his and the patient's) he relies upon to do the work of therapy. He also supposes that words are linked to emotional life and hence expressive of it with some accuracy. But he supposes too that they transcend and can even mold the emotional. The therapist may or may not also find some deeper—or poetic—significance in the fact that the use of words is an "oral" activity, perhaps related to primitive or fundamental stages of personal development.

The minister may be pragmatically aware of the indispensable importance of words for reporting and reaching and moving the elements of human experience he would touch. He may even find some metaphysical—or perhaps poetic—basis for his own reliance on words in the very status which "breath" and "word" have in the

260

philosophical and theological lexicon—especially in connection with the creative (Gen. 1:1; 2:7), sustaining (Acts 2), and redeeming (John 1) activities of God.

But there is also the risk of becoming too reliant on words. There is the temptation to frame one's relationship with others, personal and professional, exclusively in terms of the spoken word just because that is a tool that one has learned to use comfortably and well. Just as there is more to the person than the cerebrum, the human situation is more than words and is not always perfectly registered with words. God may have created by breathing His breath into man, and man may have established his dominion over beasts by naming them, but neither man nor beasts were fully known nor fully governed by words. At Pentecost, the flow of words was only preliminary to the question, "What shall we *do?*" And the key verse of John 1 is the announcement that the Word became flesh.

As applied to resistance, this reliance on words, and especially on words which describe and report, produces a single kind of response to resistance—the analytic reflection. The resistance is pointed out to the resister, verbally. The therapist or minister "calls them as he sees them," and he sees them largely in the same objective, analytic, and abstract terms in which this book, which must be limited to words, discusses such instances.

This objective verbal reflection may very often—perhaps most often—be the most appropriate and the most helpful kind of response. It is used predominantly, if not exclusively, by the therapist. It is the principal response proposed in examples in this book. But it is not the only possible kind of response to resistance. This chapter suggests three additional modes of response. These are suggested by considering two differences between resistance and other situations a minister confronts. Compared with other encounter—in which verbal reflection may be appropriate—resistance is *acted out,* and it *involves* the minister as a party. As such, it invites response which is not verbal and which is not simply a descriptive reflection.

In most situations other than resistance, therapist and patient, minister and parishioner are discussing behavior which takes place at some other time and place. The only way it can come to attention is with words. The only way it can be addressed is with words. But resistance is acted out on the spot. A person is expressing himself with behavior—often unconsciously and therefore nonverbally. This may require an equally behavioral response, communicating with that portion of the person which is being expressed without the use of words. This suggests that response to resistance may sometimes be *behavioral*, not verbal.

Since behavior other than resistance usually takes place at another time and another place and is reported, second hand as it were, to the therapist or minister, he remains an objective observer. He is not involved in the situation under discussion as a participant; therefore it remains "under discussion." He can only reflect it or reflect upon it, describe or analyze. But resistance is directed toward the minister. It occurs in a situation in which he is a prominent participant. It invites, indeed provokes, from him *reply* as a participant, rather than commentary as observer.

These considerations, then, suggest two different dimensions— verbal vs. behavioral, observer vs. participant—which can be combined to yield the possibility of four different types of response to resistance:

verbal reflection   verbal reply
behavioral reflection   behavioral reply

The terms "reflection" and "reply" are arbitrary labels, but seem as good as any to distinguish the description of behavior which the minister as observer offers from the active reaction to behavior in which the minister as participant engages.

ILLUSTRATION OF ALTERNATIVE RESPONSES

To illustrate the alternative modes of response, we look again at an incident discussed in Chapter V, the case of the parroting wife. It may be helpful to consider the possible responses in the context of the larger perspective which this book has tried to bring to bear on such incidents. So the next several pages will amount to a review of the book so far.

The context of responding

DISRUPTION. In a Bible study group, a man's comments were invariably and immediately followed by remarks from his wife. Sometimes she restated and confirmed his views. Sometimes she contradicted him. Sometimes she disregarded his comments and abruptly changed the topic. Always she seemed to need to have, as far as the two of them were concerned, the last word. In a session intended to make the Bible more understandable and meaningful for a group of persons, this behavior was disruptive. Mrs. O gave the impression of responding more carefully to the remarks of her husband than to the substance of the Scripture. As the minister became aware of this pattern of behavior, he began to feel that the message of the Scripture was sometimes lost for the group. More than once a promising line of discussion was brought to an abrupt standstill by Mrs. O's interruption of the natural flow of ideas.

For such a disruption, many remedial measures might be considered. He might consider excluding her from the group, asking her privately to change her behavior, manipulating the situation in some way to force her to change, such as by "beating her to the draw" after her husband speaks, or by changing the topic to one on which she would be unprepared to speak readily. If provoked by many similar incidents, a minister might consider abandoning such discussion groups or even his entire ministry to these people, on the grounds that they weren't prepared or sufficiently responsive.

All such reactions share the presupposition that Mrs. O's behavior is essentially meaningless, except as disruption. The only relation the behavior seems to have to the minister's purposes as a study-group leader is to block the purposes. So the only way the minister sees to pursue his purposes is to remove the block. Such responses are literally reactionary insofar as they are controlled by the disruption rather than by the minister's own purposes. The minister is led "dualistically" to cope with the disruption in a way that is different from and preliminary to the way he would implement his purposes with the group. It will take emergency police action to cope with the woman's disruption, so that he can get back to being pastor and Bible exegete and discussion leader for her, or at least for the rest of the group.

SITUATIONAL OR PERSONAL MEANING? Alternatively, the minister might consider that Mrs. O's behavior is not to be regarded sheerly as disruptive but also as having some meaning of the kind attributable to *situational* or *personal* characteristics. Perhaps her husband's behavior did, in fact, regularly require commentary or corrective, which she was competent to supply; perhaps the husband did not speak clearly or accurately; perhaps the minister as discussion leader was deficient in understanding the husband's contribution, or in changing the subject when he led up a blind alley. These would be realistic, situational "meanings." Or perhaps the meaning of her behavior had to do more with her own temperament and personality characteristics or with the private relation between husband and wife, possibly one of rivalry or hostility.

Meaning of either of these types might have suggested some response by the minister. The first most likely would have suggested some change in the minister's own tactics as discussion leader. The second might have suggested some pastoral approach to Mrs. O or to the couple on another occasion. This last response would have made use, as was pointed out in Chapter I, of the multiplicity of roles of the clergymen: encounters in one role (in this case as discussion leader) provide opportunity, information, and rapport helpful for the exercise of another role (in this case, personal pastoral counseling). Such meaning tends not to be relevant to the immediate situation in which the behavior is evoked or to the minister's role in it.

BEHAVIOR IN THE WAY SUGGESTS THE WAY OUT. Alternatively, the minister might entertain the hypothesis suggested by this book that Mrs. O's behavior is a meaningful, purposive response within the terms of the situation as he originally intended it. He can helpfully respond to her behavior within his intended role as Bible discussion leader, and not as policeman or as pastoral counselor. Her behavior may represent an important response to the materials of the Bible discussion group—perhaps to the topic and scriptural passage under discussion, perhaps to the larger constellation of clergymen, Bible, fellow church members, prayer, God, and the many connected religious associations. If her behavior, for example, represents a kind of competitiveness or a desperate desire to impress and to please, and if this reaction is evoked to some degree by the constellation of religious stimuli, then we are in the presence of some clues as to Mrs. O's status on her religious pilgrimage, her attitude toward God, church, Scripture, and clergy, and her understanding of their attitude toward her. The minister does not have to know, or even to speculate what may be the reaction behind the behavior (see Chap. V). He just has to be ready to entertain the hypothesis that her behavior represents some such meaningful reaction to the situation—of which the speculation in the above sentence provides one example. Her behavior may be the product of an unconscious mobilization of resources (see Chap. IV), representing her earnest involvement and energetic struggle; in terms of our speculation above, it could represent something like her seemingly desperate effort to prove herself (to God, to church members, to minister) worthy, knowledgeable, concerned, good. (That she wishes to demonstrate this in competition with her husband may be relatively incidental or very important; perhaps he is the only one in the group that she dares to try to "top." Perhaps other "nonreligious" rivalries with him prime her to show her reaction in this way. Perhaps he does represent for her a model of goodness and religiosity, a kind of standard of perfection which she desires to excel.)

The very inappropriateness and insistence of her behavior—the very elements which made it disruptive and resistive—become then precisely the measure of its potential meaningfulness. They provide the clue or the channel by which the minister and/or the woman may begin to discover what that meaning is.

Once a minister gets past his perception of behavior as *merely* disruptive and begins to suppose that it may be *meaningfully* disruptive, what is his appropriate response? As reported in Chapter V, the minister remarked to the woman after the meeting something about "getting two for the price of one." Why did he do this? What else might he have done?

Reflection

If the minister chooses a form of reflection, he does it in order to help the person see his behavior as the minister sees it—as resistive and disruptive, as puzzling and curiously inappropriate, as uncalled for or unaccounted for by what is visible in the situation, and therefore as especially meaningful and important. This view of his behavior which is reflected back to the person differs from other views he may have of it. It may differ quite markedly from his own sense of what is happening. In this example, Mrs. O, quite typically, tended to see (to rationalize) her behavior as appropriately contributing to and improving the discussion. She was aware only dimly, if at all, that her comments so consistently followed those of her husband. The minister's reflection perhaps provided the first occasion for her to recognize that her behavior was "special" or even "odd" or "curious."

The minister's reflection is likely to differ from other reflections the person has received "in the world," primarily because it regards any inappropriateness as a matter of curiosity and inquiry, not as a matter of judgment. If Mr. O or the other group members have reflected their view of her behavior, it probably included their sense of annoyance, and perhaps, in Mr. O's case, defensiveness.

Verbal reflection is likely to be most common. A minister might make a full and explicit statement either to the entire group or to the woman alone: "We have discovered together that our understanding of God's word is impeded by many different obstacles which we ourselves put in the way. We have discovered that God's word seems to evoke in us many different and sometimes surprising reactions. Perhaps the somewhat curious dialogue, which Mr. and Mrs. O have regularly in our study of the Bible, is an important example which would be worth considering for our general instruction. We have all gradually become aware of this regular exchange and it sometimes seems to get in our way. We may find that such a reaction is not too different from other kinds of reactions which others of us have to our

Bible study." (Such a statement might or might not be accompanied by explicit recall of the context of group sharing and group acceptance, which is presupposed.)

Preferably, most of this somber justification for intervention and statement of acceptance would not be necessary. It would already be taken for granted. In this case, a less heavy, less somber reflection might communicate the same thing and do it more invitingly. "I never have a chance to comment on anything Mr. O says." "I keep wondering why it is only your husband's remarks which seem worth commenting on; don't any of the rest of us ever say anything worthwhile?" "Sometimes it's hard to get some of you to start talking, but if I ever want Mrs. O to talk, I know how to do it; just get her husband to say something." "Do you two always deliver this one-two punch, or is it only with us?" "Like rubbing two Boy Scouts together to make a fire, there is something about rubbing your husband against the Bible that seems to make a spark for you."

Or just after Mr. O speaks, the minister might say: "I guess there are several points there which some of us might want to follow up, but Mrs. O seems to have claimed the first crack at her husband."

Behavioral reflection could be directed to the same purpose of calling attention to behavior which the pastor regards as of special importance and meaning just because it is "unusual" or not quite "fitting." There are common and readily interpretable postural means for calling attention to behavior as important and intriguing. Most obvious is the chin-on-hand, open-mouthed stare. Some responses are more subtle and subdued than this. There can be enhanced intensity of attention in both posture and expression, with body, head, and eyes focused on the speaker. Perhaps this begins abruptly with a sudden startled twist of the head, or perhaps it lingers momentarily with continued attention after Mrs. O finishes speaking—both gestures communicating a special intrigue and interest. Almost anything unusual in the minister's behavior—even a distinctive crossing of legs or gesture of the hand—may express his sense of the unusualness of the behavior.

Perhaps he may want to reflect the inappropriateness of the remark by slightly withdrawing rather than enhancing attention, eyes on the floor or on the last speaker, posture slouched, maybe even fingers drumming, etc. Perhaps he starts to speak after Mrs. O but interrupts himself with a kind of double take, with a pause and a look at her, again suggesting that her behavior is something especially to think about and reflect upon.

Repetitiousness in the minister's behavior—in any of the above responses or in any other behavior—can call attention to the repetitiousness in her behavior. This becomes a clue to her just as her repetitiousness was a clue to the minister of a certain meaningful strangeness in what she is doing. Even a standard and perhaps slightly awkward way of crossing his legs or a peculiar way of clearing his throat, or a peculiarly injected "yes," may gradually register with her unconsciously as a reflection that her own behavior is similarly persistent and noteworthy. As inappropriateness tends to call attention to inappropriateness, so does repetitiousness call attention to repetitiousness.

A minister may find himself wanting to call attention to her behavior even more explicitly by, in effect, imitating it. He may choose to answer Mrs. O's statements (or the statements of some other member of the group) consistently—just as she answers Mr. O. He may use a style different from his usual participation and more like her own efforts to "top" her husband (unless such one-upmanship happens to be the minister's usual habit and style of participation, when no such distinctive reflection would be possible). The intention is to direct her attention, and that of the group—for it is truly a general and common problem—to this quality of behavior, especially as it is intrusive, disruptive, and resistive.

Like the preceding verbal reflections, these suggestions for behavioral reflections are intended primarily to respond to "level one" (see Chap. V), the overt, manifest behavior without much, if any, regard for inferences of underlying motives. Under certain circumstances, however, the minister might think he has good reason to reflect his perception of motives. Behavioral reflection may be more suitable for this than verbal reflection, since it is less insistently explicit and more deniable if a person is not prepared to face motives.

If a minister, for example, suspects some kind of competition and rivalry involved in the behavior, he may find limited and circumscribed ways of focusing on those instances that provide clues of this competition, or of imitating this in his own behavior, as a stimulus for reflection. He may, for example find other ways of being mildly competitive, such as beating Mrs. O to the jump in passing sugar for the coffee. This may well draw her attention, her sensitivity, and her problem-solving skills to the problem of rivalry, perhaps even as she knows it in her own experience. But the behavioral reflection doesn't insist on the point enough to arouse defensiveness as might a verbal reflection of motives.

Reply

Reply, verbal or behavioral, may presuppose more often than does reflection some perception of the "meaning" of the behavior at what has been called (in Chap. V) level two and level three. If reflection is the selective identification of some aspect of behavior as important, what is meant here by reply is some effort at appropriate rejoinder. "Appropriateness" in this case is defined by the pastor's own purposes in the situation, be they pastoral, instructional, or some other means of communicating God's presence, His grace, or His demands to the people of the parish. These purposes likely pertain to the deeper meaning of the behavior. Hence the reply is likely to be addressed to the meaning the pastor intuits in the background and motives of the behavior. Reaction just to the manifest behavior, in fact, may often prove inappropriate and contradict the pastor's purposes. He may find himself offering simple recommendations for behavioral change ("Don't do that"), expressing mostly irritation over the disruption, rather than purposes of ministry.

GENERAL YET PARTICULAR. The meaning which is inferred and addressed in the reaction may be quite general (more or less what was meant by level two in Chap. V) without assuming a more specific understanding (level three). The minister may not assume anything more in particular, for example, than he would in preaching a sermon to a congregation that included Mrs. O. He may simply recognize that her intrusive behavior must represent some form of anxiety or distress or tension, some inner disruption showing itself in the manifest disruption. And his response to her may be no more particular than that of a sermon which attempted to communicate a sense of God's grace to a wide range of personal distress. In this case any of the usual ways of stating pastoral objectives would be appropriate ways of formulating the minister's purposes in reacting to Mrs. O: he wants to communicate a sense of acceptance, an affirmation of her fundamental worth—a truth and an attitude which he believes to be trustworthily grounded in God's gracious regard of her, but an attitude which she apparently does not now accept about herself.

The ways which a minister may have for expressing such attitudes or behavior are legion, obvious, yet not easy to prescribe in abstraction out of the actual living encounters. He can express his respect and esteem and regard for her, or the "acceptance" which he believes God holds for her, directly in so many words, or through gestures and expressions. He can do it indirectly in the way in which he treats her. If he listens to her, if he remembers what she says, if he shows respect for what she says—even, for example, by disagreeing with her—these are types of behavior within a discussion group which are likely to communicate this affirmation. So are such simple gestures as treating her as a social equal, not as a professional object. This might include such gestures as discussing openly with her "problems" in the church or in the discussion group, including the "problem" raised by her own behavior. Such candor is no small gesture of trust and respect.

However the minister cannot be so general in trying to express trust and esteem that it just fails to register or to be believed. "You're a fine person," or "God loves you" may really be directed at a particular "you," but it is hard for him to see himself as that kind of "you." Mrs. O knows herself, her uncertainties and her reassurances, in terms of particulars (I am, or am not, or I want to be, an acceptable mother, a brilliant conversationalist, a good dresser, a gracious hostess, etc.). These are partial ways in which she sees herself; but it is hard for her to know herself in any way except in such particulars. Here is where she feels anxieties and insecurities of a kind which prompt the sort of disruptive behavior we are discussing. Here is also where she feels any assurances. Presumably, then, the object of the minister who would offer such reassurance is to discern those particulars which *are* "ego-involved" (which are somehow identified by her with her most real or most total "self") and which are under some threat and in need of some assurance. His task may be to link these personal elements of her response with whatever particulars of the Bible or the context of Bible-study may have elicited it and which may have some answer for it.

SPECIFIC TO CIRCUMSTANCES, IF NOT TO TIME. Unlike reflections, replies usually need not follow the resistive behavior so closely in time. This is largely because the reflection tends to be directed at the manifest behavior itself (level one) and the reply at some aspect of the underlying meaning (levels two and three). To invite attention to the behavior, the reflection needs to follow it closely. But the underlying tensions and motives, we may assume, more or less persist, regardless of whether resistive behavior happens to be evident. They may be addressed equally effectively whether or not the resistive behavior is present.

We need to remember, however, that the reaction—tension or rivalry or whatever—(middle line of the diagram in Chap. I) producing the resistive expression may be evoked by particular elements of the situation. Mrs. O's competitiveness is very likely a reaction to some combination of her own background and motives, plus husband, plus some part of the constellation of Bible-minister-church members. If this is so—if the reaction is present, at least in a particular form and intensity, only in a particular constellation of circumstances—then the minister's reaction is meaningful and appropriate only within this constellation. The immediate timing of the reply may not be so critical, but the appropriateness of the situation may be. There is not much point in replying to Mrs. O's competitiveness during a pastoral call or a counseling session or a Sunday school committee meeting or a sermon, if she experiences it only in the Bible discussion group with her husband. This is the vitality and the importance of the resistive moment which makes such occasions, as they develop disruptively in the life of the church, the opportunity for significant on-the-spot ministry.

In this context it is worth noting again that all ministers *do* "reply" to the underlying meanings of resistive behavior, whether they intend to or not, and whether their reply is essentially constructive and healing or not. The minister's response, or even his absence of response, does register in one way or another with the moods and needs and attitudes and motives expressed in the resistive behavior. This is true in a more particular sense than the general truism that all of us are affecting and influencing each other all the time. The resistance is a particular gesture in which strong needs or yearnings or fears or strivings are focused. Further, the resistance is directed at the minister, to the degree that he becomes the personal representative, or sometimes even symbol, of whatever element of religion or the church is evoking the resistance. For these two reasons, he is unavoidably "on the spot," and his response to the resistance unavoidably has important impact on the motives behind it. His heedlessness (or the person's heedlessness) of the "meaning" of the resistance does not alter the inevitable effect which his reaction has on it. If he ignores and steers around her contributions, this has an effect—presumably enhancive of the threats and competitiveness she may feel by expressing irritation.

As summary, three kinds of replies need to be distinguished. At first glance they might seem to be similar, but they are likely to have very different effects. All may *seem* to reject Mrs. O and her behavior, but one, at least, actually communicates a great deal of respect and acceptance. Of the three responses, the first takes Mrs. O's remarks at face value; the second takes them as a disruption; the third takes them as a meaningful disruption—i.e., resistance. (1) A minister may argue with the substance of her contribution, or in a more mediative role as discussion leader he may point out that her remarks seem to contradict or diverge from the preceding remarks of her husband. (2) The minister may try to bypass or eliminate her habitual contributions. Responding to them primarily as disruption, he may try to ignore them ("Now let's get back to what we were saying . . ."); he may scold or try to modify her behavior ("Perhaps you ought to let someone else answer your husband sometimes . . ."); or he may directly reject her behavior by interrupting with his own remarks. (3) The minister may identify the behavior as resistance, in some such way as has been suggested.

Although all these responses are "rejecting" in some way, the last has the important characteristic of taking her remarks seriously and even more significantly, of taking her seriously. To share with her candidly his own perception of her behavior, to regard this behavior as important enough to puzzle about, and to communicate his sense that important and legitimate concerns within her are causing the behavior—these communicate profound respect and develop rapport, even though what she has to say about the Bible may be disregarded at face value.

CHOICE OF RESPONSE

The decision whether to respond to resistance at all, and if so, in which mode, must depend on the following considerations, and probably on many others.

First are the different characteristics of the *responses*. For example, verbal response tends to be more explicit and insistent than behavioral response. It is less easy to ignore. (Sometimes the minister may want to be more insistent and to demand focused attention; other times, he may want to leave more room for maneuver, including dodging.) Reply tends to be more often addressed to "deeper" levels of the resistance and what is prompting it. Reflection may also be offered to "deeper" levels, but is addressed to the simple behavioral level more easily than reply.

Second are the considerations of the *parishioners* involved: their readiness to reflect on themselves and their reactions, their expectation that their relation with the church and minister involves such self-reflection, their skill and readiness to make verbal reflection, their degree of self-acceptance and candor, their trust in the minister.

Third are the characteristics of the *minister* himself: his own skill and sensitivity; his freedom from biasing or crippling motives of his own; his familiarity with the people, and hence the likely accuracy of his hunches about them; his ability to handle disrupting situations calmly and to handle potentially unacceptable characteristics with genuine acceptance; the simple rapport he has with people, the role he usually takes with them, and their expectations of his manner and role.

Fourth is the type of *problem* involved. How serious is it? (Is it disruptive enough that it demands attention, or just tantalizing?) How potentially productive of insight and learning and maturation is it? Does it touch a more limited and therefore more manageable segment of a person's experience, or a more central and therefore more urgent segment? Is it a kind of problem from which a person can generalize and apply his learning to other matters beyond the immediate resistance? Is it significantly like behavior "in the world" or is it something peculiar to the church? What level of "depth" is required?

Finally, there is the particular *situation*. Who is present? What is their relation to each other? How much do they share in the resistance (how much does it belong to one person)? What is the expectation of the people as to what will happen on this occasion? How much time is available? What time will be available in the near future?

How these considerations interact is not at all clear. Does greater self-acceptance and trust in the minister or the minister's own sensitivity permit the greater explicitness of the verbal, or does it better foster the daring freedom and openness of the behavioral? If there is expectation that the minister's role usually involves verbal reflection, does this suggest that his handling of resistance should be deliberately consistent with this role, so as not to startle and frighten people; or should he deliberately shift roles for handling of resistance, so that this gets more attention? Do relatively unsophisticated people need a more explicit response, or will they be more threatened by it? What kind of response is better for a group and what kind for an individual? Does the answer to this question vary with the type of problem, persons, and minister? Are the type of resistance and the people's expectations of the minister such that a behavioral reflection would only "feed" the resistance and enhance it by the minister's participation in it? It would be desirable to have answers to all such questions. It would be more desirable for a minister to be able intuitively to assess all of them, without careful analytic calculation. Perhaps some can.

VIII

Some Applications of the Perspectives of This Book

1 ◆

MISUNDERSTANDING OF THE MINISTER'S ROLE

Perhaps the most annoying, persistent, and handicapping resistance which a minister faces is the difference between his and his laymen's expectations of what his role should be—what he as minister should do and how he should do it. Or to put it as he more likely feels it, the problem is their misinterpretation of his role. On the basis of his professional training and his own sense of call, the minister feels some direction and conviction about how he should proceed—which of the myriad possible ministerial activities are most urgent, and how each should be carried out. But the laymen to whom he would minister are likely to have equally firm expectations which are not necessarily consistent with his. In fact, they have *hired* him.

The issue may be whether he should wear a gown in the pulpit, whether his wife should superintend the Sunday school, whether he should discuss money or sex or politics in the pulpit, whether he should join Kiwanis or run for the school board, whether he should give main attention to preaching or to counseling or to young people or to administrative affairs, whether adult study groups have higher priority than adult fellowship groups, whether he alone is to conduct the church's "ministry," or whether he is to provide behind-the-scenes direction for *their* ministry, whether his ministry is more to the church or to the world.

When the laymen's expectations contradict the minister's, they may be true obstacles that have to be corrected before the minister can function. Or they may be "resistance" in the sense used in this book. That is, they may represent meaningful reactions to the minister and what he represents and, therefore, they may be occasions for ministry. Attention to these reactions may deal with a person's religious orientation in a way which implements the very purposes the minister once thought blocked by the laymen's expectations.

Viewing such misunderstandings of his role simply as impediments, a minister lumps them together and thinks of his plight as a massive and pervasive single problem. Each instance becomes just additional evidence that "the laymen can't understand" the church and the ministry—even perhaps that the minister is facing such difficult odds that he should get out. Viewed in terms of potential dynamic meaning, each form of "misunderstanding" becomes a separate and independent instance. One means one thing and another means something else. Each becomes a separate, manageable occasion for ministry. We can consider such misunderstandings, or role conflicts, one at a time, and what is said about one may not be generalized to another. One type of role misunderstanding was mentioned at the end of Chapter I; another in Chapter VI; another is discussed here.

Expert or fellow pilgrim?

One troublesome expectation the minister can neither live up to nor live with is the mantle of authority with which he may be endowed. The minister may feel more like a "fellow pilgrim," but he is seen by laymen as an expert, an advice-giver, one whose training, or direct pipeline to God, or morally perfect life, or some other qualification must make him readily able to pronounce judgment, dispense wisdom, and provide solutions for all problems presented to him.

This attitude appears, for example, when a person brings a problem to personal counseling. The minister may have a clear understanding of what his positive contributions can be toward the solution of personal problems in counseling. He may know what things he *can* do toward unleashing personal resources and helping a person grow mature and confident enough to deal with his own problems. He may recognize that for most problems he has no basis for accepting the lofty role of expert and authority. He may feel that offering advice as requested will only help to confirm persons in less mature and less competent stations. But how can he counsel to help people "unleash their resources" when all they do is bombard him with questions and demand clear answers? "Should we get married?" "What can I do with that teen-age daughter of mine?" "Tell me how to pray." "How can I as a Christian citizen improve our town?" "Is it all right if I find a nursing home for my aging mother?" "Why does God let these things happen to us?" "Does my husband need a psychiatrist?" "What would you do if you were me?" "I really need your advice."

"IT'S A SIMPLE MORAL QUESTION. . . . WHAT'S THE ANSWER?"

A minister is sought out by a man who is about to be transferred by his company to another city. He is troubled by the question of whether to list his home with a special agency that will try to sell it to a Negro family, or to list it with a conventional real estate broker. "It's a simple moral question. Do I owe more to the white neighbors I have now who wouldn't understand or accept this, or do I owe more to the Negroes who have had such a rotten time for so long from people like me. You have the training and experience to know how to judge these moral dilemmas. What's the answer?" The man is serious. An executive, he is accustomed to doing business this way, sizing up the questions, assembling information, then taking them to a superior or an expert for decisions. In this case he *has* summarized the moral dilemma with considerable insight and sensitivity. He is genuinely and courageously prepared to "do the right thing." He now just needs the minister to tell him what that is, since this is the minister's job.

The minister knows of ways he can be of help in this process, but his own intentions are contradicted—in fact, even immobilized—by the man's own expectations of what a minister should deliver. The minister's position is that the ethical principles, on which he might have some claim to expertness, are already clear enough to the man, and that he is already sufficiently committed to them. What is needed is further reflection on this particular situation and the clarification of his own preferences and inclinations and his sense of God's leading in this situation. The minister knows how to encourage and guide this process. That is his opportunity and responsibility. But it is still this man's opportunity and responsibility as a Christian to determine the right course in this particular situation and to make the decision. Here is real conflict and obstacle, perhaps less harsh or bitter than some the minister faces, but nevertheless posing a severe obstacle to the minister doing what he wants to and can do.

We have chosen an example in which the conflict is clear and overt. In other situations, the counselee's expectations may be subdued or disguised or not immediately expressed, but nevertheless just as real and determined: "What do you think I should do?" The man expects the minister to deliver something which he cannot deliver and is not ready to receive the ministry the minister has to offer. The minister can't minister to this man, as he feels called to, so long as this man holds his present expectations.

Correct the wrong expectation?

A direct attack against this impediment is especially tempting in this case because of the very forthrightness with which it has appeared. The man has summed up his own situation so crisply that the minister may be inclined to reply with similar directness, to "structure" this counseling situation for the man, to instruct him on the proper conception of the minister's role, and on the man's own opportunities to continue to work on the problem.

"If I thought I could answer your questions helpfully, Fred, I would. But I know from my experience that I can be of more help to you in another way. I am convinced that you have everything in you—good judgment and a good sense of what all the implications are and what the situation is really like—to make a good decision, really better than I can. But what I can do is provide some guidance in thinking through these complicated questions and be a kind of sounding-board."

This is a good speech for structuring the counseling situation. It states simply and reasonably the minister's understanding of how the counseling can proceed, and his rationale for this understanding. It doesn't reject Fred's questions as such. It affirms the minister's trust in and respect for the man himself. It instructs him briefly and persuasively on the minister's theory of counseling, and on how to be a counselee.

Such a structuring speech might even be successful in getting Fred to abandon his expectations and accept the minister's, or at least to change his behavior. Especially if repeated and insisted on, these instructions might finally be followed. Fred would shift from doing it his way to doing it the minister's way.

INEFFECTIVENESS OF ATTACKING RESISTANCE. But probably such a speech, intended to correct the discrepant expectations, would not be successful. The speech assumes that a simple lack of information or of understanding prompts Fred's direct questioning. It assumes that his expectations are "reality-based," that he asks the direct questions because he "really" thinks that is what the minister can do, that he has not previously been informed as to the minister's philosophy of counseling, that it is only necessary to restructure the situation, in order to change his expectations.

But if the counselee's earnest request for direct advice is compelled by urgent concerns within himself, then it will not be so easily modified by information and lecture, no matter how plausible and how reasonable. If the counselee earnestly wants to be told what to do in this case, his want will persist. If the plea and the question are discouraged or forbidden by the counselor at one point in one form, they will crop up in other forms. If all requests for direct advice are finally suppressed by the counselor, the need will still persist and will sabotage the counseling process. Even though he stops asking for direct advice, and even though he finally appears to be following the minister's rules, the intolerance of internal ambiguity and indecisiveness (or whatever else prompted the urgent request for advice) will still keep him from facing freely the complexities of the situation as a "good counselee" should. His uncooperative manner will still prove frustrating to the expectations of the counseling minister, though now for reasons which will be less definable because they have been forced under cover.

ATTACKING RESISTANCE CONTRADICTS MINISTRY. Whether effective or not, such an instructional lecture contradicts with ironic severity the very principles of counseling ministry which the counselor first found frustrated by the counselee. To deliver such a lecture, the minister must temporarily abandon his own principles and assume precisely the directive, supervisory role he eschews. He declines on principle to tell Fred how he should sell his house, but he does tell him how he should behave in counseling. This is the dualistic, "one-two" strategy which plagues a minister so often: you can't minister to the situation as you find it; you must first stop being a minister, arrange the situation, then minister. This is like a bowler who interrupts his game to set up his own pins. However, a bowler may find it much easier to shift from bowling to setting and back to bowling again than a minister finds it possible to shift in and out of his role. And bowling pins may adjust more easily than parishioners to being treated in two different ways by the same man.

When the minister steps out of the role that fits his expectations and intentions, he is succumbing unwittingly to precisely those expectations which he found unwelcome and frustrating. By structuring the situation and giving directions, he is meeting Fred on Fred's terms, not on his own, and to succumb to Fred's terms is only to feed the resistance. Behaviorally and actually the minister's behavior encourages what the words are intended to discourage, the seeking of further direct guidance. Here actions speak much louder than words. If the minister fits the counselee's expectations once, the counselee may reasonably feel that the minister will do it again.

At many other points in his ministry, the minister's desperate maneuver of abandoning ministry and "setting up pins" so easily puts him in the position of adopting in his behavior precisely the role he wants to deny with his words. Here is the preacher scolding and frightening his people into "loving each other." Here is the administrator calculating with a committee to plan a high-pressure promotional campaign that will make the people "more responsible" to missionary needs, or arranging with the deacons a pattern for serving communion that is "calculated" to induce a more "spiritual" response. Here is a Sunday school teacher berating a boy mercilessly to make him listen quietly to the lesson that God loves everyone. Here is the discussion group leader insisting, on his own authority, that the group should seek theological authority more clearly in its discussion.

ATTACKING RESISTANCE FORFEITS OPPORTUNITY FOR MINISTRY. The most serious difficulty with the "structuring," however, is not that it may drive the alien and frustrating expectations underground or that it encourages these expectations by actually meeting them. Rather, the chief misfortune is that a unique and important opportunity may have been missed. Fred's demand for direction *may* be just a persistent *personal* characteristic (bottom line of the diagram in Chapter I): this may be just the way he has become accustomed, as an executive, to dealing with all problems and decisions. Or, his demand for direction *may* genuinely be a *situationally* induced expectation (top line of diagram): the minister—or other ministers —despite professed intentions, may have given the man good reason to expect that he would serve as a moral expert and arbiter. But his demand may also be *meaningful resistance* in the sense of this book. He may be imposing this urgent demand in a way not entirely characteristic for him, or in a way not appropriate for this situation, for reasons of particular internal reactions. Is there something about this particular situation of selling his house which makes him unusually and inappropriately anxious to have clearcut directions, to avoid giving the complex problem the full consideration he is capable of? Does this situation make him turn to the minister with expectations which he would not otherwise impose? Does it make him "regress" into a mode of behavior which is appropriate in other situations, as in his own profession—and available to him because well practiced in them—but not appropriate in this? Perhaps, for example (and our speculation here is only to make the exposition more plausible and clear, not because a minister in the situation would need to indulge in such hunches), there may be certain ambiguities in his own feelings toward Negroes—or toward his neighbors—which he finds uncomfortable to face and which prompt him to try to make the matter one for simple, authoritative solution.

If the demand for direction represents some such meaning, and if the demand is suppressed, the meaning is lost. If the minister manages to "reinterpret" or to "structure" the demand away, he is perhaps losing his best opportunity to minister to this man. The more persistent and the more annoying the demand, the more tempted the minister may be to suppress it. Yet the more persistent and the more annoying (i.e., inappropriate) the demand, the more likely it is to have just some such important meaning.

The minister's own purposes for his ministry in general and for this counseling session in particular, and Fred's own hope for a solution to his problem, are all likely to be best served by attention to the meaning of this resistive behavior which seems at first to be frustrating these very goals. If the meaning has to do with an unwelcome, even threatening ambiguity of his feelings, then it is in facing these feelings and in their resolution that Fred will find himself more clearly able to come to a decision on his house. If something can happen in the counseling to make it possible for him to solve this immediate "little" problem—the problem that he wants the minister to decide what he can and should decide himself—then he is also likely to find that he is capable of solving the initial "big" problem, the decision itself. When a man who is accustomed to making decisions finds himself unable to make decisions which lie within his competence, he is blocked by something. This block is presumably the same one which makes him unable to be a "good counselee" for this minister.

How is a minister to respond?

First of all, what are the hints that this demand is meaningful resistance, and not a mere accidental or situational or personal characteristic? The minister notices these clues and reflects on them aloud. In so doing, he is suggesting to the counselee the possibility just as it grows within him, that there is meaning in the behavior, and that the behavior is important to attend to. He poses, for both of them, the question, "Why?"

The minister attends to his own sense of annoyance over the resistive inappropriateness of the request, and tries to spell out the basis of this irritation. He particularly asks himself, aloud, how realistic the man's demand is, how much it accords with what he might "naturally" expect in this situation or what he "naturally" is.

Minister: I think you're kidding yourself, Fred, or maybe trying to kid me, when you suppose I can answer your question just like that. You know how I operate, the kinds of things I can and can't do, and I have never led you into thinking that I can make this kind of decision for anyone else. And I know how you operate. You aren't exactly shy about making up your mind in trustees' meetings, and your judgment is usually a good one; I have been on your side a lot more often than not! When you bought that house you certainly didn't need to ask my advice. You hardly even asked Sylvia's. You told me so yourself. I'm curious. How come you were so proud of being your own boss then, and are usually good at it, but you want me to tell you what to do this time?

Although the comment serves some of the same purposes intended by "structuring" instructions (quoted on pages 279–280) as an attack on the resistance, it differs from such instructions in several important respects. First, it is a *reminder* of structuring "instructions" already delivered, of the bases which the minister has already given Fred as to what to expect. This past structuring may have been by example. It may have been by formal instructions not unlike those quoted previously; such formal instructions, inappropriate and disruptive in the counseling relation, might have been fully appropriate in another role. The minister may well have explained in preaching or on some other occasion these principles by which he is guided.

Second is the addition of the "How come?" The whole purpose of this lengthy remark by the minister was not to correct Fred's behavior, not to remind him of norms to which he was expected to adhere. Rather, it was to raise the genuine *question* for both of them as to why Fred had deviated, in this case, from norms and patterns he already held.

Third, then, the discrepancy between Fred's behavior and these norms—the degree to which his behavior was annoying and frustrating—did not have to be softened in the speech, as it does when the purpose is reproof, which has to be made gentle enough to be palatable. Instead, the *discrepancy could be emphasized and dramatized*, since the purpose was to pose this as an important enough problem to be worthy of attention. The minister reviewed all the evidence that crossed his mind as to how discrepant this behavior was, and he didn't hesitate to itemize this in the indictment.

To the minister's query, Fred replies.

Fred: Yeah, but this is a tougher one. I just feel in over my head on this one.

He seems to want to argue that his behavior is realistic and to deny that it is problematic or curious. There are at least two reasons why a man might want to insist that his resistive behavior is not resistive but is "realistic." One reason is that it "really" is realistic; in this case, despite the minister's first intuitions, there may be sound reasons for Fred's asking for direct advice on this particular question. The other reason is that it may be too uncomfortable or threatening to face the "meanings" which must be faced when one concedes that resistive behavior is motivated and meaningful. Whatever prompts the original problem of indecisiveness and in turn prompts the resistance, now prompts, as it were, resistance to acknowledging resistance.

This resistance needs to be respected, especially in the intensity of personal counseling where strong anxiety-provoking material may not be too far from the surface. This minister has done about all he can to reflect the question as he sees it. It may be that the forces provoking the problem and the resistance (for example, anxiety over ambivalence toward Negroes or toward neighbors) are so strong as not to yield to any resources available to this minister. Fred may have to hobble through this part of his life—through this attempt at counseling and through his decision about the house—without appreciably enhanced maturity or informed control over his decisions. Getting him to make the right decision in a mature, responsible fashion is not ultimately the minister's responsibility. The minister has reflected the problem as clearly and as accurately as he sees it. If Fred is to recognize and tackle it maturely, it is not further argument that will make this possible. The minister's inclination is to be silent at this point (since he has reason to think that Fred will understand that his silence is intended to give them both a chance to think, not as a gesture of rejection of Fred's remarks).

But the minister also senses a certain ambiguity in Fred's phrases. The phrase "over my head" may be half consciously a kind of recognition that this plea for help has some distressing personal dimensions. The minister decides to reflect this possibility, but with an ambiguity matching Fred's, rather than with literalness, so as not to insist.

Minister: Yes, I think this may be a deep one for you, but I still say you are a good swimmer.

Fred: Well, what do you think it is?

Fred abandons the denial, the claim that his question is realistic, and accepts the minister's view that it may be curious. But the resistance continues, perhaps abetted by the degree to which the minister has, in spite of himself, assumed the role of an authority. Fred continues to want to deal with the situation without himself getting involved. He concedes that there is a "problem," even apparently that it is within himself, but he would like to keep the problem something external and objective, something the minister can handle as expert and outside observer. This further suggests that there is something about the internal and subjective which is stressful.

This particular counseling minister is not tempted by the invitation to psychologize. His only choice is to continue to reflect things as he sees them.

Minister: There, you're doing it again. You're still asking *me*. But that's not like you.

To the previous clues of the meaningfulness of the resistance can now be added this degree of persistence. The same kind of plea for objective expert guidance crops up on different though related matters.

Fred: God, you're relentless!

Fred turns the tables and starts reflecting the counselor's behavior. This is continuing resistance to the degree that he is still talking about the counselor and not about his own problems. It does have a realistic component: the minister *is* relentless. But it is also an implicit acknowledgment of the terms and tone of the present situation as the counselor has depicted it. It is more tribute to the counselor than rebuke, more acknowledgment than denial; Fred is moving closer to the counselor in feeling and in understanding, not away from him. Another counselor, more timid, more exclusively concerned with maintaining a "warm relation" and with "acceptance," might understand Fred's exclamation more as a "break" in relation, and he might move to apologize and to reassure. This counselor is encouraged by this confirmatory response and waits to see what will happen next.

After a short pause, Fred speaks, half to himself.

Fred: Almost as relentless as Sylvia.

Is this a peeling off of the resistance and getting down to "real" problems? Or is the reference to his wife additional resistance, a cover story, designed unconsciously to distract them both? Is it continuing to evade whatever all the resistance has been serving to evade? How much is a nagging wife a "real" problem, and how much is the mention prompted by resistive motives, exploiting a slight basis in reality? The minister could ask this question aloud ("I can't tell whether that's really a question or whether you're trying to get us off the track"). He could answer the question for himself by jumping on the question of the wife as though it were truly important, or dismissing it as resistance. Or he could wait to see what happens next. He waits. The bait not taken, Fred continues.

Fred: I wonder whether I'm really as wishy-washy as you both seem to think.

Here for the first time, he talks, or almost talks, about himself. He raises a troubling question about his own behavior. To be sure, it is still externalized to the degree that he considers it as an accusation made by others. But the degree to which he exaggerates, at least far beyond anything the minister has actually suggested, implies plenty of concern proceeding from within himself, too. (That he does exaggerate the accusation and that he feels it as an accusation at all might move some ministers to apologize, to explain that they weren't accusing him of being wishy-washy, or otherwise to try to "restore harmony" to the relationship. Among the counselors so inclined would be those who really had meant some such rebuke and those who are unusually motivated to maintain harmony on the surface.) Our minister chooses to reflect the sense of the problem as expressed, and the strong feeling with which it was expressed. The "troubling" exaggeration is probably an important clue.

Minister: You say "wishy-washy" with quite a sneer.
Fred: I keep myself tuned up with a high-power system, and people still think I'm indecisive. Maybe if I weren't so efficient most of the time, you'd let me ask a few questions now and then.

The bitterness, still largely directed outward, continues to show, and seizes principally on the preceding incidents in the counseling conversation. Yet the counseling relationship is still strong enough to tolerate the bitterness, which again is so much greater than warranted by anything which has actually happened in the conversation that it betrays sources outside this conversation.

But along with the bitterness is disclosed a glimpse of some tensions within Fred. One now gets a hint that the contrasting patterns of behavior which the minister had called attention to may reflect conflicting tendencies within the man himself. The minister's reply partly reflects this.

Minister: You make being such an efficient powerhouse seem more of an effort than you usually let on.

Fred: Yeah, it took me a long time to get myself tuned up.

Minister: Why bother?

Now they are launched on an extended counseling session touching what might be called Fred's "self-image," his self-confidence, his studied attempts to enhance his self-esteem, the pleasure he derives and the difficulties he encounters in maintaining such a pattern of decisiveness and authoritativeness.

In the end, these proved by no means unrelated to the initial question of selling the house. It turned out, for example, that Fred was far more concerned with others'—in this case the neighbors'—opinion of him and their recognition that he was doing the "right" thing than he normally let on. Part of his reason for so urgently wanting the minister's endorsement, one way or another, was to make it clear, to himself and to the neighbors, that he was doing the "right" thing. Furthermore, his attitudes toward Negroes were not unaffected by this same cluster of feelings. Rather, his attitudes closely reflected, in their ambivalence, his own ambiguities of self-esteem and of concerns for dominance and deference. These were also evaded or masked by the intellectualized emphasis for the "right." These important components of his decision could not have been tackled or even recognized if the minister had not respected the point at which they cropped out and intruded as resistance into the counseling relationship. With greater clarification of these interfering feelings to which the resistance pointed, he was better able to move to responsible decision.

Beginning about at the point of the minister's "Why bother?" the conversation with Fred became personal counseling, dealing with the second and third levels described in Chapter V, and perhaps requiring sensitivity and skills not possessed by all ministers. But before that point, counseling is not going on, only preliminary preparation for counseling. No special skills are required. And above all, no "deep" levels of personality are involved. The minister is discerning and reflecting only the most obvious elements of the dialogue. Any minister would experience the same frustration and sense of discrepancy—"role conflict"—that this minister did. But many would move beyond this in one direction or another. This minister simply stopped with the most elementary impression, and reflected that. That was all that was required.

If the minister had paid more attention initially to the *form* of the resistance, he might have garnered more clues and had less use for his more general speculations about ambivalent feelings toward Negroes and neighbors. Of the many different forms of resistance which Fred might have used to avoid a meaningful discussion of the problem of selling his house, the form which he did use proved to be quite characteristic and significant. He might have resisted by an intellectualized and generalized discussion of the problems of prejudice, or by a criticism of the neighbors for their narrowness, or by asking the minister for a kind of historical survey of similar instances in his own experience. That he resisted by demanding authoritative direction from the minister and demanding this guidance in terms of what was "right" could be clearly seen, at least in retrospect, as representative of the very pattern of conflicting concerns which made difficult both his decision about the house and the discussion of this decision. In the counseling relationship intended to discuss the decision he acted out one set, at least, of the tensions which that decision produced.

2 ◈

THE ADMINISTRATIVE JUNGLE

CAUGHT IN THE JUNGLE

"I wanted to develop a meaningful program, and close pastoral relations. And I could have. But we all got bogged down in the machinery of the church. Like quicksand, it just sucks you in. You can't help yourself."

One young minister's discouraged reflections after two years in a parish speak for most men a few years into their ministry. Indeed, his remarks are almost so common as to be cliché, rather than prototype, were they not reported with a keenness and an earnestness which stamps them with the authenticity of his own tormenting experience.

His happened to be a church with a large stately building and a proud history in a city neighborhood which had held out against engulfing deterioration but was now encircled by blight. The church membership was a fraction of what it had once been. It was comprised mostly of the families of blue-collar and white-collar workers who had long histories in the church. Although the morale of the church was low, it and the neighborhood had gone down about as far as they would. The neighborhood was about to be saved by an urban renewal program, which would halt deterioration and assist restoration. The population of the neighborhood, and presumably of the church, was likely to become increasingly integrated, but with a spirit of optimism and community morale fostered by the urban renewal program. But this new minister's experiences were not primarily determined by these specific characteristics of his church. They might have happened, and indeed are reported, in any type of church.

By "program" this minister mostly meant three specific projects: a Bible study, theological discussion group; a self-study group of church leaders to discover the role to which the church was called for its coming years; and a group of educational, social service, and recrea-

291

tional activities intended to minister to the immediate neighbor-hood.

By "closer pastoral relations" he said he meant "a more intimate and genuine relation with the people as they really are with all of their hopes and all of their problems, big and little." He cited an example in which a sermon on race relations had angered a deacon. And for this he blamed himself, because he had not been sufficiently close to the man or sufficiently sensitive to his need, for the sermon to communicate genuinely with him. He also mentioned the "dis-tance" which he felt the people put between him and themselves. He felt they had come to regard him more as a busy administrator, more as they probably regarded their bosses, and less like the close confidant which he himself wanted to be. He particularly regretted this distance in the case of the young people. He was especially distressed over the instance of one girl who had become pregnant but who had not come to him for any help. He had not known of the problem until after a serious break with her family. He felt that this was the kind of problem which he could have been helpful in meeting and to which he wanted to devote his time, but he simply had not been permitted to develop the previous relationship with the girl which would have made such a ministry possible.

By the "quicksand" of busy machinery he meant at least two different things. First, his own time, energy, and creativity and that of his laymen were drained by activities in the church which seemed irrelevant to the above purposes, but which seemed to be required by the structure of the church. The commission structure required by his denomination seemed to generate committees and meetings and agenda which did not contribute, even indirectly, to the purposes that he most keenly felt for his ministry. The persistent momentum of women's groups, men's clubs, and Council of Churches generated fairs and luncheons, dinner meetings and committee meetings, a joint Thanksgiving Day service, and an annual meeting which similarly showed no signs of contributing to the minister's earnest hopes, but which almost thoroughly drained him and his people. Some activities, such as stewardship campaigns and the building maintenance com-mittee, seemed to the minister to provide some necessary, instrumental contribution to his purposes, but so indirect that he still resented, or at least regretted, their demands.

Second, by the "machinery," the minister meant the terrible barrier of cranking and pump-priming activities that seemed to stand between him and the achievement of his purposes. Even when he did shake free of clubs and committees to work on one of his own projects, he found himself so busy with arranging and recruiting and explaining and training that he never felt past a beginning. A Bible study group, instead of meaning serious and vigorous grappling with the themes of Holy Scripture, meant heart-breaking hours of recruiting group members, arranging a meeting place and time, ordering study books, delivering study guides to members, explaining elementary things about the Bible, and otherwise trying to *prepare* people for significant discussion. Even to develop a "pastoral relation" seemed to mean agonizing hours of scheduling evenings in the parsonage for members of the church, helping his wife get the parsonage ready for these evenings, arranging times for pastoral calls, and going through hours of small talk and social conventions without often getting to a more intimate and intense relationship.

Chop away the jungle?

Caught in such a jungle, a minister's immediate and natural impulse is to slash away at the snares which entrap him. He is in no mood for the proposal of this book that the existence of the administrative machinery may have more inherent relation with his purposes than he first realizes. If the administrative snarls lie across his path, he is far more inclined to dispatch them than to consider how they may actually define the path. He understandably feels the machinery to be a quite independent and unwelcome intrusion. His sights are focused on his purposes (e.g., theological sensitivity) and on the means which seem most obviously appropriate for achieving them (e.g., Bible discussion). The machinery seems to arise from outside the focus of attention, from denominational procedures, from traditions and customs in the church, from the need for a Council of Churches to sustain itself, from the lethargy or indirection or irresponsibility of the people. He may be set on a path of ministry. But if snares emerge from the side to block his path, he cannot go on. He must temporarily—or permanently—abandon the path, turn to the side, and attack this jungle growth.

He may attack demands of the denomination and the Council of Churches directly, by repudiating their authority for him and for his church, or by attempting to transform their demands into ones more congenial to his own purposes. He may even feel called to abandon his original goals permanently and to devote his entire career to working, perhaps as a denominational executive, to reconstruct denominational structure more consistently with his goals. Presumably he expects clergymen who follow him to benefit from the work he has done in clearing a path.

He may attack problems of lethargy and irresponsibility with scolding and with appeals. He may try to reduce the drain on time and energy by devices for improving the efficiency of office procedure, by hiring more secretarial help, by recruiting laymen to share the administrative burden. He may adopt more efficient fund-raising procedures. He may "free" himself by turning this over to his laymen or to a professional fund-raiser; he may even decide to "free" other ministers by becoming a professional fund-raiser himself. He may renounce the claims the women's society or the men's club make on him to attend meetings. He may even move toward trying to abolish these organizations altogether.

These all may be thoroughly legitimate and effective ways of meeting the problem. To shift from metaphor to more formal language, such counterattack on the underbrush alongside the path assumes that the problem lies in the objective situational context: if the situation is modified, the obstacle will be removed, and ministry can proceed. In some instances, such an assumption may be quite accurate. The administrative machinery grows strictly out of objective requirements. There really is money to be raised. There really are plans to be made, appointments to be arranged, obligations to be met, denominational requirements and quotas to be fulfilled, people to be marshaled and aroused. Just to be a responsible part of the institution of the church requires it. One does these things because he has to. To avoid doing them, one must change some objective part of the circumstances.

Most suggestions on administration which one hears in seminary or reads in practical guidebooks recommend such direct attacks on the problem of machinery. When the administratively burdened plight of the minister has been bewailed in the literature of the last decade or so, it has not been questioned whether such machinery is realistically required by the circumstances. The need for it has simply been taken for granted, and circumstances have been blamed. Recommendations for remedy have suggested various revisions of structure and procedure, in the local church and in the denomination, calculated to change the circumstances so as to relieve church, minister, and sometimes laymen, from burdens of frustrating machinery. The literature has seldom, if ever, considered the possibility that there is more relevant meaning in the administrative snarl, for example, that churches and churchmen engage in so much machinery not because they have to, but because, in some disconcerting and discernible though unconscious sense, they "want" to.

STAY THAT HATCHET!

The administrative counterattack to the administrative obstacle is the first and easiest response to give. But, we have to ask, are the situational circumstances always to blame? Just how demanding and insistent "really" are these claimed obligations to the situation, and how much are they convenient pretexts or rationalizations? How much is the administrative counterattack to the administrative snare really justified by the objective nature of the situation? Or how much is the counterattack a kind of blind, angry reaction against the obstacle? How much is the counterattack justified by its objective effectiveness; does changing the situation really remove the obstacle? Or how much does the counterattack fall victim to the jungle growth and nourish it, rather than rooting it out? By accepting the premises of objective need for the administrative machinery, and succumbing to its tactics, does the counterattack only foster the obstructive machinery? How much does the assumed objective need stand the test of such questions as these as they may be asked either of the administrative machinery or of the administrative counterattack on the machinery: Do all effective churches or effective ministers do these things to this degree? What would happen if we just didn't (if we just didn't, for example, meet denominational requirements and quotas, or fight requirements and quotas; if we just didn't plan everything so thoroughly with meetings and double-check with phone calls, or campaign to streamline meetings and calls)? Viewed quite objectively, do these activities actually accomplish as much or make as much difference as one may subjectively feel while he is in the midst of them?

Is all of the snaring administrative growth really a product of the objective context in which the minister is trying to follow his path? Or is some of it unknowingly seeded or nurtured by the minister himself? Realistically, what are the consequences of failing to hold a meeting or to attend one, of failing to make a phone call or to write a memorandum, of failing to meet a denominational prescription? Perhaps the consequences are not disastrous or even serious. Perhaps meetings and phone calls and quotas are made not because they have to be but just because they are there or because they are attractive distractions. They easily present themselves as something to be done if one is otherwise prompted to find "something to be done." Whenever the minister's path ahead becomes obscured or his steps faltering, the administrative jungle growth is temptingly present, offering easing distraction or reassuring sense of achievement— whether one is tending the growth or chopping away at it.

What happens when ministers and churches do undertake reforms in the circumstances that are blamed for requiring the machinery? Ministers hire secretaries, resign from Council of Churches committees, get laymen to form telephone squads, get a lay leader for the discussion group, and otherwise rearrange the allegedly oppressive circumstances. Ministers may change churches, or even careers. Then what happens? This is one way of "testing the reality of the situation." To the degree that the situational assessment doesn't test out as "real," then (1) we must challenge the effectiveness of the administrative counterattack, and (2) we have a clue to the richer meaning the resistive obstacle may have. If the chopping attack on the jungle growth doesn't clear away the growth, one ought to stop the chopping and take a new look at the nature of the growth. Maybe the roots are not off on the side of the path where one is chopping, but more clearly lie along the path, perhaps even helping to mark the path, or pave it.

Sometimes the problems indeed disappear with the change in circumstances. The minister may find himself relatively free to pursue his own purposes more directly, to exercise his ministry as he feels called and trained to perform it. Other times the longed-for freedom does not come. The new secretary now has to be supervised and "kept busy." There are tax and hospitalization forms to be arranged, office procedures and schedules to be established, systems for answering the phone and making appointments to be settled. With the secretary there, letters get answered which otherwise would have been neglected with no great loss. There are employment policies to be established—hours, pay, vacation, sick leave, and questions of lines of authority; these may even require additional time of boards and committees.

Any of the other changes in circumstances may bring, instead of freedom for ministry, occasion for machinery. The telephone squad has to be recruited, trained, and reminded. The longed-for new self-study group one finally gets started takes it own kind of cranking and organizing. And so on. The distant green pastures, when reached, prove full of the same old thistles.

THE JUNGLE CHARTED

Clues to meaning

Persistence, then, becomes one of the clues that the situational assumption is inadequate and that the obstructive machinery has more meaning to yield up. The above calls attention to persistence over changing circumstances during a period of time. But persistence might also be a notable clue when the machinery is seen to develop consistently over varying circumstances in which a minister finds himself at one time. He may be involved with different people of various degrees of initiative, responsibility, and sophistication. The activities are of varying urgency and of varying complexity. Yet if he finds that he, or his laymen, are tending machinery with equal intensity in all of these various circumstances, this too may be a clue that the machinery is not completely a response to the circumstances.

A more powerful clue may come if the machinery seems to develop regularly and systematically in connection with certain kinds of situations but not others. For example, a minister might find that all occasions requiring him to scrutinize the purposes of his ministry and the nature of his vocation seemed to be accompanied by "busy work" or other potentially resistive behavior, but not, say, occasions for dealing with familiar and limited material, such as a Bible chapter. This would be the kind of systematic association which would be a noteworthy clue.

Intensity may be another indication of surplus meaning, meaning beyond that which can be accounted for by the circumstances, meaning from somewhere within a person's or an institution's reaction. Perhaps details are checked out and plans are made with thoroughness and determination, even with a vengeance. The agenda for the meeting is prepared in meticulous detail and parliamentary procedure is followed scrupulously. The minister, the head deacon, the board of deacons, or even a denominational office, prepare a page of step-by-step instructions for the ushers and another page for deacons serving communion, and still another page of detailed procedure to be left on the pulpit for visiting ministers during the summer.

The loving care with which the machinery is tended invites a psychological diagnosis such as "compulsiveness." But this is not accurate, if the behavior is not generally characteristic of the people concerned. They may not be "compulsive" in most of their affairs. If they were, their behavior would require a separate kind of understanding—as a "personal" factor (bottom line of diagram in Chap. I) —and response—perhaps pastoral—but would not warrant consideration as meaningful resistance in our terms. We are considering instances in which the compulsivelike behavior appears in specific reaction to particular circumstances.

A whole denomination may attempt to prescribe procedures in intense detail and to provide for all exigencies by carefully arranged commissions and constitutions and designations of authority.

A denomination such as the Methodists invites, at least at first glance, a hypothesis along the following lines: perhaps the kind of intense religious, more or less "raw," unadorned spiritual experience which John Wesley discovered and fostered may be so disquieting— or perhaps so elusive and easily lost—that it must be accompanied by safeguards of *"methodism"* which have also been characteristic of Wesley and his followers. If something like this were true of a denomination as a whole, or of churches or individuals within it, this would be an example of the fact that resistant behavior may imply sensitivity and other important religious resources. When the disturbing and holy presence of the Lord was keenly felt in the Ark, it was safeguarded and surrounded by regulations and procedures. The warning corollary might follow that a church thoroughly relaxed and casual about the machinery might be one that just didn't feel its mandate keenly enough.[1]

Inappropriateness, above all, becomes a clue to prospective meaningfulness. In one sense, intensity is only another form of inappropriateness; arrangements and procedures which in mild form would not seem unrealistic, or frustrating and disrupting, or meaningful, in such intense degree assume these characteristics of resistance. The frustration in the fact that a minister (or a church board, or a church) does not find himself pursuing the kind of activities he intends to is itself a hint that something important and potentially relevant is intruding.

[1] To try to apply such hypotheses, derived essentially from the psychology of individuals, to institutions, of course runs the risk of overlooking many complicated factors. Among these are the differences between those who found an institution and its patterns and those who simply follow; the particular factors which are involved in the selection and self-selection of leadership and bureaucracy; and the inherently situational grounds for "machinery" arising out of institutional structure.

Meaningful response

What kinds of "meanings" congruent with the minister's intentions may be suggested by such clues as these, and how may he respond to them?

RESISTANCE REFLECTS AVOIDANCE. The minister may note the persistence, insistence, or other inappropriateness of the administrative machinery. He may note that it seems consistently related to particular types of situations, such as his moves toward self-study, biblical and theological sophistication, community responsibility, increased personal rapport. There is apparently something about these intentions which is distasteful or threatening or burdensome, or for some such reason is being avoided and warded off by the machinery.

Here the reflective response would seem easy and obviously constructive. As a matter of curiosity and question, the resistive behavior is noted, its inappropriateness clearly implied, and its association with particular stimuli mentioned.[2]

Say, for example, that the pastoral call consistently gets bogged down in talk about church business: "Every time I try to get to know you better, it seems we get to talking shop. I wonder why? I'm at least as interested in you as I am in church business, and I know that you have more interesting things on your mind." The emphasis is on taking the "why" question seriously. The minister now wants to talk about why they always end up talking about church business. (The corresponding question the minister might ask himself is, "Why do I talk church business?" or "When I set out to make calls, why do I get so involved in mapping my route, or why do I suddenly think of so many urgent phone calls that I don't really have time for good calls?")

The church council may decide that members are already too preoccupied with commissions and committees and club activities in

---

[2] For the present there seems no need to distinguish between resistive machinery-tending behavior or machinery-attacking behavior in which the minister engages, and that of others. The minister may as profitably raise the same questions for himself as for others, in case he is the one showing the resistance.

the church for them to consider this year a Bible study discussion group or a self-study group. Or the council chairman may think these questions should be considered through more formal channels by a subcommittee, with its report and a full memorandum from the minister as a special item on the agenda of a future meeting. These responses may be persistent and regular and intense enough to suggest meaningful resistance. Then the minister has plenty to talk to the people about: Why are they responding in this way at this time?

In focusing such questions on the resistive behavior, in call or in meeting, the minister may well find that he is following, unwittingly and without design, the same intentions he thought blocked. He is establishing in the call a more intimate personal relationship. He is pursuing in the board a kind of self-study. Under most circumstances, his attention to resistance may jolt people out of a kind of lethargy into more honest awareness of the way the world is, including their own responsibilities in it.

RESISTANCE ILLUSTRATES NEED FOR MINISTRY. It may be that the minister discovers a different kind of congruence with his purposes as he considers the context of the resistance. The resistance may not so much demonstrate opposition to his intentions as it illustrates the warrant for them in the first place. For example, the minister's ambitions for a Bible study group must have grown out of some evidence that these people were evasive or misinformed or otherwise deficient in their handling of the Bible. Perhaps, for example, they didn't respond to biblical content in his sermons, or perhaps they simply failed to show the sense of Christian norms for their lives that should derive from Bible study. When he proposes Bible study, and they take recourse to machinery, this might simply be another illustration of the same need. It is more easily missed because it involves their immediate shared experience, but it is also more potentially instructive and useful for the same reason.

If the chairman of the business meeting (or the minister himself) handles the customary opening devotions so perfunctorily because he is preoccupied with preparations for the business of the meeting, or if members are flipping through agenda documents and making notes during devotions, then they may be acting out the very thing the minister really wants to address himself to in his devotional message. Right here and now in concrete shared experience may be a key instance of the religious need the minister wants to discuss in more abstract and remote terms. It would be particularly ironic, but not at all uncommon, for a minister to let such an episode pass unremarked at the outset of a meeting called to consider the need for Bible study. The minister would be passing up the living instance in order to get on to the planned abstract discussion.

INFERRING MEANING FROM CONTENT OF RESISTANCE. The above has suggested reflections on the *context* of the resistance. Similar possibilities of reflection occur with the *content* of the resistance—again assuming that it shows such clues as inappropriateness, persistence, and intensity.

What is implied by the particular form of resistance which administrative machinery is? If resistance is to be applied, why does it assume this form and not some other (such as simple avoidance, or meandering discussion, or a change of topic)? The answer to this question, like others, lies partly in the objective reality of the situation. Church affairs provide plenty of opportunity for pouncing on administrative business as a form of resistance. Perhaps sometimes the answer lies entirely in this objective reality: church business overwhelmingly forces itself on a person if he is the least bit inclined to look for some means of resistance. But even when this is true, to let the matter rest there may simply beg the question. Is there some meaning in the fact that the heritage of the institution provides not only stimulus to spiritual growth but also such an insistently available form of resistance to this stimulus as is notoriously provided in church machinery? Is it possible that we now have church machinery so readily available as a form of resistance because our fathers in the faith developed it as such and passed it down to us as part of our heritage?

What significance may be inferred from the fact that the machinery becomes used, rather than alternative forms of resistance? Some general hypotheses come to mind, some of which have already been implied.

For one, the machinery of church business has about it the characteristic of reducing the mysterious to the manageable. Telephone calls, committee agenda, instructions for ushers, keeping financial records of the church, and all the rest, are understandable, controllable, manageable matters. As such, they may be highly reassuring to one who is faced by the vastness, largely an undefinable and ambiguous vastness, of the demands and assurances of the gospel, of the mission and ministry of the church, of the intensity and challenge of personal vocation.

Beyond this, machinery may express defensive pride by changing mood and posture from one of awe to one of authority. Instead of being cowed before the majesty of God and His summons to a life of faith, one is able to move into control over that tiny fragment of God's mission which he finds in church business, forgetting that it is a tiny fragment. Confrontation with the lofty may provoke even a kind of retaliatory, vengeful defensiveness. In the neat, regular lines of telephone-call memoranda, of agenda for the trustees' meeting and instructions for the ushers, one may again find a paradigm of Christ hanging on the Cross.

There is, too, a possibility that the grinding of the machinery brings a certain sense of reassurance and justification. The tasks first made manageable and now managed, the visible evidence of achievement (important because visible even though not grand), may bring real satisfactions. In these may be assurance of one's worth, one's faithfulness, one's responsiveness to the demands of God, even perhaps of one's having earned good will in the eyes of God.

These are general suggestions of possible meanings in such busy machinery, meanings which would take specific form and character in specific situations. If some such meaning is suggested by the reliance on machinery, this may be relevant to the minister's purposes in one of two ways. Just as was said earlier about meaning inferred from context, the nature of the resistance may show him a reaction to his purposes, or it may illustrate the needs which have prompted these purposes.

He may find in the form of resistance a clue to others' reaction to his purposes. If efforts toward closer pastoral relations or suggestions of self-study seem to enhance the reliance on the machinery, then this may not only tell him that his purposes are being resisted, but also suggest something about why. If such efforts produce a self-restitutive, self-enhancing reaction (as we suggested above that administrative machinery is), this raises the possibility that the closer pastoral relation or the self-study is in some way threatening the degree to which a person feels in control of himself or his environment or assured of the favor of God, or whatever else it is that the machinery seems to be trying to restore for him.

But it may be also the other way around. It may be that he has formulated his purposes in reaction to just the quality of life or need which is represented by this particular resistive recourse to machinery for apparently self-justifying purposes. It may be that any one of his professed purposes—the pastoral relations, the Bible study, the self-study, the community outreach, was prompted by his awareness of the degree to which these people did seem narrowly self-reliant. He might have sensed this from the way they talked about themselves and their work in the course of pastoral calls or from some other observations. He can now also sense it in their relations with church business. Here may be most apparent for all to see and acknowledge and respond to precisely the concerns and needs which the minister has wanted to address with his planned program.

The minister can respond to such resistance without abandoning the role he intends for himself. He doesn't have to shift into becoming administrative repairman, psychologist, or anything else. It will be consistent with his role and become a natural part of the relation he already has with the people if he can simply reflect the situation as he sees it—some of his own efforts or their common purposes have been thwarted by their behavior—and ask them to think about it with him. If he is in the midst of developing a pastoral relation, his reflection and theirs will be an extension of this. If he is in a more "official" meeting, his reflection and theirs will be an extension of this. It will be similar for behavioral reflection, if he chooses, for example, to adopt the kind of exaggerated or caricatured machinery-tending role, so as to stimulate and provide focus for their common reflection. Also, if he chooses reply, rather than reflection, whether the reply is behavioral or verbal, he is presumably undertaking to quiet the fears or otherwise address the needs which he sees represented in the resistance. He will be doing this in the same context and relationship in which the resistance appeared. He will speak as administrator to council or study leader to study group. He will find ways to answer them in the same coded "language" they have used to speak to him in resistance.

3 ◈

BIBLE STUDY GROUP

DISPERSION AND DISRUPTION

A minister opened a regular meeting of a small Bible study discussion group with some leading questions about the planned topic, the Holy Spirit. Basing his questions on several assigned readings in Acts, including portions of Chapters 5, 16, and 19, he asked what the members regarded as appropriate signs of the influence of the Holy Spirit in their lives.

A woman responded immediately with questions about Ananias' death (Acts 5). How could such a thing happen? Did this mean instant judgment? If so, exactly what had he done wrong? Her question was echoed by others and a variety of answers was offered: He was probably an old man anyhow. He was shocked at being so suddenly found out, especially in front of others, embarrassing and unusual treatment for a rich man. Maybe he got so angry at Peter or at his wife, because he thought she told on him, that he had a heart attack. His sin was that he had withheld some of the money. His sin was that he didn't trust God or the church and saved some insurance for himself. His sin was the deception. And so forth. This discussion lasted over half an hour and was far more diffuse and rambling than this attempt to list the "main points" might suggest.

The minister felt baffled and bewildered because this exchange of exegetical opinion seemed not to be getting anywhere or to have any relation to the planned topic or his opening questions. As common as was this type of experience, he was without a clear strategy of response. He sometimes joined in the discussion, trying to clarify questions and to improve the exegesis of the passage. He sometimes deliberately stayed out of it, hoping it would either spend itself or develop a discernible point of focus which he could then clarify. He made one effort to break off the discussion by pointing out that the reading he had suggested had been only of the first four verses of

306

Chapter 5 and that they were picking up Ananias' death from the fifth verse.

Finally, in an impulsive effort to break the stalemate, he jumped into a pause with the question, "What about some of these other passages?" The members followed his suggestion, but not as he intended. One immediately picked up the reference to speaking in tongues in 19:6, and there ensued a discussion of this topic very similar to the previous one: How could such a thing happen? How was it to be interpreted? What about people who claim to "speak in tongues" today? There were also some questions about interpretation of dreams, stimulated by 16:9. The discussion just did not get off the ground, in the direction that had been planned or in any other direction.

DIAGNOSIS AND REMEDY

In situational factors?

The minister could not get the discussion where it "should" be. Was something wrong in the *situation?* Perhaps some technique or circumstance needed to be changed so that discussion would be fruitful and meaningful. Perhaps better preparation by the minister was needed—a sharper, more focused presentation that would stimulate discussion, perhaps more sophistication or skill in "group techniques." Perhaps there was a need for better preparation by the members, perhaps a different study book, more insistence that they read the assigned chapters, more pointed study questions at home. Perhaps the minister should have tried to recruit more members or more prestigious members in order to improve morale of the group so they would take the material more seriously. Perhaps morale would have improved if refreshments had been deferred from the beginning to the end so that people wouldn't have felt so chatty and informal. Perhaps the minister should have provided a more formal and longer introductory statement, more like a lecture. Perhaps he should have taken less responsibility and asked one of the group members to lead off each time. And so on. Any minister, lay planner, professor, or

writer of practical guides can come up with all these and many more
solutions to "improve the discussion."

All such reactions agree in assuming the meaninglessness of the
discussion as it took place: it was pure obstacle and impediment.
They disregard the actual discussion except as something to be
improved or remedied. People are not where they should be, and the
distance between where they are and where they should be provokes
only maneuvers for moving them across the distance. The distance
does not invite inquiry—as this book suggests—as to why they are
where they are. The "solutions" share two important characteristics
of the discussion itself: (1) they "miss the point," and (2) they
search for specific manageable explanations and clues and solutions
where none is called for.

Perhaps, of course, there *is* some circumstantial "reality-base" to be
considered before one supposes that the obstructive digression may
be meaningful "resistance." Perhaps, for example, the presentation
by the minister and his leading questions have simply fallen flat; they
may have been too vaguely stated, or irrelevant to any concerns of the
people.

Not only in the situation

However, if he takes another look, the minister may find good
reason to have second thoughts about his rush to situational diagnosis
and manipulation. For one thing, the very variety of solutions that
flood his mind, especially the contradictions among them, should
remind him that wherever all these possible solutions may come from,
they don't arise out of careful study of the evidence of the situation.
They *all* can't be needed situational reforms, and the fact that they
all flood his mind should suggest that he is not in fact actually deriving these possible remedies from close appraisal of the situation.

For another thing, the minister may well recall his past experiences
with juggling just such situational solutions. He has, in the past,
looked to one such maneuver after another, first with great hope that
it will provide remedy, then with resignation that it has not. After
repeated failures to find a successful panacea, he may be ready to

recognize that his own understanding of the nature of man and of ministry, and his own purposes in the study group for deeper confrontation of self and of Spirit preclude, and are contradicted by, this kind of superficial situational manipulation. What is needed is a way to minister in the situation, not a technique for preparing the situation for ministry.

Evidence concerning the degree to which the situational "reality-basis," is responsible for the disappointing discussion is in practice difficult, even awkward, to come by. It is a matter of degree rather than absolute difference. A difficulty in communication takes two sides. At some point, members' response to the minister's unclear presentation becomes denial. If they wanted to try harder, they might get it. No minister ought to have to make an ideal initial presentation or be responsible for arranging absolutely optimum conditions for discussion; such is not required by any doctrine of ministry, much as ministers may personally feel it their obligation. If the study group members cannot follow the minister's points and his questions, the responsibility must always be to *some* degree his ("reality"), and to *some* degree theirs (motivated resistance). Ideally, one might imagine some ways to test the relative degree of each of these components. How much do the members objectively *not understand* what the minister is getting at and how much do they *not want to pursue* the subject? A minister may find ways to make probes to assess how well they objectively understand what he is getting at. (This may even be simultaneous with his interpretation of the resistance.) "Did you understand what I was saying? And since you did, why didn't you follow it?" As always, establishing the limits of the degree of "reality" *is* to define the degree of subjective problem remaining. The practical difficulty is for the minister not to make such a test probe seem to be a *demand* to discuss.

The above strategy of probing *reality* was intended to bring the elements of resistance and reality into sharper confrontation so that minister and members alike might discern the relative contribution of each. The same purpose might be served by probing the element of *resistance* more directly. The minister may reflect his sense that avoidance is taking place: "You don't seem to want to take the Holy

Spirit too seriously or too personally." Or, he may venture a hunch, at a little deeper level, as to the general discomfort which may lie behind the avoidance: "It's not too comfortable to think of God so directly touching our lives as talk about the Holy Spirit implies." If he wants to leave more room for the people to move and choose, he may say, instead of "It's not too comfortable . . . ," "It's not too easy. . . ." "Easy" is ambiguous as to whether it refers to intellectual or motivational factors. Here again the practical difficulty is to let the group members recognize the probe as expressing genuine tentativeness, curiosity, and acceptance of the avoidance, rather than as a demand for a change. They can do this only (1) if it is that, and (2) if they have some past experience that leads them to expect the minister to respond in this way. If an answer to this is a fairly bland, "What do you mean?" or some form of "Maybe, maybe not," or a kind of pat agreement that has the effect of closing the subject and moving on, or a flat disagreement that also closes discussion, or an abrupt change in the subject, this kind of resistive-repressive response may be more direct evidence that the previous behavior was also resistance in action.

In personal factors?

Perhaps persistent personal factors are in control of the occasion, deflecting the person's behavior from what it should and could be. (Here we are at the *bottom* line of the diagram in Chap. I.) The people may be using the scriptural material to reflect urgent personal concerns. This explanation might either supplement the *situational* explanation above or be independent of it. Perhaps people found that these scriptural passages—as Scripture often does and as it is supposed to do—mirrored some elements of their own dilemmas. In talking about Ananias, they were speaking of themselves. Perhaps such personal engagement with the Scripture passages quite properly took over the discussion from the planned, but irrelevant, topic, and should have been respected, encouraged, and assisted. The minister could have more explicitly focused the concerns which the people expressed and the solutions they found.

For example, perhaps someone had feelings that he deserved immediate punishment like Ananias'. But he wanted to reassure himself that God is not really so harsh, and that Ananias' case was somehow different from his own (e.g., Ananias was already an old man; his sin was different; things aren't like that any more). Or perhaps it was a more diffuse fear of death or tragedy which was evoked by the Ananias story and for which a person was seeking reassurance through explanation. Or perhaps somebody actually identified with Ananias and through this discussion was indirectly confessing his own faithlessness in withholding or deceiving or mistrusting God. Perhaps the Ananias story awakened particular misgivings someone had concerning his own relation with the community and his responsibility toward others.

This question too—whether such discussion of the biblical account reflects such personal concerns—requires, like the situational question, a relative rather than an absolute answer. We suppose that any such discussion must have some personal motivations of this kind behind it. Why do people say *these* things about *this* passage? It's not purely chance or random; it must have something to do with personal reverberations which the passage sets up in their own lives. The question is how importantly or problematically these concerns loom in the present discussion. Are such anxieties and bids for assurance the major thrust behind these remarks? Do they provide the main thing to be sensed in what is going on here? Or, instead, are these relatively minor or incidental or essentially solved problems which are being evoked here in the service of some other purpose, such as resistance? Assuming that Mrs. S's first remarks about Ananias reflect *some* apprehension of personal judgment to be visited upon her, the question still is: Is such a question a major, prominent, "real" basis? Or are the remarks prompted primarily and principally by resistive motives? Does Mrs. S, in order to serve resistive purposes, have to have something moderately interesting and relevant to talk about? Is it for this purpose that she recalls a little stray, mild, lingering apprehension? In the case of Mrs. A in Chapter II, the question was similar: Was she really and seriously worried about being diagnosed as severely ill, or was this an essentially already resolved query which she found it convenient and plausible to talk about, in the service of resistance. The corresponding question concerning the situation was: Was the minister's less than precise and relevant opening statement the principal "cause" of the wandering discussion? Or did it just provide a convenient occasion for people already motivated to resist the main point?

Not only in personal factors

The available clues, although not decisive, tended to suggest in this Bible study discussion group that such discussion was not primarily, or at least not discernibly, based on earnest and pressing personal concerns of this kind. The best evidence came, though inadvertently, in response to the minister's abrupt shift from one Scripture passage to another. There was no inclination to persist in a return to the Ananias story. Explanations of glossalalia would be equally useful for resistive purposes as attempts to explain Ananias' death, but hardly as good for handling fears and guilts evoked by the Ananias story. Though less dramatically discernible, it was this same kind of shifting and meandering and distractibility *within* the discussion of Ananias which was simultaneously frustrating as "pointless" and also a clue that the motives were more to cover than to express. People were easily distracted from one theme to another and no clues to clear focus emerged. The only thing the many diffuse comments had in common was that they were persistently staying *off* the intended topic and *away* from leading questions. The very point which most annoys the minister and makes the discussion seem meaningless becomes, in fact, an important clue to its meaning.

Additional evidence was provided by the bland response evoked by the minister's tentative probes in this direction. When he offered some interpretations about "people these days sometimes feeling that they stand in Ananias' place," and about the "commonness of the sins Ananias seemed guilty of," these evoked neither confirming reaction and interest nor the kind of rejection which might make him feel he had touched something genuine but too sensitive. The reactions tended to be more on the order of a polite pause.

MINISTRY TO THE RESISTIVE REACTION

From considerations along some of the above lines, the minister in this case felt that he was dealing with something like resistance. Rather than not comprehending or not finding relevant his leading questions about searching for signs of a spirit, he began to suspect that they may have found this line of question too pointed, something to stay away from.

The immediate *context* of the resistance was the Bible passages and his own questions, and the larger context was the history of the study group. The minister was aware that the members may have sensed from their past experience with him something of the direction of his own answers to his questions, and that it was these "answers" they were forestalling and resisting. The "signs of the Spirit" the minister might be preparing to emphasize would stress freedom, absence of clearcut moralistic criteria, involvement in "secular" responsibilities.

However, rather than context, the minister was more impressed with the form and *content* of this resistance, although this was related to what he inferred from the context. He was impressed with the degree to which the discussion consisted of attempts to control and manage and analyze ambiguous and uncommon experiences, specifically those of Ananias' sudden demise, the phenomenon of glossalalia, and dream interpretation. This kind of response seemed to him to be not strictly an accidental reaction to the general question of the appropriate marks of the Christian life, especially in the light of their expectation of his opposition to attempts to tie the Spirit into neat packages. Were they *demonstrating* in their search for petty certainties their own answer to the question of the quality of life in the Spirit? Were they engaging, in this behavioral and unconscious way, in a dialogue with the minister about the nature of the Christian life?

He attempted to develop this interpretation, to point out to them that they seemed to be searching for specifics and turning away from his questions which might lead them toward the more threatening

criteria of openness and ambiguity. He suggested that they seemed to
fear matching their lives against such criteria as the simple trust of
the early Christians, that their behavior in fact was a kind of negative
instance of what he regarded as proper signs of the presence of the
Holy Spirit and a Christian life.

This kind of response stuck to religion appropriately and to the
existing role relationships (see Chap. VI). It did not venture into
deeper psychological interpretations, such as of specific fears or
other grounds for their resistance.

But another kind of response might have been more appropriately
faithful to the criteria of tentativeness (see Chap. V) and acceptance
(see Chap. III). The minister might simply have called attention to
the problem as it has been presented here and as he perceived it at the
time. There had been an initially announced and agreed upon topic,
appropriate Scriptures, an official presentation, and some leading
questions, all of which may have had their defects, but which seemed
reasonably intelligible and, so far as he could tell, were understood by
the group members. However, as they could readily see, they had
spent over an hour in meandering discussion on incidental portions
of the narrative which seemed to have some interest and some
relevance, but apparently not enough to be getting them anywhere in
their discussion. He thought this was curious and probably had some
significance. What did they think? Is there something about signs of
life in the Spirit which is difficult? Is there something that makes it
easier to try to figure out what happened to Ananias and why?

If there has been resistance as we have surmised, the people will
also recognize it, and maybe even be troubled by it. In focusing on
the resistance, the minister focuses on something real and vital. The
"problem" of why they responded as they did is inescapable, and
probably also welcome. It also, incidentally, gets them on the topic
he wanted all along. The resistance itself provides confidence for
supposing that the people do sense the difficulty as the minister does,
that they are bothered by it, and that they want to and can talk about
it (see Chap. IV). For the resistance itself, understood as above,
suggests that they are sensitive to key religious questions and are
already in internal "dialogue" with them and about them. Otherwise

they would not have been so ready to resist the initial questions. The resistance also suggests, by its form, that they have considerable familiarity and facility in discussing biblical and presumably other religious matters.

This would be *verbal reflection* (see Chap. VII). *Behaviorally*, the very nature of the minister's statement in making this reflection might be provokingly dogmatic or provokingly ambiguous. The style of his remarks might suggest the minister's own norms of openness and freedom. He might continue the dialogue in the behavioral terms they have used.

A *verbal reply* might be simply a statement, using biblical materials, of the grounds for trust, reassurance about the acceptability of openness and indecision. This would bypass the overt resistance and be addressed directly to the fears the minister suspects prompted the resistance. A *behavioral reply* would be his own demonstration of openness in trust and his own ability to live with himself and not to be embarrassed before them over making open-ended ambiguous statements—not even in boldly plunging into what he thought was the heart of a matter, the resistance in this group, without knowing all the answers in advance.

4 ◈
COUNSELING: A MISUNDERSTANDING

In the course of premarital counseling, a couple reported to a minister that the girl was already pregnant. In the ensuing counseling, they discussed with candor, insight, and maturity a range of problems which this posed for them and their marriage: guilt over their sexual relationship, shame at "having" to get married, community and family reaction seven months hence, doubts over whether they were marrying because they loved each other or were forced into it, the financial and emotional difficulties of having a child so soon, how "wanted" the child was, etc.

Throughout this extended discussion about the implications of the pregnancy, one matter was not touched on which seemed to the minister an obvious question to raise. Was one of them particularly to "blame" for the baby, for having taken inadequate contraceptive precautions? Under the circumstances it seemed to the minister inevitable that the boy and girl would each be raising the question within himself. That they were not discussing it with each other, at least not in his presence, seemed an important omission. Was it possible that one felt such intense, although perhaps unconscious, guilt for having "blundered" in some way and was secretly blamed by the other? Were such feelings, if they existed, more anxiety-laden, threatening, and unfaceable together than the many other troublesome implications of the pregnancy which they had faced freely? If so, what was the reason that this problem was more troublesome than the others? For example, could thoughts of blundering with contraceptives evoke some crucial, lingering sense of inadequacy or immaturity for marriage? Could it represent some important area of mistrust and failure of communication between the two?

Was omission resistive?

The counseling minister might have regarded the silence on this topic itself as a form of resistance. One could justifiably suppose that

316

it was so inappropriate *not* to discuss such an "obvious" question that the inappropriateness was "meaningful." The supposition of meaningfulness could be supported because the silence touched such potentially important matters, because it persisted through several counseling sessions, because it persisted through a number of occasions on which they discussed their sexual relations and the conception of the baby, occasions on which it might be expected to arise. That is, it was a persistent and intense silence. The minister might have posed the problem of resistance, as just discussed: "There is one question which it seems to me you 'ought' to have discussed. But you haven't mentioned it. I am not particularly interested in whether you discuss it or not, or what the answer may be. I am wondering whether there is any important reason that we ought to think about together as to why it hasn't been raised. Maybe our discussion here has been thwarted in some small way by something which will thwart even more important relations later if we don't do something about it now. Anyway, I have been wondering whether either of you has feelings that one or the other should have done something different to prevent the pregnancy. And more important, if you do have such feelings, is there some significance in the fact that you haven't expressed them?"

Through such intervention, a counselor might expect a reaction ranging somewhere from an intense denial ("You're really on the wrong track there!") through a casual, puzzled, nonchalance ("Well, I don't know; I never really thought about that much; it just sort of happened this way . . ."), to an earnest outpouring of bottled-up feelings. The counselor would be more interested in either the first or the last kind of reaction, than in a genuine nonchalance which suggests that he really is on the wrong path.

In the actual counseling that took place, the pastor did not respond in this way. This is partly because he did not understand the omission so clearly as a potential resistance. It is partly because he felt that the omission might not be interpretable as meaningful resistance, but perhaps due to a "reality," "situational" factor: namely, that despite the minister's expectations there had not been any actual occasion for the topic to come up naturally. What he actually said could be con-

strued as an attempt to test out the degree of this reality factor. He
suggested the topic. The couple's reaction could be construed as
evidence that the omission had been meaningful resistance, not just
"reality-based" in the sense that the topic hadn't suggested itself.
Their "overlooking" of the topic persisted despite his suggestion.

He said, "I have been wondering whether you have any feelings
that one more than the other was responsible for the pregnancy?"

The girl replied immediately, "No, we both wanted to sleep together . . . to have a sexual relation, and we both equally enjoyed
it."

MISUNDERSTANDING DISRUPTS COUNSELING

She has misunderstood his question. She has taken the minister to
refer to the sexual act, not to contraception. This misunderstanding
provides a disruption. It impedes the progress of the counseling as he
had planned it. Such misunderstanding is a minor disruption, and a
very common one. Nevertheless it is precisely the kind of disruption
with which this book is concerned. This "misunderstanding" is the
resistance to be discussed here.

Attack the resistance?

The most "natural" reaction to such disruption is to undo it, to
overcome it as expeditiously as possible, so as to proceed along the
planned course of counseling. The minister will explain that this is
not what he meant by the question; he will make the question
clearer. He is assuming, without thinking about it, that the defect is
"situationally" produced and therefore can be situationally corrected.
"I was referring to the use of contraceptives, not the sexual relation
itself." The question made more explicit, and the couple directed to
reply to it, the counseling can now proceed.

The fact that such explanation and direction deviates from his
usual counseling role and manner is perhaps not greatly important. It
is only a slight and temporary deviation. The counseling relation and
its progress would really not be disrupted by this particular lapse into
directiveness.

But much of importance and relevance to the counseling is lost if the misunderstanding is allowed to pass simply as an unfotunate disruption to be quickly overcome. Such a "misunderstanding" may have important meaning behind it. It may be the point at which vital feelings, intensely relevant to the purposes of counseling, even though temporary and in disguise, have broken through an important but less vital and less intense level of discussion.

Clues to meaning

Clues to special and important meaning in the girl's response lie, first of all, in its *inappropriateness;* it is inappropriate in at least two respects. First, she has misunderstood the question, and her fiancé has let the misunderstanding stand. To be sure, there is some prospective "reality-base" in her misunderstanding. The counselor's phrase "responsible for the pregnancy" was not unambiguous. There is never any absolute and authoritative judgment as to what is "appropriate," "realistic," "normal" behavior, and it is no more forthcoming in this fairly trivial decision than in more substantial decisions of normalcy. But it seemed to this counselor that in the context of this conversation with these people, his phrase, viewed as objectively as possible, conveyed more of the meaning he intended—concern with contraceptives—than the meaning she interpreted. This judgment was enhanced by the following consideration.

Second, her response was inappropriate to the degree that what she was now reporting had already been extensively discussed. Their feelings about their sexual relations, past and future, had been so thoroughly explored that for her now to respond as though this were a new topic was a particularly odd misunderstanding.

Beyond these two types of inappropriateness is another clue in the promptness and *intensity* with which she replied. There is also another slight clue in that she, rather than he, was the one so quickly to reply. For her to answer a major question and to do so with such firmness and intensity was not entirely characteristic of their established pattern of behavior in counseling. Each of these clues deserves to have the question, "Why?" raised about it.

One might infer meanings from the *context* of the resistance: Does she unconsciously detect the reference to contraceptives and, equally unconsciously, feel motivated to avoid the topic? The question of contraceptives in general, or of their use of them two months ago in particular, may be too sensitive and anxiety-laden to face. This might be for one or more of many possible reasons. There might be a sense of ignorance and unreadiness which touches off more general feelings of immaturity or unreadiness for marriage. Perhaps she blames herself for not having done what she knew she should. Perhaps she suspects or feels or fears some unconscious desire on her part to have the baby and thus trap her boyfriend into marriage. Perhaps she mostly blames him for not having prevented the pregnancy, but also feels guilt or anxiety over blaming him. Any one of these or other feelings could be behind a move to avoid the question of contraception. Any one of them could have important further ramifications in their relationship. But there is no clue simply in the fact of avoidance as to which if any such interpretations are valid ones. Speculation, much less certainty, about these motives may hardly be necessary. It is only necessary to recognize that some meanings of this importance may be involved.

From the *content* of her resistive response, one might find clues to different types of motivations. Her comment is a rehearsal of the problem of guilt over the sexual relations—a problem which seemingly had been fully faced already in the counseling. What could it mean that she so inappropriately reverts to it now?

Possible meanings of misunderstanding

a. It might mean what has just been suggested: She wants to avoid the question of contraception reasonably implied by the question. And in the service of this resistive motive she exploits the ambiguity of the question, which leaves a loophole for answer. She employs as the content to fill this loophole a problem which has been a real one in their discussion.

Her alertness to the threatening question, to the loophole in it, and to the means of utilizing the loophole represent important skills and resources which are usually used to productive advantage in the counseling. Her relatively clumsy recourse to a more or less obviously inappropriate (because already discussed) topic may suggest her desperation at this point. A person normally so skillful and resourceful who is clumsy at one point of resistance must be clumsy for a reason. The reason may be that she is so desperately threatened in this instance that full use of her resources is precluded. It may also be that there is some unconscious wish to be "caught" in the resistance, to have it discovered and dealt with.

b. To revert to this topic might also mean something quite different. It might suggest that she feels the minister has not fully understood their feelings about their sexual relations, or that these feelings have not been as thoroughly dealt with as the counselor may think. In a seemingly smooth counseling relation, such resistance may be the best hint the counselor gets that there are certain elements of mistrust or a lack of rapport. These will certainly influence and interfere with further counseling unless they are dealt with. If they do exist, they cannot be dealt with unless they are exposed by following back the particular clue of this awkward and inappropriate "repetition."

c. Perhaps the first possible meaning that comes to mind in considering the content is that there is lingering unresolved tension over the sexual relation—past or future—which is still easily triggered by such a relatively light stimulus as the ambiguous question. Does she feel guilty or fearful more profoundly or in some different way from those so far discussed? Such possible speculation is supported, in this instance, by one additional clue in the content of her statement. This is the mildly awkward way in which she referred to their sexual relation, first using the euphemism "sleep together," then changing to the formal phrase "sexual relation." Both euphemism and formality are evasive of actual emotion-filled expression, and the shift from one to the other suggests some lingering difficulty in "facing" the fact.

MINISTERING TO MISUNDERSTANDING

Whether any of these speculations is appropriate, however, can emerge only from further consideration and discussion. This can most effectively be motivated and guided by the counselor's reflection of the resistive behavior exactly as he sees it; it is an important puzzle to be solved, important for the sake of further counseling and for the sake of meeting their mutual goals in the counseling. In the nature of the counseling role, verbal reflection is most likely the appropriate response.

Counselor: Well, this is something else interesting. I meant one thing by my question, but you seem to have understood me as meaning something else. Should we look at that misunderstanding a minute? Does it mean anything important that we need to know?

He points to what has happened as directly as seems to be necessary to invite their attention to it. He does not begin his half-formed speculations about the meanings of the misunderstanding. It is just that in the smooth flow of counseling, a disruption has occurred, and disruptions may be especially important to consider; his own speculations, if any, about the dynamics behind the disruption serve only the purpose of emphasizing that it is potentially important.

The minister does not even define the nature of the misunderstanding as explicitly as he might: "I meant contraceptives but you understood sexual relations." He does not want to put words into their mouths; if they do recognize a misunderstanding, how *they* define it will be important. Furthermore, there is some need to test the "reality-basis" of her misunderstanding, to leave open the possibilities that she "really" did think he meant the sexual relationship, or at least that she still wants to claim this.

Girl: Oh, I see. You mean should one of us have done something. I thought you meant, did one of us want the sex more than the other?

She acknowledges the "misunderstanding." She shows that with this slight prodding she is able to see the distinction between what the minister intended and what she answered. If she identifies the distinction this clearly after the vague reflection of the minister, she probably sensed it, to some degree, when he first posed the question. (If his reflection on the misunderstanding had explicitly identified the distinction as he saw it, then we could judge less well from her reply whether she had probably sensed the distinction from the beginning.) Although she recognizes the distinction and the misunderstanding, however, the flat casualness and the matter-of-factness of her reply comprises a kind of denial that there is any special meaning in the "misunderstanding."

This response makes the minister feel justified in pressing her just once more by emphasizing that her reply has been inappropriate, puzzling, and potentially meaningful. It is not just the "misunderstanding" itself which seems to want explanation; that could have the "reality-basis" she now seems inclined to want to claim for it (or to hide behind).

Minister: But I thought we had pretty thoroughly discussed your feelings toward your sexual relations. I already knew that you both wanted it and enjoyed it.

He wishes to expose her resistance more fully as resistance, appealing to her own motives to face herself, to avoid resistance, and to be curious about it. If she still wishes to resist and to deny meaning to the resistance after this one additional probe, her needs for such resistance and denial had better be respected for the time being.

Girl: Well, Jerry always took care of that, but one night. . . . Really, though, I'm sure I'm as much to blame as he is. I probably led him on and I didn't stop him. . . . But then, it might not even have been that night. Something might have gone wrong some other time, too. . . . Anyway, that's all past now. . . .

She starts out dutifully (in response to the counselor's mild urging) to give an account of the baby's conception, at least her account. Apparently, she does harbor blame toward Jerry, but she breaks this off to express something like misgivings for blaming him. In turn, this combination of powerful emotions—blame of Jerry vs. guilt over blaming Jerry—proves too much to face and she cuts off the whole discussion.

By now she has so fully exposed and demonstrated this conflict—to speak vs. to resist speaking—that the minister has simply to reflect what she has shown.

Minister: There seem to be real thoughts and feelings there but it isn't easy to get them out.

Girl: Maybe this is something Jerry and I need to talk together about before we talk with you.

Under other circumstances, the minister-counselor might be more inclined to check out the degree of "reality" behind such a statement. How much real mistrust of the counselor and counseling does it reveal? In this case it seems to him obvious that whatever small component of "real" mistrust there may be, its dominant meaning is as a desperate resistive plea. He says as much.

Minister: I might take that personally, but I think what you really mean is that you don't feel like talking about it at all.

Girl: Well, it is hard. I don't even know how much I should be thinking about such things, much less talking about them, much less talking about them to you.

Here is a real outpouring. The counselor reflects this and expresses uncertainty about what she means by "these things." It soon develops that she is experiencing serious uncertainties, perhaps fear, as to how much "strength" and "initiative" she has to supply to the marriage. She feels some doubt over whether Jerry has enough "strength" to "take care of me and the baby," and whether she knows just how to fill a wifely role—how much to be a helpless clinging vine and how much to be a comrade in arms and a tower of strength. She wants to take her part in making moves and decisions, but doesn't want to push too much. She fears she may be inclined to nag or try to dominate Jerry if she thinks he isn't doing enough. But she can hardly help it.

These kinds of misgivings and concerns about their relationship obviously have important implications forward and "centrifugally." Here is an element important to the rest of their life together. It is precisely a goal of counseling to deal with such things, and it is possible that nothing else in the counseling relationship was as important as the attention given to this problem.

These concerns also have important implications "backward" and "centripetally." This concern over where responsibilities started and stopped was apparently behind her reluctance to "tattle" on Jerry, even behind her reluctance and resentment at having to think about this question at all. Why hadn't Jerry figured out what had happened, explained it to her, and taken the responsibility—like a man! It was related to the fact that she was the one doing the speaking in this instance, hurriedly, intensely, hardly letting him get a word in, and also reluctantly and without saying much. It was related to the episode of the contraceptives itself, and to the confusion and anxiety then over who should do what. Should she have left it up to Jerry to "take care of that" or should she have taken more initiative herself, as she apparently inwardly felt inclined to do? Should she have taken more responsibility for stopping him "that night"?

The problem of her reluctance to speak, when diligently but calmly followed, thus exposed some very important matters. Rather than going off on all of these implications, the counselor kept the discussion closely on the immediate question which most directly concerned them then and there. This was simply the question of the "resistance," the impulses and anxieties she felt about discussing the question, and eventually Jerry's own feelings about having her pursue this conversation.

This—what each of them thought the other should be saying and not saying—became the problem they shared, discussed, and eventually reached some tentative decisions about. Little was said, except by indirect allusion, about each of the centrifugal or centripetal implications, all the other instances past and future in which this problem might loom. Their own "little" problem *in* counseling carried the load of the others lodged within it. It seems likely that their own attempts in new situations in decades ahead to work out this problem was given help by the concerted, candid attention to the question of who should and should not be saying what in this particular counseling hour.

IX

Resistance in Worship:
A Summary

The "problem of worship" is usually analyzed for or by the minister in some such terms as these:

Worship is intended to be an intense and rich experience in which persons express their deepest and loftiest feelings before their Creator. With themselves thereby opened and receptive, they feel God's guidance and grace anew in the lives they have thus laid before Him. In the churches' experience forms and language have developed which enable persons to express themselves most fully and to apprehend God's leading and presence most richly. Persons can worship more fully with the aid of these forms and language than without it. But these forms and language require training and practice and discipline to be used suitably. Otherwise, there is misunderstanding or nonunderstanding, inattention or nonattendance, "wanderings of mind" or "empty forms." The people do not fill their proper role as members of the worshiping congregation, or permit the minister to exercise the role he feels called to and trained for, as leader of the worshiping congregation, if they have not learned how to use the forms.

To this "problem," two types of response are most common. One is to change the forms of worship to make them more suitably matched to the readiness of the people. The other is to change the

326

people to make them more suitably matched to the forms. These responses correspond, in terms proposed here, to adjustment of the objective situation and adjustment of the persons who enter the situation. Both strategies regard persons' resisting reactions—the "wanderings of mind," etc.—as without significant meaning, as only something to be overcome.

The former may involve modest local rearrangement of the elements of worship, perhaps experiments with lighting and with music and with visual material in the chancel. Or it may, on a grander scale, be called "liturgical reform," and involve the minister in writing for church papers or experimental liturgies or in attending meetings of liturgical committees of his denomination or of Councils of Churches.[1]

The other response is perhaps more feasible, more justifiable, and more common. This is the education of persons. They must be taught how to worship if they are to do so suitably, meaningfully, and reverently. They must be instructed in the appropriate rhythms and modes of the worship service, the rich, historically imbued meaning of the words they recite and the symbols they share. The proper purpose of each part of the worship service must be explained to them. People must learn hymns which are more meaningful in language and more reverent in music than the gospel hymns they learned in childhood. Or else they must be helped to learn the "good old hymns" so loaded with power. They must learn to have a communion table separated from the back wall. Or else they must learn to respond to the higher liturgical meaning of an altar. They must be urged to be reverently quiet from the moment they enter the sanctuary, or else they must be urged to be more spontaneous and more vigorous in their worship participation.

[1] In these terms, liturgical reform which is prompted to adjust the forms of worship to the existing needs and idiom of present-day men needs to be distinguished from that "reform" which would revise liturgy to correspond more closely to some other norms, usually derived from more ancient practices. The former, for example, might involve the replacement of pastoral and agricultural imagery with symbols more inherently meaningful for urban and suburban Western man. The latter only enhances the task of educating people to make use of the forms.

Once the congregation is elevated to a suitable understanding or once more suitable forms are adopted—once the intrusive resistance is reduced—they can worship. Then the minister can lead worship. Meanwhile, in either of these remedial strategies, he is likely to feel that he is out of his *metier* and engaged merely in preliminary preparation. Either activity, reform or education, may be reasonably satisfying to a minister. Or either one may seem an annoying necessity. But whether he is designing new liturgical forms, or whether he is harrying people into adhering to forms which should already be firmly a part of their tradition, he is likely to feel this a distraction from his ministry as worship leader. Ironically, the more keenly he feels the importance of worship, the more keenly he will feel sensitive to the deficiencies in the congregation's worship, and therefore the more likely he is to be drawn into such preparatory, "non-worship" activities.

Appraisals of remedies

The following things can be said about these common and perhaps characteristic strategies for solving the "problem of worship."

1. They *do* distract the minister. His feeling that he is drawn into a secondary, less vital engagement is justified. He stoops to the level of the resistance and fights the battle on its own terms: He would worship and lead worship; inattention or misunderstanding or apathy or superstition keep members of the congregation from worshiping; instead of proceeding to worship—with these people as they are—the minister abandons worship; he becomes committee member or liturgy writer, adult educator, pleader, and goad. He is talking about worship but not worshiping or leading worship.

2. They assume that the defect and hence the remedy lie in the "objective situation" or else in the habits or understanding or attitudes of the persons themselves. If the reaction of a person to the worship situation is not as one expects it should be, then an appropriate change in the situation or in the person will improve the reaction.

In any particular instance, this assumption may be quite justified. Perhaps even in most instances of difficulty in worship the difficulty may be "realistically" based, in this sense. It may be entirely accounted for by the obsolescence of the worship forms, people's inexperience with the forms, etc., those matters which are being attacked by these solutions.

There are, however, exceptions. In any particular instance, the question needs to be raised as to whether this assumption, so easily made, is, in fact, warranted. Are the forms really that obsolete and inappropriate, or is this only a convenient pretext, a rationalization to cover a more difficult, complex, and perhaps uncomfortable explanation? Are the inattention, the straying thoughts, and other evidence of estrangement from the worship experience really greatest for the most obsolete of the forms? Or does this evidence of estrangement persist even when newer forms are introduced and even when persons are instructed and trained? Are people really as inexperienced and unpracticed in using these forms as one might like to think? Have not most of them had a lifetime of experience and much previous "instruction"? Perhaps they can be said, in some sense and perhaps unconsciously, to "know what they are doing" when they turn aside from full engagement in the worship experience. Do the minister's new educational efforts or his efforts at reform essentially just repeat without avail what has already gone before? Do his efforts at instruction only meet a further estrangement, which has been described elsewhere in this book as a "talking past," in which people deflect, without seeming really to understand, what he is trying to say to them? Is there a kind of relentlessness or intensity about the inattention or the wandering of mind or the superstition or other insistence on inappropriate forms? This would suggest that the resistance is not simply a passive absence of proper direction, but rather has a purpose and a direction of its own. If the instances of resistance are not correlated simply with obsolescence or with inexperience, do they seem correlated with something else that would suggest that they are a meaningful response? Do they occur, for example, especially at moments at which persons are asked to affirm their faith, or at moments of abject self-dedication?

Questions like these raise the possibility of resistive reaction: The obstacles may not be due entirely to particular deficiencies in the *situation* or the *persons*, and may therefore not be appropriately remedied by simply giving attention to the situation or to the persons.

3. These appraisals and strategies assume that these resistive reactions are without pertinent meaning. They assume that the resistance is not responsive to the forms of worship but is only a kind of barrier laid across their path. They assume that people do not perceive the significance of the worship forms. The possibility is not considered that the significance of the forms *is* apprehended and is responded to in a particular—and revealing—way in what appears as resistance. It is not considered possible that the constellation of church and worship, and the many mental associations they bring to mind, actually evokes specific reactions which find expression (as well as disguise) in the resistance. If women chatter across pews during the prelude, this is just women's chattering (the bottom line of the diagram in Chap. I), or this is just their failure to understand the reverential purpose of the prelude (the top line of the diagram). If a man is more conscious during the offering of the ushers' efficiency or inefficiency than he is of "offering himself" before God, this may be his own compulsiveness or waywardness of thought or it may be because the forms of the offering are not sufficient to grip him. But there is no consideration of the possibility that the chattering or the concern for the ushers' efficiency may actually be an important expression of these persons' reaction to the reverential purpose of the prelude or the symbolic meaning of the offering.

4. Furthermore, this "rejection" of their reaction is communicated to people. In an experience which is supposed to provide for the full and honest expression of oneself, the very feelings and thoughts one may be having at the time are ruled impermissible. The educational or the reform efforts say to people: The reactions you have, the spontaneous but not obviously relevant thoughts and images which come to mind during sermon or prayer, Scripture or hymn, are not acceptable.

An extreme form of this rejection is in the "training" of children for worship. This so often consists of telling the children what are the appropriate reactions to have to the standard worship materials and, further, telling them that they should not have the feelings they do have during the church service. Their childhood concerns and their natural childhood reactions to the worship experience must be left at the door, and they must spend years of Sunday mornings practicing the sounds and gestures which, they are assured, will be meaningful when they are adults. But whatever childish fears or enthusiasms or concerns they may feel like giving expression to during worship— even those they may feel like expressing *especially* during worship— must be suppressed.

5. The alternative is that the real feelings expressed in and by the resistance may also be captured and lifted up in the worship as important parts of the people who are placing themselves before God in their own way.

Let us consider, then, several elements of the morning worship service which do not often appear in handbooks on worship but do often appear in a minister's experience. Perhaps there is less disparity than there first seems between such episodes and the views of the handbooks.

In discovering episodes of resistive worship, however, there is a particular problem facing us and any minister. The resistance is easily private and undetected. Communication in worship is so onesided and the congregation's role so passive that their own reaction to the worship experience seldom gets opportunity for overt expression. Even if there is considerable resistive failure to follow the aids of worship, the congregation has so little opportunity to demonstrate this that a minister may—especially if he wants to—proceed unfalteringly, as though the congregation were fully worshiping as they intend to and as he wants them to. There may be important, dominating resistive reactions, but the minister may never know it. Only with a few subtle hints in attention, in vigor of participation, in after-church comments at the door is there much chance for overt expression. On the other hand, a minister, without too much difficulty, can explore, if he wishes to, the mind of his congregation as well as his own mind and learn more directly about the reactions to worship.

PRELUDE TO WORSHIP

On entering certain churches, persons customarily cross themselves, kneel, recite a prayer, or otherwise begin to worship with the aid of traditional postures and forms. Upon arriving at the place of worship in other churches, persons begin their worship with other characteristic, even "traditional" acts: they head immediately for the vacant pew nearest the rear—or else to their "own" pew. They greet each other with sociable chatting. They read through the events of the week on the calendar.

What would be in greater contrast? One set of actions facilitates worship—at least when "properly" and "meaningfully" used. The other set of reactions obstructs worship. Or so we most naturally suppose. But is this always as true as it seems?

Sitting in the rear and socializing during the prelude must certainly seem to any minister to be pure obstruction. The spectacle of empty front pews and noisy inattentive rear pews as he rises for the invocation scarcely enhances his own sense of worship and hardly testifies to a responsive readiness for the worship experience he has planned.

To such impediment, a minister may respond with anger, despair, or other emotional reactions, which he may express to the congregation, his wife, or his fellow ministers, or which he may keep to himself except as they find indirect expression.

Change the people

Alternatively, a minister may make a more reasoned attack on the problem in order to remedy it. If people can be coaxed closer to altar and pulpit, if they can be trained to be quiet and reverent, the congregation's worship will be enhanced. Perhaps music or lighting or interior decoration needs to be improved to set a more reverent tone. Perhaps reminder placards at the door or in the pews, perhaps cords blocking the rear pews, perhaps cushions supplied only for front pews, will provide the situational remedy. Perhaps cajoling is necessary in the newsletter, by the ushers, and from the pulpit. Perhaps the people just need more time to become accustomed to worship, so the prelude should be extended and invocation delayed, or they should be greeted reverently in the narthex or allowed to chat there, as a kind of decompression chamber, before being admitted to the sanctuary.

This may well be a correct type of appraisal and such measures may well be effective in some, and perhaps in many, situations.

Change the service

But a minister may overcome his feeling that rear seating and chatting are sheer frustration and obstacle. He may be ready to "accept" such behavior as a legitimate and necessary part of the persons as they come to worship. Women may need to, and should, greet each other, exchanging pleasantries and gossip; this may be the nature of women. If people simply feel more comfortable sitting toward the rear, why shouldn't they? There is nothing inherently irreverent or otherwise wrong in coming before God in worship as one who is overtly sociable, chatty, and uncomfortable about sitting forward. There is even New Testament endorsement for humility in worship. If this does interfere with the existing worship service, then the worship service needs to be changed so as to accommodate these personal realities, not vice versa.

A minister may find ways to accept and embrace these personal traits within the worship service. It is his priestly function to help these people feel themselves, *as they are,* lifted before God. If what they are includes these sociable or gossipy or shy characteristics, to acknowledge and express these characteristics may be accurately and truly representing them as they are. The minister may decide that the invocation ought to acknowledge that the congregation is gathering for worship with feelings still resonating from the rush to get to church on time, from the quickly exchanged gossip, from whatever slight embarrassment or unevenness may have been involved in finding seats. In a more "behavioral" gesture, he may make sure that the worship obviously accepts these characteristics by arranging the chancel, pulpit, lights, and loudspeaker to be sure that all parts of the service are clearly visible and audible in the rear and even above the chatting.

Similarly, one could argue that the priestly function also requires the minister to acknowledge, embrace, and lift up reactions to interruptions, whenever these are insistent and generally shared. When a pastoral prayer is interrupted by a persistently crying baby or a low-flying airplane or a cacophonous piano in the Sunday school room, the minister abdicates part of his responsibility if he chooses to pretend that everyone's thoughts are not on the distraction. The minister is now praying for and on behalf of a congregation, who are all troubled, in one way or another, by a distraction. This is, in some ways, the most "real" thing about these people at this time; it is certainly what they most share as a congregation.

Such an attitude toward these "frustrations"—representing the difference between acceptance and rejection—may often be appropriate and constructive. It is hardly inconsistent with the theme of this book. In fact, there may be places where the book seems to be recommending this. But to be as precise as possible—and perhaps even more precise than is warranted—this is not exactly the perspective which the book has intended to advance. It is the difference between the bottom and the middle lines of the diagram proposed in Chapter I.

The attitude just suggested above is concerned primarily with acknowledging adequately the characteristics of persons as they come to a worship service. These are characteristics which they possess generally and exhibit in many other situations. Indeed, an important reason for acknowledging these within worship is so that the effects of worship can "generalize" to these same characteristics outside of worship.

For example, the tendency to gossip, like all other characteristics of a person, needs to be brought into church so as to share in whatever transformation the presence before God may bring. Perhaps there is such a thing as learning to chat and gossip in a Christian way and with a sense of responsibility before God. Presumably this can be more likely developed when such behavior is brought, with full status, into God's presence.

But strictly speaking what has been proposed here—represented by the middle line of the diagram—is the suggestion that one may interpret resistance as a reaction of particular persons to a specific situation. This is what warrants the suggestion that the resistance may turn out to be highly relevant to the minister's purposes in the situation. Purely "imported" personal characteristics, not specifically evoked by the situation, might sometimes prove relevant to a minister's purposes and provide occasions for fulfilling them, and sometimes not. In counseling or in priestly roles, where presumably *all* feelings and thoughts of persons are more or less appropriate for the minister's attention and reply, it is easier to establish the relevance of such personal characteristics than when the minister is exercising a more narrowly focused role, such as in administration or even in preaching and teaching.

Resistance as a worshipful response

Not unlike crossing oneself or genuflecting, chatting and heading for a rear pew may be a habitual, expressive, and meaningful response to the situation of worship. In a sense, this may be the way in which they do begin to worship. If the meaning of these opening worship responses is different from that of crossing oneself or genuflecting, this is all the more reason that it needs to be understood.

A minister can find such a hypothesis plausible and begin to sense some clues to meaning if he makes such observations as the following. The people do not show signs of being so "sociable" or "shy" in other situations, even in other situations in the church. There is an insistence on the behavior: people shake off the ushers' and minister's suggestions to change. They may even exaggerate the behavior: they make a beeline for a rear pew; or they look around for persons to talk to, even reaching across several pews, more than is convenient, and more than is polite to other people.

Perhaps the minister notices some regularities. For example, people move front more readily when the congregation is standing and they are less noticeable. But they won't move during silent prayer, even at the ushers' urging and even though with heads bowed they would be equally unnoticed.

Perhaps the clinging to the back pews and the chatting seem to be enhanced, rather than reduced, when the minister arranges a more solemnly worshipful atmosphere before the service, with robed choir and minister present all during the prelude and with a modest candle-lighting ceremony. This might seem paradoxical—certainly irking. But it may seem less so if one considers the possible interpretation that these reactions are in some sense responses to the worship stimuli and therefore are enhanced when these worship stimuli are made more prominent.

POSSIBLE INTERPRETATIONS. Considering such clues as these from the context and content of this particular resistive behavior, the minister might consider hypotheses along these lines:

The total range of stimuli connected with coming to church—including the special Sunday morning schedule at home, the better clothes, the members of the congregation, the church building, the scene of worship, and all the associations these experiences have ac-quired from childhood on—elicits a particular mood which may be thought of as coming into God's presence. Almost inevitably one is reminded of ideals and goals which he has held for himself and which others have held for him. These reminders may result in some uneasy feelings, conscious or unconscious. (Whether they deserve to be called guilt feelings or not may be a question. That label may be too specific.)

The rear pew might be both refuge and protection from the full force of such reminders, including perhaps especially the gaze of oth-ers. It may also be an expression of how one feels about oneself in this context (perhaps as though one deserves to be "sat in a cor-ner").

The chatting might be a distraction from some of these reminders and also an attempt to force evidence of others' good will. It might also turn out to contain a surprisingly large ingredient of confession: "It was a rat race this morning and I really yelled at Helen." "It's

Sunday morning again and I still haven't called on those new people." "Thanks, your hat looks nice, too, but I'm not at all sure I should have spent as much as I did for this." "Did you see the paper this morning . . . ?" "Did you see the way Wanda snubbed us? It makes me furious, but I guess she has a rough time with Charles these days." "I felt ashamed to be running right past that Negro church again."

Perhaps the personal uneasiness evoked by worship stimuli may be more specific. Perhaps reverential participation in worship seems to presuppose a belief or faith which a person feels he lacks. Perhaps "going forward" still is reminiscent of a time in adolescence when the minister and his parents wanted him to "go forward" to answer an altar call and he didn't; or else he did, and didn't "mean it."

Ministering response

Perhaps some such "awe of the holy" or "guilt feelings" are involved in this behavior. Perhaps they are not. Perhaps a minister feels some grounds for sensing the content of the feelings; perhaps not. Perhaps he develops hypotheses like those above, perhaps others, perhaps none. They are suggested here as a way of recognizing that *some* such meaning—this or another—may well lie behind such persistent and insistent resistance. But it is enough for the minister to respond only in terms of the outer and more visible signs and to let inferences as to their meaning be developed by persons themselves, either consciously or unconsciously.

VERBAL REFLECTION. The minister may, in conversations with individuals, with small groups such as deacons, or with the entire congregation, find ways of expressing his conviction that this behavior, just because it is inappropriate and "unlike" them, must represent some meaningful and important part of their reaction to the worship experience. "This is how some of us choose to 'warm up' for our worship, to make our first approaches to God. And that is all right. Sometimes I wish I understood a little better what it means." For some people, to some degree, off and on, this may invoke a certain degree of reflection and insight. At least some of the feelings may become closer to experience and expression in the context of the worship.

Most of the people, as well as the minister, may never really understand what these feelings are. The behavior itself may even become a kind of symbol which can be overtly utilized in the worship, even though no one—except, as it were, the person's own unconscious perception—knows exactly what the symbol is referring to. One can imagine the minister telling some persons privately—assuming rapport and understanding—that some prayers were being offered for those in the rear pews, or that the minister was praying during the prelude for those who were chatting, and for whatever that meant! This might even become a kind of "inside joke,"—again assuming rapport and acceptance—acknowledged as with a notice on the morning calendar that the rear pews are reserved for "those that require them." Or that the prelude is the time for persons to begin their worship "each in his own way." Such tactics can easily become perverted into forms of mild coercion—if that is what the minister really wants. But they also can be forms of genuine acceptance and invitation to openness, if *that* is what the minister really intends.

BEHAVIORAL REFLECTION. It is plausible to foresee some behavioral reflection, although in the context of worship this easily runs the risk of sacrificing rather than extending the minister's role as worship leader. Conceivably the minister might find ways in his own pre-worship behavior to express a kind of aloofness or an undue sociability, which would help to reflect and focus the congregation's behavior. If he adopted some such tactic as flitting about the narthex before the service, conversing, and seemingly hesitant about taking his proper place in the chancel, he would have to be prepared to have this discussed, first critically, then perhaps analytically. In very particular circumstances, such a strategy just might serve the purpose of shaking people loose to the point of exploring with new keenness and sensitivity the significance of the worship and some of their reactions to it. But on the whole, worship does not seem to provide much opportunity for behavioral reflection.

Reply. On the other hand, worship provides almost ideal circumstances for reply—both verbal and behavioral. As the minister or as minister and people together develop tentative hunches about the state of approaching worship which is represented by this behavior —an awe of the holy or discomforts of guilt or whatever—he can raise these up and make replies to them with the language of worship. This, after all, is precisely what his purpose is. If the resistance is expressing confessions or apprehensions, this can be articulated in the service and replied to with the needed expressions of acceptability to God, His forgiveness, etc. The language of worship traditionally has just the characteristics required for such reply by the minister. It can be highly penetrating and evocative, yet it can be ambiguous and general enough to avoid the threat, the offensiveness, and the undue directiveness of offering specific hypotheses about specific people. The language of worship should be able to reach past disguise, to touch and reply to people's pressing and troubling feelings, even when these feelings are otherwise not able to find more direct expression. However, it can do this only when these feelings exist and when they are ready to be so reached. In the language of worship, unless the minister ventures to replace it with the language of psychology, he cannot *insist* on his hunches of interpretation.

AT THE DOOR

The minister's most immediate encounter with members of his worshiping congregation comes after the end of the formal service, typically at the door. This may be a difficult and disappointing time for both parties. The minister is likely to want this encounter to provide something—an extension of the worship service. The themes of the sermon are still resonating. He would welcome serious "feedback," continued discussion or meditation on these themes, perhaps just some clear indication of how they registered and were received. He may hope for continued closer access to the lives of these people whose intimate concerns have hopefully been touched and shared in the worship service. Perhaps in some sense the conversation can provide additional personal moments of confession and absolution, thanksgiving and praise, intercession, renewed vocation and resolution to service. The people, too, are likely to be wanting this personal extension of worship.

Yet in the face of such hopes, what often happens is a timidly murmured, "I enjoyed your sermon," or effusive, "That was just wonderful!" a hearty joke, an eager foray into some bit of church business. No personal involvement with the themes of worship, Scripture, sermon, prayer. No encounter between persons at a level and on concerns presumably reached in the worship service itself. This is resistance.

Ministers may feel this disappointment in varying degrees, may respond with varying emotions, may learn to live with it to varying extents. If they attempt to understand and remedy it, the most natural approach is likely to be in terms of the situational conditions: There simply isn't enough time or privacy for the right kind of exchange. If the minister (more like a college professor after class) would stay in front of the pulpit to greet those who really want to see him, there would be more leisure and privacy. Perhaps an assistant, or a deacon, could provide more formal greeting at the door. Perhaps a coffee hour would help people linger. Perhaps a postworship discussion session in the lounge would be rewarding.

Or if he doesn't blame lack of time and privacy, perhaps the minister decides that his own personality is at fault—still a "situational" diagnosis. He may feel he is not warm enough, or open enough, to bring people out in a meaningful encounter. Perhaps firmer resolves to be warm, perhaps coaching from his wife, perhaps a Dale Carnegie course, perhaps psychotherapy—these might remedy this defect.

So goes the catalogue of situational diagnoses. If not to these, one may naturally turn to what the bottom line of the diagram in Chapter I calls "personal" explanations: The people may be too timid or too superficial; some kind of formal or informal training is needed to help them overcome these defects.

Perhaps more significant personal concerns intrude and are to be heeded. Perhaps an illustration mentioning the plight of retired persons in convalescent homes or a biblical analogy referring to the relation between father and son is seized upon out of context. This is "resistance" to the main point of the sermon, but it may be suggestive. Even though the comments are casual and general, the minister may have reason to sense that such a topic touches a personal dilemma. And he may take care to make himself especially sensitive and especially available for personal counseling. Or a man may gratuitously and irkingly insist on apologizing for missing church the preceding Sunday, or Bible study on Thursday. The minister may feel this represents a more general sense of guilt, and he makes himself available to help the man deal with it. Or if the apology is accompanied with the explanation, "Things were pretty hectic at home then," the apologizer may be bidding, consciously or unconsciously, for pastoral attention to his family situation. These are instances of persistent personal concerns of relevance to the minister—at least in his pastoral if not in his preaching role. They are not particularly elicited as *reactions* to the worship service itself. They might equally well turn up in administrative or other situations whenever the minister might happen to mention convalescent homes, a father-son relationship, or a missed appointment. That they do happen to emerge in the context of the worship relationship facilitates another relationship, that of counseling. This is legitimate—and from the general point of view of this book—welcome.

But it is not precisely what this book is proposing. The resistance to more intimate after-worship encounter may have a meaning *as resistance*. It may, in some sense, be a person's reaction to the worship service. It may be expressing in ways to be decoded some reaction which is in fact feedback and continuation of this experience in worship. This is more likely if the response is *especially* "timid," *especially* "effusive," *especially* "hearty," or *especially* "eager"; if it is especially disappointing of the minister's expectations; if it seems otherwise uncharacteristic of the relations between minister and parishioner; if the resistance persists, perhaps in shifted form, even after the reforms of increased privacy and of increased friendliness on the part of the minister; if it seems paradoxically to be greatest when the worship service has seemed most meaningful or the sermon most successful.

Ministry at the door

With these possibilities in mind, a minister poses a question to a group lingering after church, about half comprised of young people. "This business after the church service always seems quite an anticlimax. I get pretty involved in things during the worship, and I think maybe the rest of you do, too. Then we get together out here by the door and there is a lot of small talk. I don't think any of us very often gets to say what's on his mind out here, so I don't think we very often really 'get together.' Do you ever feel that way?" The reaction is first pretty complete silence, then a couple of murmured denials, "No, I'm always glad to see you."

Then one man offers, "Well, what do you expect, with such a long line of people. There isn't time to say anything, is there?" He is joined by a chorus, seconding this idea and offering other "situational" explanations. Their readiness to explain the situation seems to represent their recognition that it exists more or less as the minister has pictured it. After a while, the minister reflects this and goes on mildly to challenge the adequacy of their "situational" explanation. "You seem to feel the same thing I do and have some ideas how we can fix it. But I'd have to think about this a bit. For example, it still seems to happen here at the end of the line, when there isn't so much of a rush. We still have trouble getting around to saying anything as important as what may really be on our minds."

New, still essentially "situational" explanations are offered, and the minister in turn challenges the adequacy of each of these. "When we have tried coffee hours, really about the same thing happens, doesn't it?" "You don't have that much trouble telling me off other times; why do you always say that bit about 'enjoying the sermon'?" "The sermon isn't really any more intellectually profound than other things you do discuss."

"Well, you always seem so busy." The simplest rationalization now stripped away, other explanations come forward, which are probably still mostly rationalizations, but may have a larger component of significant meaning also represented. The minister still challenges. Fortunately their rapport is such that what he means as mostly a statement of reality does not seem to be personally defensive or scolding. "When have I ever been too busy to have a smoke with you?"

"Well, you know, I don't really mean you. I mean all ministers seem kind of hard to get to." The argument now shifts from the minister personally to his role.

The minister asks for clarification and specification. This is partly because he really does want this young man to make himself clearer. It is also partly as a way of testing the reality of the contention; how much evidence is there to support such a statement? And how much does the statement cover something else? "What do you mean by that?"

There is now give and take among the small group as to how much this "accusation" is justified. The consensus seems to move toward the conclusion that the statement as made is not really justified. Among the remarks in the discussion which the minister feels to be going significantly "deeper" are the following:

"I think it may be especially when you fellows dress up in these robes and get to be 'holy men' that you seem hard to get close to."

"Some things are easier to talk to you about and some things are easier to listen to you pray about."

"It's a lot easier to answer my children's questions about sex than about God."

By challenging those statements which seem patently rationalizations and "cover stories" and by reflecting sympathetically the comments which seem less like rationalizations and more "meaningful," the minister does, in fact, guide the discussion toward deeper levels. But the interpretation which emerges is theirs, not his. There is some discomfort in being forthrightly "religious." Talking with a minister otherwise is easy enough and passively participating in worship is, too. But taking an initiative raises uneasiness—even just a conversation which presupposes some religious premises and familiarity raises uneasiness. The minister reflects what they seem to be saying.

About this time members of this group begin to excuse themselves. The minister feels warranted in a final reflection, "It's even hard to talk about why it's hard to talk about religion." The "touché," called back over a shoulder, confirms the minister's interpretation that the departure itself is to some degree resistant.

This twenty-minute discussion has moved far, perhaps farther than one can expect most such discussions to progress. There is testimony and confession of uneasiness in approaching religious symbols and forms. This begins to touch what was called in Chapter V "level two." What may lie below this level, what produces this uneasiness —guilt over approaching the symbols of goodness, guilt over uncertainty in the faith, whatever—has not been touched and may never be with these people, at least not overtly. One can reasonably suppose that in this conversation each of them has come closer to expressing such troubles. And the closer one comes to expressing problems, the more likely one is to find them dissipated in the light of better judgment. The materials of the worship service itself offer an instance of such "better judgment" which may help to reduce such concerns and anxieties.

The minister's calm assuring manner in discussing the subject also provides a kind of behavioral reply. For these people, the handshaking confrontation with the minister at the door now becomes, in place of the mild embarrassment, a symbol—very importantly, a shared symbol—of the uneasinesses they feel in approaching God and of some of the assuring replies which are available for this uneasiness. If it is exaggerating to suggest that the handshake may become an important symbol of grace, it does not exaggerate to suggest that it does become a meaningful extension of the worship service to which it is now appended.

COMMUNION

If a minister makes the slight effort to discover what reactions of mind and feeling his congregants actually have during worship, he may wish he had not. The "wanderings of mind" or even the emptiness of mind which he discovers may not be recognizably related to the moods, rhythms, and experiences described by the doctrines and theories of worship. Far from reverence, thanksgiving, penitence, and renewal may be instead a preoccupation with the day's events. Far from a singleminded concern with one's relation with God the Creator, Sustainer, and Redeemer may be busy attention to the mechanics of the service ("What page is the next hymn on? Did I bring enough money for the offering today? The minister pronounces 'Thee' peculiarly in the prayer. Better not leave my gloves on my lap or I'll forget them when we stand up next. Who was that starting to read the minister's part of the responsive reading? It's easy to do. Why can't the ushers keep in step?")

If a woman seeks out the minister to confess and remedy her inability to "concentrate" and "really worship," the minister may have to look no further than his own mind during worship to discover that her "problem" is not unique. (What may be unique and a noteworthy clue is that she does regard it as a "problem" and seeks help.) In any case, however, the point here is not to contend how widespread or not may be such resistive distractions to worship. The point is to raise questions about the attitude a minister may take toward such resistance when and if it does appear.

Here are some of the thoughts experienced by one man during a communion service. It happened to be a service according to the Methodist order, in which each member of the congregation takes a turn at the altar rail. "It looks like it'll be my turn in two more groups. But I can't tell for sure. The ushers are trying to take people from one side, then the other, but they aren't very well coordinated. Johnson can't seem to count off the right number of people to send up front. He waits to see how much space the first ones leave, then he sends some more. This could take all day. The people can't seem to get the idea they're supposed to go up one aisle, then back the other. I'll do my part and get up there quick. And I'll fit in close at the rail, too, so they can get a full quota in. Some of these women shouldn't wear such tight skirts on communion Sunday. I suppose I should be thinking more about the minister's sermon and trying to feel some of 'God's mercy' that he was preaching about. What page was he reading from a minute ago 'We do not presume. . . .' I wonder who made this up. Why do they stick to this way? Do they ever change it?"

Preaching for more worshipful attitudes

A minister attempts to prepare people for communion in various ways, in formal training classes, in private counseling, as an incidental adjunct to such other activities as a deacons' meeting, with written statements in newsletter or morning calendar, perhaps in his personal prayer for members of the congregation, and in his sermons. Let us suppose that he was aware of this communicant's line of thought during communion, that this was common enough to take note of, and that he wanted to address himself to it in the morning sermon preceding communion. How might he do this in a sermon?

A sermon might scold such resistive reactions to the meaning of communion. A sermon might explain the norms of the appropriate subjective experience during communion. It might urge, cajole, or command people to conform to these norms, as though their distraction, if not a deliberate assault on the meaning of communion, were at least an act of will. A sermon might, in the fashion of handbooks of mystics, or of hypnotists, suggest devices of discipline—thoughts and objects to focus attention on, procedures for systematically emptying the mind of diverting thoughts.

A sermon might pay close attention to the substance of the particular thoughts and respond to them seriously at face value. The minister might explain that efficiency of crowd control is not important or possible in the communion service. He might explain the sources and the intended purposes of the parts of the service, and something of the denominational procedures by which they become instituted and modified. Such strategies in a sermon would be intended to subdue and quiet the distractions by removing the stimulus which aroused them, or at least making the stimulus seem less troublesome and arousing. This would correspond to administrative action to improve the ushers' efficiency or to control standards of women's dress so as to diminish these causes for distraction.

Alternatively, the sermon might adopt the strategy of trying to make the elements of the communion service more vital competitors for attention. The minister might set out to "make God more real," the congregation's faith "more vital," the symbols of the service more compelling.

Whatever merits such strategies have, and however "successful" they may be, they are caught *in* the resistance. They are responsive to it and controlled by it in its own terms. They regard the fact of resistance as a kind of procedural problem, a matter of means. The minister largely abandons his preaching and priestly purposes and uses the sermon to adjust the procedures. If attention can be drawn back to the communion service, *then* that service can have its effect. Discussing procedures for disciplining one's thoughts, or answering questions, the minister becomes as distracted—as far up a side road—as the man whose thoughts he would return to the main track.[2]

Though such reactions seem to be reasonably direct attacks on the resistance, there is serious question about their effectiveness, although this, of course, is a matter for empirical decision in any particular case. Frequently, two things may be true about such responses to resistance. (1) They are offering the man answers which he already has. Most of these injunctions and explanations he has heard before. Most of them he can and even does on occasion offer to himself. If the resistance persists anyway, these attacks must not be touching its real roots. Nor will one more repetition. To attack resistance with these is more valid logically than psychologically. (2) Even if they are effective in subduing particular forms of distraction, they are not effective in subduing the distraction itself. The man may no longer be distracted by ushers' inefficiency or curiosity about the service. But he is likely now to be distracted by something else, perhaps by the force of the minister's scolding. The resistance has simply shifted ground.

Celebrating the resistance as worship

There is another possible attitude toward these distracting thoughts, which regards them essentially as positive reactions rather than as negative deficiencies. They are "positive" not in the sense that they are favorably valued or any the less regretted as distracting people from total involvement in the experience of communion. They are regarded as "positive" in the sense that they are acknowl-

---

[2] This very fact, that in many actual responses to resistance, a minister himself tends to share in the resistance, perhaps deserves to be looked at more carefully, and not just scolded and scoffed at. It would be more consistent with the theme of the book to ask—acceptingly—what meaning it may have for a minister himself to succumb even in rejoinder to resistive distraction to the celebration of communion.

edged as responses which a person is actively, responsibly, purpose-
fully (though perhaps unconsciously) making to the particular situation. His response is not a deficiency somehow to be corrected by
fuller information and instruction, or a more adequately directing
and arousing situation. He is already responding fully as a person to a
fully perceived situation. This is not less true, even though the
response, or the person and perceived situation it implies, is different
from what the minister or even the man himself might hope.

This full meaningfulness of the resistive response is a hypothesis to
be considered. In any particular case, the hypothesis may seem re-
futed. It may simply not be true that the information or the point of
view which would subdue the distraction is already fully available to
the man. It may be true that when the distraction is directly attacked, the problem is solved. But the hypothesis is supported if
there are clues to meaningfulness at hand. These might include the
insistence and persistence already noted. They might include unusual
emotional accompaniments, perhaps a kind of exaggerated annoyance
with the ushers or with the tight dresses, or perhaps a complete
absence of any emotional feeling which might be expected if ushers
or tight dresses were arousing enough to provide distraction. They
might include such apparent anomalies and inappropriatenesses as
the fact that a man who was thoroughly distracted throughout the
communion service still insists on attending regularly.

The "meaning" of these distracting thoughts may lie somewhere in
the broad range of regarding them as a symptom of some important
area of alienation between the man and God. He comes to God's
altar and to the symbols of God's love, but can't quite face them
(second level of Chap. V), perhaps for some reasons of unworthiness
or guilt (third level). The fact that the resistance assumes the form
of distraction (rather than, say, a compulsive attention to the forms
of the service) and the fact that in content the distractions have a
very large component of "ought" suggests this.

On the other hand, the "meaning" may represent some primitive
form of personal worship reminiscent of the story of the widow's
mite. There might be some sense in which this man's concern for
efficiency and decorum is such a prominent part of himself that in

some sense this is what he has to offer God. If he, as a person, is going to be present at the Lord's table, it has to be in some form of concern for efficiency and order. If the worship forms do not otherwise provide for such an expression on his part, it may be that his "distraction" is his way of providing new forms.

Or the "meaning" may be something entirely different. Neither the minister nor the man needs to know what it is. If the minister does have grounds for sensing such meanings, he may find ready occasion in the sermon to offer *reply* to them, without ever mentioning explicitly either the distracting behavior or his understanding of its roots. But *reflection* may also be effective in the sermon. The minister simply needs to take seriously the hypothesis that whatever a person does at the time of communion, he is responding with some important part of himself in a meaningful way to a significant encounter with and perception of the elements of worship.

Following such an attitude, the sermon will deal *with* these "distractions," not attempt to subdue them. The sermon will not be devoted completely to such experiences; this again would be to subjugate the sermon. But in the course of preaching, say, on the widow's mite, or "the Sabbath was made for man," candid acknowledgment may be made, by way of illustration, of the kinds of preoccupation and distraction people do bring to their worship. These will be made to seem perfectly matter of fact, acceptable, and important. Hopefully, a Christian minister does not find it rare to be preaching on the theme that God welcomes and makes use of the unlikely and unofficial and unorthodox materials that people bring to him. Bread and wine were once humble and unlikely ingredients, and Jesus' peculiar handling of them in the Upper Room was something of a distraction itself. Perhaps the distracting thoughts, and the vital personal "meaning" they may have, are closer to the essential themes of the sacraments than the standard subjective mood persons are trained to expect of themselves in this somber ceremony. On that possibility, they deserve to be welcomed and even celebrated. Perhaps the man has the right to have his own worldly, intrusive thoughts symbolized by the elements of the table.

For a man to feel himself thus known and accepted at the

communion table is an important step, but only a beginning. These "distracting" thoughts and the corollary question "Why distraction?", once they are welcomed rather than fought, should evoke additional reflections and associations. Whatever "meaning" they have for the man will come closer to acknowledgment, closer to expression, and closer to God's presence. What more does a minister expect from his celebration of the sacraments?

INDEX

INDEX

General Index

Abby   see Van Buren, Abigail
acceptance   5, 20–2, 55, 62, 65,
   83–5, 89–107, 166, 193, 198–
   9, 203, 219, 237, 252–5, 266–7,
   270, 272–3, 285, 287, 310, 314,
   330–1, 333–4, 338
achievement, cultural demands for
   111–2, 113, 115–7, 118–120
Adam and Eve   136–8, 149, 156,
   175, 178–181
aggression   75–6, 122–3, 125,
   142, 179, 192, 264, 288
ambivalence   x, 64, 164–5, 168–
   175, 188–9, 196, 210–1, 233,
   249, 286, 299, also see Conflict
ambiguity, and intolerance of ambiguity   128, 191–2, 202–3,
   313–4
American Association of Pastoral
   Counselors   228
American Foundation of Religion
   and Psychiatry   228
archery, as analogy   181

Auld, Benjamin Frank, Jr.   46,
   77
authority   172, 240, 277–290

Barth, Karl   11–2
Baruch, Dorothy   23
behavioral response   261–2, 267–
   9, 273–4, 304, 315, 334, 338,
   344
Bonhoeffer, Dietrich   11
bowling, as analogy   281
Brehm, Jack W.   168
Brothers, Dr. Joyce   188
Brunner, Emil   11

childhood,
   as basis for religion   230–3,
      also see Church school,
   as analogy   24, 104–5, 108–9,
      113, 138
Cohen, Arthur R.   168
Colby, Kenneth M.   51
commitment   153–7, 165–175

353

Index of Applications to Church Activities